The Quality of Mercer's

By the same author

James Joyce and Medicine
The Enigma of Tom Kettle
An Assembly of Irish Surgeons
etc.

THE QUALITY OF MERCER'S

The Story of Mercer's Hospital, 1734–1991

by
J.B. Lyons

with a Preface
by William A. Watts

GLENDALE

First published in Ireland
by Glendale Publishing Ltd.
1 Summerhill Parade
Sandycove, Co. Dublin

British Cataloguing in Publication Data

Lyons, J. B.
    The quality of Mercer's : the story of Mercer's
    Hospital, 1734–1991
    I. Title
    362.110941835

ISBN 0907606962

Origination by Wendy A. Commins, The Curragh, Co. Kildare
Printed and bound in Great Britain by
Biddles Ltd, Guildford and King's Lynn

*To the former Nursing Staff
of Mercer's Hospital*

Ech mans day stands prefixt, time short, and swift with cure-
    less breatch
Is lotted all man kynd, but by thyr deeds thyr fame to stretch:
That priveledge vertue gyves.

Thomas Phaer's translation of Virgil's *Aeneid*

Contents

Illustrations

1. Mary Mercer's Stone House. (From Brooking's Map of Dublin, 1728.)
2. William Stephens, MD.
3. Francis Le Hunte, MD.
4. Page from Minute Book.
5. Portrait of the composer, William Boyce, by Thomas Hudson. (Courtesy of the Bodleian Library.)
6. State Lottery Ticket, 1751.
7. Mercer's Hospital, 1762. (From Peter Wilson's *Dublin Magazine.*)
8. Edward Hill, MD. (Courtesy of RCPI.)
9. A letter from Dr Hill.
10. Plan of the RCSI's original premises to the rear of the hospital.
11. Title-page, 1835.
12. Francis L'Estrange, Philip Bevan, Edward Ledwich.
13. Richard Butcher. (Cartoon by Spex.)
14. Butcher's saw.
15. Sir Joseph Napier, Bart.
16. Address to Mr. O'Grady, 1889.
17. Programme of the Mirus Bazaar, 1904.
18. Female medical ward, 1808.
19. Operating theatre, 1908.
20. Sir John Lumsden.
21. Mr Charles Maunsell.
22. Mr Seton Pringle.
23. Medical Staff, 1934.
24. Sir William I de C. Wheeler.
25. Dr R.J. Rowlette.
26. Mr T.G. Wilson.
27. Mr T.A. Bouchier Hayes. (From a drawing by Sean O'Sullivan.)
28. Sister Mary T. Moore. (Mercer's, 1975–1983)
29. Topping-out. (Mr D. Kneafsey, PRCSI, and Mr J. Hegarty, Contractor.)
30. Department of General Practice. (Professor William Shannon.)
31. The Mercer Library, 1991.

1. *Mary Mercer's stone house. (From Brooking's map of Dublin, 1728.)*

2. *William Stephens, MD.*

3. *Francis Le Hunte, MD.*

Abbreviations and Acknowledgements

Acronyms such as TCD (Trinity College, Dublin), RCSI (Royal College of Surgeons in Ireland), RDS (Royal Dublin Society), hardly require explanation but the forerunner of the RCPI (Royal College of Physicians of Ireland — the KQCPI (King and Queen's College of Physicians of Ireland) — does puzzle many.

Library staffs at TCD, the National Library, the RDS and the Colleges of Physicians and Surgeons extended their customary helpfulness and tolerance. The Bodleian Library supplied a portrait of William Boyce whose forgotten anthem 'Blessed is he who considereth the sick and needy' was splendidly restored by Marion Doherty.

The portraits of William Stephens and Francis Le Hunte are taken from Kirkpatrick's *History of Dr Steevens' Hospital* and for processing these and other illustrations I am grateful to Philip Curtis, Bairbre Guilfoyle and Patrick Nolan. Mrs M. Bouchier-Hayes has permitted the use of Sean O'Sullivan's drawing of her husband. Sybil Mellon's beautiful rendering of 'the old Mercer's' is reproduced by courtesy of the artist and serves to remind us of what that lovely little hospital looked like towards its close.

Gillian Smith's typing skills were called on repeatedly. Mary O'Doherty assisted in ways too numerous to mention (only that well-worn cliche actually does justice to her helpfulness) while the book was being written; she also read the proofs and compiled the list of medical staff, a venture in which complete accuracy can never be guaranteed because of the inherent unreliability of reference works.

Others whom it is a pleasure to thank include Professor Kevin Breathnach, Dr Seumas Cahalane, Professor Davis Coakley, Mr Desmond Dempsey, Ms Beatrice Doran, Dr John F. Fleetwood, Sister Eileen Martin (now Mrs Dooley), Dr F.O.C. Meenan, Sister Mary T. Moore, Dr Eoin O'Brien, Dr M. ffrench O'Carroll, Dr Liam O'Sé, Dr Marcus Shrage, Professor William Shannon, Mr Tom Turley, Professor William A. Watts.

Publication was generously supported by the Mercer's Hospital Foundation.

Department of the History of Medicine,   J.B. Lyons,
The Royal College of Surgeons in Ireland,   MD, FRCPI
123 St Stephen's Green,
Dublin 2.

At a meating of the Managers of Mercers
Hospital May the 28th 1736

Philip Percival Esqr in the Chair
Arch Deacon Whittingham
Present Dr Madden   Mr Daunt
         Mr Dobbs   Mr King
         Mr Hall   Mr Mathurin

The Treasurer gave in an Acct of Cash receiv'd by him for the use of the House
amounting to Four Hundred and twenty Six pounds eleven Shillings and 2½ as also of
his Disbursements for the same Amounting to One Hundred and Thirty three pounds
nineteen Shillings and 9½ by wch it appear'd that the sd Treasurer has then remaining
in his hands belonging to the House the sum of Two Hundred and Ninety two pounds
Eleven Shillings and sixpence

No Orderd That the Following Abstract of the said Acct be entred in these
Minnutes as a Memorandum till such time as proper books are
provided and the Treasurers Accounts passed in form

An Abstract of the Treasurers Acct
to the 28th of May 1736

Treasurer to ye House Dr	£ s d	Per Contra	£ s d
By Cash arising from ye Tickets of ye Musick	402 18 2½	By Expences for ye Musical performance as specified	2 6 7
By the Ld Primates Subscription	11 10 0	By Mr Wesley as pd Do for	14 18 2½
By Sr Richard Warburton baronet	3 0 0	by Sigr Scrughmini for	1 0 0
by Mr Meredyth	1 3 0	by Saml Mathews for	5 13 0
by Mr Beady's subscription	3 0 0	By Mr Hall for	50 0 0
by Mrs Graydons ½ years Interest of £100	3 0 0	by Do for	60 0 0
	£ 426 11 2½		133 19 9½
		By Ball in ye Treasurers hands this 28th May 1736	292 11 5
			£ 426 11 2½

Mr Dobbs informd the Chair yt he had recd by Tickets & that he had disposed of the sum of
Two Hundred and fourteen Pounds eight Shillings, but could not make up his Account to the
House because there were still some Tickets in his List disposed off and not paid

Resolvd that as soon as Mr Dobbs and Dr Stephens have given in their Accts of Tickets
in full, the neat profit arising from the Musical performance be exactly computed and
communicated to the Publick by inserting a Paragraph to that purpose in the Newspapers

Preface

We are fortunate that Professor J.B. Lyons, that eminent historian of Dublin hospitals, was available to write the history of Mercer's Hospital where he himself served as a consultant physician until its time of closure. The hospital began due to the charitable gift of the rather shadowy figure of Mary Mercer, about whom very little is known. Her generosity resulted in a hospital that survived for 249 years until, like other small voluntary hospitals of its vintage, it became the victim of pressures to amalgamate and to save costs by moving to new buildings. Our staff dispersed, mainly to St James's Hospital, and happily those who wished to continue to work in the medical services were able to do so. Professor Lyons records the happy circumstance that the buildings of the hospital were acquired by the Royal College of Surgeons in Ireland and are now used for the instruction of medical students and for the provision of community medical services, the original buildings having been extensively and elegantly refurbished. The capital which resulted from the sale of the hospital has been invested by the Board, transformed into the Mercer's Hospital Foundation, to pay for the development of geriatric services at St James's Hospital and the teaching of community medicine and provision of community services by the Royal College of Surgeons in Ireland and by Trinity College. The Board was very conscious that the original purpose in establishing Mercer's Hospital was to care for the sick poor of Dublin and the interests of the Foundation reflect that understanding. The medical problems of the old and of the sick poor in the community are among the least adequately provided for still today. Thus out of the sadness of closure much good has emerged.

Professor Lyons dedicates his book to the nursing staff of Mercer's Hospital. The quality of nursing was always a subject of pride to the hospital, but we should not neglect all of those members of the hospital staff and of its Board who over the centuries gave honourable and good service to the community in which they lived. This is what our book records and commemorates.

W.A. Watts
Chairman of Mercer's Hospital Foundation
and Provost of Trinity College

5. *William Boyce by Thomas Hudson.*
    (Courtesy Bodleian Library.)

6. *State Lottery Ticket, 1751.*

Introductory Note

Harry O'Donovan, script-writer to Jimmy O'Dea and co-fashioner of 'Biddy Mulligan the pride of the Coombe', came now and then to Mercer's with asthma. 'You'll go home this afternoon, Harry?' a doctor asked on one occasion when treatment was completed. 'Provided the quality of Mercer's is not strained,' he punned.

The events of two centuries and a half cannot be presented in a short book. A fast-sketching artist might encompass them in a fresco depicting the history of Mercer's and its times. This would include the arms of Dublin University and the motto of the Royal College of Surgeons in Ireland, *Consilio Manuque*, wisdom and handicraft. At the risk of overcrowding his tableau the artist would show the city's narrow, cobbled streets, the commodious Georgian residences of the well-to-do declining into sordid, unhealthy tenements and the fine squares favoured by professional men attracting the devotees of commerce.

The picture should feature an icon of St Stephen, for the hospital stands on ground hallowed by the medieval chapel of St Stephen which supported a lazar-house. The political symbols would include Shelley's 'fane of Liberty converted to the Temple of Mammon', the smouldering General Post Office, the Four Courts shattered by fraternal discord, the tricolour over Leinster House. Decorative scrolls would record the names of Jenner, Lister, Roentgen, Florey, Fleming and other general benefactors.

The broad brush strokes necessary to recreate such a pageant of history are not emulated here. As the subtitle is intended to convey, I have endeavoured to offer the story of a hospital in an account which could begin, 'Once upon a time ...' and by good fortune seems likely to merit the traditional ending: '... and they all lived happily ever afterwards.'

8.   *Edward Hill, MD. (Courtesy of RCPI.)*

Mr President —

Your messenger informs me that I may draw upon the treasurer of the Col. of Physicians for Ten guineas. — What can be the motive for such a Grant? If it be meant as payment for four months labor in arranging and preserving from destruction the Library of the School of Physic; I should insult the Self-esteem which I have ever maintained, & will never forfeit, did I not instantly reject the despicable pittance.

Again, if I am to consider it as an honorable acknowledgement of a public benefit, and not as an oblique indication of disrespect, I deem it so greatly unworthy the Col. to bestow, and me to record such an acceptance, that 'twere much better it had never been proposed.

I must therefore peremptorily decline to avail myself of their munificent intention.

I am, with the most friendly regard, yours truly —

E.H.

To Dr Callanan —
Prest of the Col. of Physns.   Dect 9th 1820

7.   **Mercer's Hospital, 1762. (From Peter Wilson's Dublin Magazine.)**

9.   *A letter from Dr Hill.*

Chapter One

1734–1784

THE MERCER CONNECTION

Like any other *nosocomium*, Mercer's Hospital was a place of hope and agony. Opened in 1734 it was one of a number of eighteenth century institutions provided to supply medical care for the poor and destitute. This welcome amenity was possibly the material expression of an evangelical spirit but it can be argued that it derived primarily from medical insights. When Dr Richard Steevens, a leading Dublin physician, died in 1710 he left his fortune 'to provide one proper place or building within the city of Dublin for an hospital ...'[1] His purpose was not effected until 1733 and meanwhile in 1718 six Dublin surgeons had adapted a little house in Cook Street for the care of 'the maim'd and wounded poor'.[2] This forerunner of The Charitable Infirmary in Jervis Street had only four beds but gained room for four or five more patients when moved to a larger house in Anderson's Court in 1723 and accommodated fifty patients on the Inns Quay in 1728.

The new charity built in St Stephen's Churchyard could not have been more appropriately placed inheriting the site occupied in the fourteenth century by the lazar-house of St Stephen, its function thus in some degree a continuation of the good work done by St Stephen's Hospital, just as the contributions to medicine made by the library and the professorial department of general practice recently opened fulfil, albeit in a different manner, the work interrupted when Mercer's was closed in 1983.

The story of Mercer's Hospital, then, really begins with the earlier foundation referred to by that interesting man, Richard Stanihurst (friend of the jesuit martyr, St Edmund Campion and translator of three books of Virgil's *Aeneid*), in his 'Description of Dublin' — 'this was erected for an hospitall for poore, lame and impotent lazars, where they abide to this daie'[3]— and I shall borrow the words of T.P.C. Kirkpatrick who reminded those assembled in

1934 for the bi-centenary celebration that they stood on holy ground:

> As early as 1230 there was here a chapel dedicated to St Stephen, and in a Memorandum Roll (17 Richard II) of 1394 it is stated that one Blena Mocton, or Ellen Morton, had lately endowed the aforesaid chapel for the maintenance of such citizens of Dublin as might be smitten with leprosy. She had placed her charity under the supervision of the Mayor of Dublin, and she endowed it with certain tithes from the monastery on Hoggen Green, with three acres of meadow round the said chapel, and with lands at Ballenlower in the County of Dublin, now Leopardstown. At the time one John Scrope was appointed Custos of the Chapel.
>
> In the records of the City for the year 1491 there is a resolution of the Corporation stating that every free man or woman of the City, who was a leper, was to be taken into St Stephen's Hospital, situate within the franchises of the City, without any payment, and that anyone who attempted to make a charge for the admission of such a citizen was to be liable for a fine of forty shillings.[4]

The ancient laws of Dublin decreed that 'the election and choise of the custos of St Stevens is gyven unto the Mayor and aldermen' and that he 'shoulde be a borne chylde of this cittie...'[5] In 1604 it was agreed that 'James Carie shall have the custoshippe of Saint Stephins during his lyfe, condicionally the petycioner doe bring in and deliver to the Maior before the post assemblye all evidens, mynumentes and writtinges which he have concerning the hospitall ... and to repaier the hospitall.'[6]

The lazar-house eventually tumbled to ruin, a casualty, perhaps, of the wars of the Commonwealth. Nettles grew in St Stephen's Churchyard[7] and in the early 1720s the minister and church-wardens of the parish of St Peter, on learning that a benevolent spinster lady, Mary Mercer, was looking for a site on which to build a house for the shelter of poor girls, decided to help her. They had already offered the churchyard to one James Knight to build there a house 'to contain four rooms for poor decayed Christians' but he had failed to fulfil the project and on 25 February 1724 the ground was given to Miss Mercer on a lease for 999 years at a pepper-corn rent dating from 25 December 1723.[8]

Her father, George Mercer, a native of Lancashire, had come to Dublin as a pensioner at Trinity College on 28 July 1663 at the age of eighteen; in the following year he was elected scholar. He became a Fellow, an honour then reserved for the celibate, on 30 May 1670 and was appointed Medicus on 9 September 1671 although he did not take a medical degree until 1681. This versatile man was Senior Greek Lecturer, too, and in due course Vice-Provost. But his academic career ended ingloriously for we read in the College Register for 8 June 1687: 'A letter from the Archbishop of Dublin was presented to the Provost, and senior Fellows whereby it appear'd that Doctor Mercer was married ... The same day at another meeting in the afternoon Doctor Mercer's senior Fellowship being voyd Mr Benedicit Scroggs was co-opted, and admitted Senior Fellow.'[9]

It seems that the obligation of celibacy was sometimes set aside by general connivance, the wife passed off as the Fellow's sister. Presumably a spiteful acquaintance was responsible for Mercer's deprivation for marrying Miss Mary Barry. It has been stated that Dr Mercer died in December 1687 but the College Archivist, Ms M.C. Griffith, has found evidence to the contrary. In the early part of 1688 Mercer was still alive and at law with the College. He refused to hand over deeds and documents which had come into his possession while acting as agent for the College; he claimed that he had been unfairly deprived of his fellowship while in the country on College business and that he 'in Equity and Justice ought not to have been put out of the said fellowship in that Unwarrantable Manner', without such proper proof of the marriage as the statutes and customs of the College and the laws of the kingdom required; furthermore he was owed over £42 as stipend for his work as agent and had executed a bond to the Master in Chancery on the College's behalf and must be indemnified. On 24 February 1688 he replied to the Provost:

My occasions kept me abroad on Wednesday night and yesterday soe that I could not answer your letter before today. I am as ready to restore your papers as you are to pay what is due to me; I do not desire to put you or myself to trouble but if you please will reserve the difference to your counsell, or any other indifferent person that you will make choice of.[10]

Unable to proceed against the recalcitrant doctor at common law (not knowing the number and particulars of the papers) the Provost and Fellows sought a subpoena with *duces tecum* for the said documents. How or when the dispute was resolved is not known.

Further information about the Mercer family is meagre. Dr Mercer may have died a comparatively young man. His widow survived the turn of the century and her will was proved in the Prerogative Court in 1703. The date of birth of their only daughter is unknown. After her parents' death this philanthropic lady was affluent and remained unwed.

Mary Mercer's inheritance included an estate and lands in West Derby, near Liverpool. She purchased some lots in Dublin's Abbey Street area 'whereon severall houses are built' and dedicated her wealth to the care and education of poor girls. Hence the stone house built at her direction in the disused churchyard.

The charitable intentions of Jonathan Swift, Dean of St Patrick's since 1713 ran in a different direction; he wished to provide a hospital for the mentally ill and his friend, Sir William Fownes, a former Lord Mayor of Dublin, writing to the Dean on 9 September 1732, recommended to him 'a very proper spot' for the purpose at the end of King Street and let to Leigh, a builder or bricklayer.

> Also there stands to the front of the street, a large stone building called an almshouse, made by Mrs Mercer; though by the by, I hear she is weary of her work and does little in supplying that house or endowing it.
>
> Perhaps this ground may be easily come at through Leigh's heirs; and by your application, I know not but Mrs Mercer may give her house up to promote so good a work.[11]

Swift's hospital was to be opened quite some distance away in 1757 but at about the time that Fownes wrote his letter a hospital was being planned by a group of men who evidently met with Mary Mercer. She relinquished to them in 1734, as trustees for the new charity, the stone house in Stephen Street[12] and one suspects that ill-health rather than being 'weary of her project' led her to this decision. Be that as it may, a pertinent entry in the Dublin Assembly Roll confirms that progress had been made.

> Dean William Percivall, minister of Saint Michan's, Doctor William Jackson, minister of St John's, William Stephens,

doctor of physic, and William Dobbs, surgeon, in behalf of themselves and several other persons, setting forth that there is not in this city any public charitable provision for lunatics, or such other poor people whose distempers are of tedious and doubtful cure, such as persons afflicted with cancer's, king's evil, leprosy and falling sickness, etc., and that Mrs Mary Mercer hath with great charity given up a new building at the lower end of Stephen's street, facing William street, for the above use, but the said house not being finished, and no provision for cells for raging lunatics, which must be strengthened with arches and other necessaries being wanted, which is computed to amount to about £200 at least, and therefore prayed that this city would give their charitable aid and assistance to carry on a work so evidently necessary: whereupon it was ordered that the receiver-general of the city revenues, on the Lord Mayor's warrant, do pay the within memorialists £50, sterling, for the uses in the within memorial mentioned, the same to be allowed the treasurer on his accounts.[13]

The trustees nominated in the foundation deed of May 20th 1734 were the Protestant Archbishops of Armagh and Dublin, the Bishop of Kildare, the Lord Mayor and high sheriffs of Dublin, the ministers of the parishes of St Peter, St John, and St Michan, the Dean of Christchurch, Dr Jonathan Swift, Dean of St Patrick's, and five medical men, William Stephens, Francis Le Hunte, Hannibal Hall, William Dobbs and John Stone.

Mary Mercer died in her house in Great Ship Street on Tuesday March 4, 1735, and was 'very decently interred at Christchurch' two days later.[14] One of her servants, Samuel Kathrens, had witnessed her will which left the bulk of her fortune for the creation of a charity school and nothing whatsoever to the hospital.

By this will and testament, she bequeathed her soul to Almighty God and to her executors left £3,000 for the purchase of lands etc. to be conveyed to trustees who shall 'give employ and bestow the rents issues and profits of the said lands' for the support and instruction of twenty-five poor girls until they were ready for employment as apprentices; the funds realised from properties in West Derby and Dublin were to be similarly employed. She left an interest in £1,000 to her cousin, Mary Barry, for her lifetime or until such time as she married. The sum of £2,000 was to be

invested to provide 'care and relief' for indigent persons living in
local parishes. Her cousin was to receive 'all my wearing apparrell
and household furniture of what nature or kindsoever with the
gold diamond ring my said uncle Paul Barry was pleased by his
last will and testament to bequeath me.'

Mary Mercer's school for the education of poor Protestant girls
(the sectarian stipulation, as Michael Quane pointed out, was
imposed not by Miss Mercer but by her trustees) was endowed and
erected at Rathcoole, County Dublin, in 1744 and opened in the
following year at Michaelmas with twenty pupils. By 19 June 1747
twenty-five pupils were supported and this number was gradually
increased. In 1823 the trustees of Mercer's charity school agreed
to move to a building erected near Castleknock by the Morgan
bequest and within two years the move had been accomplished.

The house in Stephen's Street which has carried Mary Mercer's
name for more than two and a half centuries stood in a good neighbourhood. Nearby William Street, in modern parlance, was an 'up-
market' street. Esther Johnson (Swift's 'Stella') and her friend
Rebecca Dingley had lived there at one time and St Stephen's
Green with its fashionable Beau's walk offered a pleasant recreation area which Swift urged his lady friends to use. 'Why don't you
walk in the Green of St Stephen?' he asked them in a letter from
London. 'The walks there are finer gravelled than the Mall.'[15]

THE OPENING PHASE

When Mercer's Hospital opened on 11 August 1734 with beds for
ten patients its first governors were: Dr Clayton, Lord Bishop of
Cork (and later of Clogher); Dr Jonathan Swift, Dean of St
Patrick's, who rarely if ever attended; Archdeacon Whittingham;
Dean Madden; Dr William Stephens; Rev James King; Hannibal
Hall, William Dobbs, John Stone. The physicians were Drs Stephens
and Le Hunte who attended in turn on Mondays and Fridays, the
surgeons were Hannibal Hall, William Dobbs and John Stone.
They gave their professional services without charge.

William Stephens (b. 1692), whose forebears had held public
office in Counties Wexford and Waterford, studied medicine under
the great Boerhaave in Leyden, enrolling as 'Hibernus' on 3 September 1716 and defending his thesis *De Elixir Proprietatibus* for
the MD degree in 1718. He returned to Ireland following his election as FRS, married in 1721 and was conferred MB and MD at
Trinity College in 1724. He was admitted a Candidate of the

College of Physicians becoming a Fellow on St Luke's Day 1728 and held presidential office in 1733, 1742 and 1759. He published *Upon the Cure of Gout by Milk Diet* (London, 1732) a translation of *De Furia Podagrae Lacte Victa* by Johan Dolaeus (Amsterdam, 1705).[16]

Stephens and Le Hunte were among the fourteen founders of the Royal Dublin Society.[17] The latter held a second post as physician to Dr Steevens' Hospital where Stephens was elected governor on 21 April 1743.

Dr Francis Le Hunte, a native of Cashel, was president of the College of Physicians in 1729 and 1741. He inherited an estate of £1,200 a year when his brother, Richard Le Hunte, MP, died in 1747. Then, as reported by the *Dublin Journal*, he 'retired from the business of his profession and enjoyed his friends with a cheerfulness and good nature.' His neglect of his duties at Steevens' caused the governors on 4 December 1749 to ask Stephens to take charge of the hospital 'till such time as Dr Le Hunte shall think fit to return to a personal attendance on the same.'[18] When Le Hunte died at Brennanstown, County Dublin, in 1750 — 'universally esteemed for his great knowledge in his profession', according to the *Dublin Gazette* — he was replaced as visiting physician to Steevens' by William Stephens who appears to have left Mercer's in the mid-1740s when appointed physician to the Royal Hospital where in 1747 he had living-quarters.[19]

Dr and Mrs Stephens' home was in Stafford Street with a country house in County Wexford. They had two daughters and when Fanny Stephens married in 1753 her dowry amounted to £1,700. Stephens died suddenly in Wexford in 1760 of 'gout in the stomach'. His portrait in the library at Steevens' Hospital prompted Kirkpatrick's remark that it was unlikely that he had ever tried the milk diet for his gout.[20]

Rev Dr William Jackson drew the corporation's attention in 1735 to the lack of a supply of piped water 'whereupon it was ordered that the memorialist have liberty to affix a branch of three quarters of an inch diameter to the main in Stephen street, for the use in the above petition mentioned, the same to be laid in without any expense to the city, and to continue during the city's pleasure.'[21]

A record[22] exists of the governors' meetings since that of 28 May 1736 on which occasion the following attended: Hon Philip Percival (chair), Archdeacon Whittingham, Dr Madden, Mr Dobbs, Mr Hall, Mr Daunt, Mr King and Mr Maturin. The treasurer reported that he had received £426 11 2½ 'for the use of the House' and had disbursed £133 19s 9½d. Mr Dobbs said that he had disposed of tickets for the musical performance to the value of £114 8s. The poor-box was then opened and contained thirteen shillings and four pence. The chairman recommended for their consideration one of the performers at the recent concert held for the benefit of Mercer's 'as a Person unable to bestow his Trouble Gratis' and it was resolved that he should be paid (18s 6d) and his name concealed. A petition was read from Mary Mercer's former servant, Samuel Kathrens, the first house steward, 'praying Lodging in the House for himself and his Wife and an Augmentation of his Salary.' The matter was referred to another meeting.

The petition from Kathrens was deferred again in June and subsequently rejected. Soon he was dismissed 'as in every way unqualified for the office of House Steward.' He was replaced by Robert Donnelly, a former patient, as Clerk of the House. Meanwhile it had been ordered 'That the Revd ArchDeacon of Dublin be applied to, for a Greater Compass of Ground to enlarge the House.'

Mrs Elizabeth White was engaged as housekeeper in January 1737 at £8 per annum. She was to be allowed nine pence daily to provide a dinner for the clerk, apothecary and herself, small beer included. She was to buy the meat required for consumption in the hospital and 'give out the Coals to the Several Nurses to be used in the several wards.'

On 28 October 1737 the Lord Mayor came to the Board with the good news that the late Captain Hays had left a legacy of £500 to the hospital. Very soon the governors had to consider how to answer the surgeons' plea that 'a Bagnio & Fluxing Room are much wanted.'

The term 'fluxing' or 'salivating' relates to courses of treatment with mercury which when prescribed in large doses, usually for venereal diseases, caused salivation measured in pints or quarts, the amount of saliva produced being directly related to the expected curative outcome. Mercury, which Dioscorides called Hydrargyrum, or water of silver, could be given by mouth, by 'unction', or by fumigation. Corrosive sublimate was the preferred form for oral use. The 'Neapolitan Ointment' was used on the skin—the patient stood before a good fire and rubbed the ointment into the feet up to the ankles; two days later it was applied from the ankles to the knees and on the fifth day the rubbing was continued up to the buttocks. If ptyalism did not ensue by the fifth day a further rubbing up from the buttocks was needed and if a free flow of saliva was not established by the ninth day rubbing was extended to shoulders and arms. Fumigation, though effective, was dangerous. The patient, his head covered with a blanket or cloth, sat before a fire and when a suitable preparation was thrown on the coals he inhaled the fumes.

The elaborate preparation required has been outlined by Kirkpatrick:

> The patient was to be bled from the arm to the quantity of about twelve ounces, in order to attenuate the blood, so that there might 'be room for it after it is rarefied by the mercury'. The patient was also to be purged 'lest intestine commotions should be raised in the same time as the salivation'. In addition to these the patient was to bathe for an hour every morning and evening, if he was strong, but if weakly once a day. In either case the stomach was to be empty at the time the bath was taken. The number of bathings varied according to the constitution of the patient, but each morning in the bath or in bed, the patient was to take 'a draught of clarified chalybeated whey, turned with an infusion of germander, water-cresses, chervil, &c. or broth made of chicken, or a piece of veal, boiled with diluting, cooling, vulnerary herbs, such as wild savory, saxifrage, agrimony, spleen-wort, maiden-hair, water-cresses, &c.' When the salivation was well established bleeding and purging were again employed and 'the clothes wherewith the patient was covered during the time of the friction' were to be taken off. Great care was to be taken during the whole process to prevent the patient taking cold.[23]

Dr Steevens' Hospital did not fit up its fluxing ward until 1757 but at Mercer's the desired facility was provided without delay. As the regimen entailed keeping a blazing fire and an abundance of hot water the chimney of the fluxing-ward was a source of trouble. A salivation usually lasted for from twenty-five days to a month.

On 2 June 1738 it was ordered that Alice McCann, a nurse who had been in disgrace two years earlier, 'be carried before the Lord Mayor to be punished for seducing the Patients in the House and that she be discharged the Service of the House.' In the following year it was noted 'that a great quantity of Medecines and Druggs belonging to the House were Stolen with a large quantity of Old

Linnen by James Dun and Elenor Ware who have made their escape and absconded to avoid due punishment.' Nurse Ware must have been a flighty Eve for after this incident the governors recommended, 'That it be an instruction to the Surgeons not to appoint any Nurse for this Hospital under the Age of Forty Years.'

Towards the end of 1738 the governors were negotiating 'with the several Persons concerned in the Ground adjoining to the Widows Houses' and having purchased it they set about providing the hospital's first extension using the legacy left by Captain Hays. A sermon preached at St Andrew's Church on 13 February 1739 and divine service performed in the cathedral manner with *Te Deum Jubilate* and two new anthems composed by Handel were events designed to recruit support 'there having been a very extraordinary expence this year by an Additional Building which will contain 30 more Sick Poor.'

The new building was completed by 1740 and stood to the west of the original structure its facade receding some ten feet. An attempt to call the institution Mercer's and Hays's Hospital was soon abandoned. Perhaps it was this new acquisition that prompted the governors to a more business-like approach. 'Memerandum, To Inquire where Mrs Mercer's deed of Conveyance of this House to Dr Stephens, Dr Hall, Mr Dobbs & other Trustees etc is deposited, and whether it is registered or no ... Memerandum, To privide a Strong Box with two locks, wherein to deposit Deeds and Papers belonging to the House.'

Rice Gibbons 'having signified his inclination to attend this Hospital as Surgeon' was duly elected, becoming a governor on 3 May 1740 in which year Dr John Anderson (d. 1787) also joined the staff. Joseph Shrewbridge was appointed surgeon and governor in July 1744.

Hospital statistics were given in a newspaper advertisement in November 1745 for the benefit of potential subscribers:

> Patients lodged & taken care of in the Hospital last Year: 264
> Now under Cure in the Hospital: 56
> Out Patients who have received advice and Medicine in the House: 2294

		£	s	d
Annual Expences of Mercer's Hospital:	1741	522	9	8
	1742	570	10	0
	1743	519	8	3
	1744	474	4	9½
	1745	604	3	0½

Within little more than a decade from its foundation the hospital's good name was attracting patients in numbers that caused over-crowding and in 1746 the governors felt obliged to insist 'that except Cases of Sudden Accidents no Patients from the Country shall be received till the Recommenders shall have applyed to the Physitians & Surgeons & shall receive their Answer that there is a Vacancy for the Admission of such Patients.'

A committee was formed in February 1748 to consider the most effective way of achieving the status of a Body Corporate and Dr Bartholomew Mosse came from the Lying-in Hospital in March to discuss the State Lottery. Mrs White, the housekeeper, moved to the Hospital for Incurables and was replaced by Mrs Jane Dover. In the following year it was agreed 'that a Shed be built to contain & preserve dry Straw & that a Convenience be made for contain-ing a few Tons of Scotch Coals for the Bagnio.'

Dean Hutchinson reported to the trustees and governors on 10 November 1749 that he had asked Counsellor Stannard to prepare a bill to incorporate the trustees and had offered him a fee of ten guineas. The lawyer returned the fee to the hospital and undertook to prepare the heads of a bill. The desired incorporation was effected by Act of Parliament in 1750.

The diligence of Mr Kenny, the apothecary, was rewarded by £5 extra in May 1751 but by November this office was vacant and in consequence there was 'a great Damage to the Hospital'. The medical staff was encouraged 'to accept of a young Apothecary if he inguage himself to continue in the Service of the Hospital for Seven Years or for such time as they shall judge proper'; a Mr John Boyd was appointed. Dr Woods resigned his post towards the end of 1752 and was replaced in January 1753 by Dr Anthony Relhan who in 1755 was elected president of the King and Queen's College of Physicians of Ireland.

A feeling of dissatisfaction articulated by the medical staff as early as 1751 concerning space and conditions within the hospital led to a critical review of the situation on 30 March 1754. The governors had before them a document signed by the physicians and surgeons:

> We the Physicians and Surgeons attending the Sick and infirm in Mercer's Hospital are unanimously of oppinion that the said Hospital is a very inconvenient Building for the purpose it is converted to, that the House is by many Degrees too small for the Number Lodged in it; that the Wards are too low and narrow and ill situated with respect to the Doors and Stairs and by which means the Hospital is render'd unwholesome to the Sick who suffer more in it than is generally apprehended; that the officers are so dispos'd of in the House as not to know much less to remedy abuses committed in the Oeconomy of the House that the charity is deprived of the Advice and assistance of some of its principal Governors on account of the offensive smell prevailing in the House and lastly that the Physicians and Surgeons are exposed to great danger and inconvenience from the Stench in the House and the ill contrived Situation of the Apothecary's Shop which is the only Room they have to examine both Physical and Surgical Patients promiscuously in.
>
> We therefore the Physicians and Surgeons purpose (with the concurrence of the Governors of this Charity) to pull down the present Hospital and to rebuild it in such a manner as may effectively remedy the Evills complained of without any diminution of the present Fund.[24]

It was agreed that these recommendations be implemented and it was ordered 'that a House be taken as soon as possible for the reception of as many Patients as it can contain during the rebuilding.'

Following the usual custom which, incidentally, was to lead to an impasse in a future troubled situation, the new physician, Dr Relhan, became a governor. He attended meetings regularly and the minutes show that soon he was entrusted with financial transactions. 'Dr Relhan is desired to attend at Dicks Coffee House on Friday the 14th of February Instant of One Hundred Pounds a Year Fee farm Rent & to offer for it Six & twenty years Purchase in Behalf of Mercers Hospital.'

He acted for the hospital in the contemplated purchase of lands at Saucerstown in July 1756 and advised against it. He was next empowered to 'receive from the Treasury the £500 granted by the Parliament towards Building the new Hospital.' Before long tongues were wagging. The doctor had not handed over the monies to the treasurer and after October 8th he ceased to attend meetings. On 11 January 1757 the governors resolved, 'That it is the Opinion of this Board that Doctor Relhan be proceeded against with the utmost Expedition.' In the event, however, the process of law was unnecessary and in February the treasurer acknowledged receipt of the grant from the errant physician.

This unedifying episode ended Dr Anthony Relhan's connection with the Board of Governors. According to Kirkpatrick, he left Dublin in 1762 or 1763 to practise in England.[25] Dr Samuel Clossy replaced him as physician and was elected governor on 3 April 1672. Clossy's service to the hospital, regrettably, was brief. His *Observations on Some of the Diseases of the Parts of the Human Body* was published in London in 1763 in which year he sailed for the New World. He hoped to gain an appointment at a military hospital planned for New York. This failed to materialise but Samuel Clossy is today remembered as one of the principal founders of New York City's first medical school at King's College, the forerunner of Columbia University.[26]

The building project, meanwhile, had gone ahead speedily and by 1 October 1757 it was ordered, 'that a Person be sought for proper to take care of the Fires in the new House till it be fit to be opened.' In November it was agreed to advertise 'that the new House is now opened for the Dressing and taking care of the Extern Patients and that on Monday the 14th Instant a few beds will be ready for receiving the Interns in Extraordinary and Pressing Cases and that they hope to have ready for a general reception against the first day of December next.' A petition presented to parliament disclosed that 'the unhappy failure of the bank by Messers Wilcok and Dawson' where the funds were lodged had left the institution in straitened circumstances.

Arrangements were made in May 1758 for the city plumber to lay a pipe to supply the hospital with water. The new building's façade, as Noreen Casey has pointed out, had two unusual architectural features. 'It has three storeys over a rusticated ground-floor basement. It is also unusual in having an attic storey above the main cornice.'[27]

The deaths of John Stone (1756) and Rathborne Mills (1759) — the latter leaving a legacy to the hospital — depleted the surgical staff creating vacancies to which Gustavus Hume and Henry Morris were appointed in 1760. Dr Archibald Hamilton was appointed physician and was joined by Dr James Span in 1768. Dr Edward Hill, a talented and unusual man who was to hold his post as physician until his death in 1830, joined the staff in 1773.

Concerned by rising costs, the governors on 26 January 1765 asked the medical staff to consider how these might be reduced. The result of the deliberations remain unstated but on 14 February 1767 it was decided 'That a Machine for Electrifying be provided for the use of the Hospital.' The governors were relieved of this expense when one of their members, the Earl of Lanesborough, presented the necessary apparatus. The acquisition of a piece of ground contiguous in Love Lane — 'to Air the Patients in this Hospital' — was discussed. The Dean of Christchurch was asked on what terms he would lease it but these were eventually declined.

When John Howard, the author of *The State of the Prisons in England and Wales* and the greatest authority on conditions in penitentiaries and hospitals, paid a fifth visit to Ireland he was favourably impressed by Mercer's:

> The governors of Mercer's Hospital have lately adopted a new and salutary contrivance. One pane in each of the upper sashes is taken out and its place supplied by a fine wire lattice painted green; which rendered all the wards (at my visit in 1783) fresher and more agreeable than those in any other hospital in the city though this is situated in the closest part of it.[28]

Praise from such a source must have gratified those at the helm at Mercer's with responsibility for its pilotage in tempestuous times.

MERCER'S AND MUSIC

As has been mentioned, Mary Mercer did not endow the hospital. Her legacies, as we have seen, included £2,000 for the indigent sick in local parishes. Hopefully the governors asked the ministers and church-wardens to apply the bequest to the poor in the institution. It is unlikely that their request was heeded but they coped successfully with the thankless task of fund-raising, investing the surplus in properties and securities.

In 1745 when the hospital accommodated sixty-three in-patients, the annual expenditure was £604 3s 0½. The outlay for a quarter's provisions was as follows: 'Mr Audbert, Baker, £12 9s 4d; John Toole for Oatmeal, £1 4s 2d; Anne Price, Huckster, £1 4s 1½d; Geo Lanouze, Grocer, £1 6s 3d; Alice Anderson, New & Buttermilk, £31 3s 4½d; Eliz Richardson, Butcher, £6 3s 11d.

Subscriptions, occasional contributions and legacies helped to make ends meet and at one time Mercer's, the Charitable Infirmary and the Lying-in Hospital participated in a State lottery.

Music was a major source of income for Mercer's. The performances usually took place in St Andrew's Church. They were splendid occasions attended by the Lord Lieutenant. A Captain's guard was mustered; stewards from the nobility and gentry carried gilt and white rods respectively; matting was laid in the nave, carpets and cushions were provided for distinguished guests; Parliament and the Law Courts were adjourned.

In this association between Mercer's and the world of music, the hospital was the gainer but may have contributed something too, as shown by the Trustees' action in lending 200 guineas to the Philharmonic Society to buy an organ, the loan to be repaid by 20 guineas annually, the hospital retaining ownership of the organ 'after such time & notwithstanding the payment of the said Principal'.

Handel was a notable benefactor. The first reference to the hospital's indebtedness to him relates to his *Te Deum Jubilate* and two Coronation Anthems which, on 13 February 1738, 'were performed at St. Andrew's Church with the greatest decency and exactness possible, in the presence of their Excellencies the Lords Justice and eight hundred Persons of the first quality and distinction'. To complete the occasion, a sermon was preached by the Rt Rev the Lord Bishop of Kildare. The same compositions were performed for the benefit of Mercer's on 16 February 1740, when the sermon was given by the Bishop of Ferns.

George Frederick Handel, the son of a barber-surgeon, was born in Halle, Saxony (now West Germany) in 1685.[29] He was intended for the legal profession but his precocious talent as a musician determined the direction of his career, despite his father's initial discouragement. He was appointed organist to a local Lutheran Church in 1702 and next joined an orchestra in Hamburg. He visited England in 1710 and 1712 and eventually took up per-

manent residence in London. His genius as a composer was never
in question but few artists are without detractors. Handel and
Robert Walpole were lampooned together in a popular periodical,
the latter for taxing tobacco, the former for the high price of his
oratorio performances. And through his management of Covent
Garden he lost a fortune.

Watkins Shaw has described in *The Story of Handel's Messiah*
how the composer sat down in his London home on Saturday,
22 August 1741, with Charles Jennen's libretto before him, to start
work on his great anthem. Six days later he completed Part One
and by September 14th the entire work was finished. Handel's
amanuensis, Johan Christoph Schmidt from Ansbach, then made
a fair copy of the manuscript, the 'conducting score' which the
composer carried with him when he set off for Ireland early in
November. He had received an invitation in February from William
Cavendish, third Duke of Devonshire, the Lord Lieutenant, to
give a series of concerts in Dublin in 1741–1742 with the assurance
that they would be well supported.[30]

At Chester where he was delayed when his ship could not sail
because of contrary winds, Charles Burney, then a schoolboy, saw
him 'smoke a pipe over a dish of coffee at the Exchange Coffee-
house'. He applied for permission to use the organ in a nearby
church, intending to try out some of the music to be played in
Ireland. He asked if any of the members of the choir could sing at
sight and a printer named Janson was recommended to him, but
with unfortunate consequences.[31]

During a rehearsal Janson broke down. Handel admonished
him in several languages and asked him in broken English: 'You
schayntrel! tit you not dell me dat you could sing at soite?'

'Yes, sir — and so I can — but not at first sight.'

Handel arrived in Dublin from Parkgate, the port near Chester,
on 18 November 1741 and took lodgings in Abbey Street. Maclaine,
an organist, and his wife, a soprano, also crossed to Dublin for
Handel's Irish season. Signora Avoglio, an Italian soprano, arrived
on November 24th and Mrs Cibber, an English actress and mezzo-
soprano, on December 3rd. The latter played Indiana in Steele's
The Conscious Lovers at the Aungier Street Playhouse on December 12th, her first appearance on the Dublin stage. She filled this
part again on February 9th for the benefit of the Charitable
Infirmary.[32]

Little is known of the Maclaines but those who heard him play the organ in Chester on his way to Dublin were so impressed that they felt that until then they had never heard the instrument played properly. Christina Maria Avoglio who had appeared in London 'from nowhere' in 1740 was to pass from the public notice just as suddenly four years later.[33] Mrs Susannah Cibber (*née* Arne) was to become Garrick's leading lady and possessed a stage presence that made up for what Burney called her 'mere thread of a voice'. At twenty she married the recently-widowed Theophilus Cibber, a profligate actor-manager, and immediately regretted it. The husband facilitated his young wife's love-affair with John Sloper and subsequently sued the Berkshire squire for criminal conversation but was awarded £10 instead of the £5,000 he sought. Eventually Susannah Cibber lived with Sloper and bore his children.[34]

According to Horatio Townsend, a barrister-at-law and governor of Mercer's, who published *Handel's Visit to Dublin* (1852), the great musician spent much of his time while in the Irish capital playing the organ at St Michan's Church. He frequently called at the house of Alexander Lee, a music-seller on Cork Hill. In later years Lee claimed erroneously that *Messiah* was composed in his house, led astray, perhaps, by the time Handel may have spent under his roof engaged in revising the original score.

Preparations for Mercer's annual benefit performance were already under way and Dr John Wynne, Sub-Dean at St Patrick's Cathedral, was deputed by his fellow-governors to get the sheets of music for the performance from Matthew Dubourg, Master of the State Music, and empowered to give guarantees for their safety. On November 21st the governors 'Ordered that Mr. Putland, Dean Owen and Doctor Wynne be and are hereby desir'd to wait on Mr. Handel and ask the favour of him to play on the Organ at the Musical Performance at St. Andrew's Church.'[35]

The benefit concert was held on December 10th. Handel's *Te Deum, Jubilate* and two new anthems were performed with 'a Grand Anthem compos'd on the occasion by Mr. Boyce ... at the request of several well-wishers to the Charity.' It is not known whether Handel did play the organ or not but on December 12th the board of governors 'Ordered ... that Dr. Wynne be desir'd to thank Mr. Handel for his attendance.'[36]

The gratification afforded by Handel's presence may explain why the governors failed to record their debt to William Boyce until 2 January 1742 when it was 'Ordered that the thanks of this

Board be given to Mr. Boyce for the Anthem he favoured us with for the last performance at St. Andrew's Church, and that Dr. Owen be desir'd to acquaint him therewith.'[37] The anthem created specifically for Mercer's Hospital by William Boyce (1710–1779), a London composer, was the suitably named 'Blessed is he that considereth the sick and needy.'

> Blessed is he that considereth the sick and needy
> The Lord will deliver him in the time of trouble.
> The Lord will preserve him and keep him alive
> And he shall be blessed upon the earth.
> The Lord will strengthen him upon the bed of languishing
> Thou wilt make all his bed in his sickness.
> And when I am in health thou upholdest me
> And shall set me before Thy face forever.
> The blessing of him that was ready to perish came upon
>   me
> And I caused the widow's heart to sing for joy.
> I was eyes to the blind and feet was I to the lame
> I was a father to the poor.
> Blessed be the Lord, God of Israel, from everlasting to
>   everlasting.
> Hallelujah, Hallelujah, Hallelujah.[38]

Boyce's splendid anthem was to be performed again and finally for Mercer's benefit on 12 December 1745 at St Michan's Church. Later it may have lost identity through confusion with the same composer's 'Blessed is he that considereth the poor', or have been overshadowed by the availability of Handel's great work. Whatever the cause it sank into oblivion until triumphantly restored in a performance before a delighted audience in the Royal College of Physicians of Ireland on 14 November 1990.

Early in January 1742 the governors made successful representations to ensure that the choirs of both cathedrals would combine in the hospital's interest for performances of the Philharmonic Society. The Dean and Chapter of St Patrick's agreed to co-operate on the understanding that the authorities at Christchurch

> will concur with them in permitting the Choir to assist at Mr.
> Handel's. They think that every argument in favour of the
> one, may be urged with equal strength, particularly that

which with them is of the greatest weight the advantage of
Mercer's Hospital, Mr. Handel having offer'd and being still
ready in return for such a favour to give the Governors some
of his choisest Musick, and to direct and assist at the
Performance of it for the benefit of the Hospital, which will in
one night raise a Considerable Sum for their use, without
lessening the Annual Contribution of the Philharmonick
Society or any of their other funds ...[39]

The hospital minutes confirmed this agreement on 27 January
1742 but behind the scenes Jonathan Swift, the irascible Dean of
St Patrick's, indignantly denied that he had given licence 'to
certain vicars to assist a club of fiddlers in Fishamble Street ...'
Swift forbade his subordinates 'to appear there, as songsters,
fiddlers, pipes, trumpeters, drummers, drum-majors, or in any
sonal quality ...'[40]

A change of mood, or perhaps Dr Wynne's tactful interference,
resolved the *contretemps*. The cathedral choirs continued to offer
their charitable services together and when Mr Putland reported
on 4 March 1742 from a committee 'appointed to consider of a
Performance design'd for the Benefit of this Hospital, the Infirmary
and the Prisoners of the Marshalseas', he requested that a
deputation should seek the participation of the combined choirs.

Handel's series of concerts were fully subscribed but when Mrs
Cibber was taken ill early in March a performance of *Hymen*
arranged for March 10th was postponed for a week and as the
diva's recovery was delayed a further postponement until March
24th was necessary. By then the great event of Handel's visit to
Dublin, as we now judge it, the first performance of *Messiah*, was
scheduled for April 12th in Neale's Music Hall in Fishamble
Street, and postponed at the request of 'several persons of
Distinction' until April 13th, preceded on April 9th by a public
rehearsal; in anticipation of a large attendance ladies were
requested to come without hoops, gentlemen without swords.

The enthusiastic audience of 700 on April 13th gained about
£400 for the charities, Mercer's Hospital, the Charitable Infirmary
and the prisoners of the Marshalseas, many of whom were re-
leased when their debts were paid. The band was led by Matthew
Dubourg. A critic credited Signora Avoglio with having performed
her part 'to Admiration' and Swift's friend, the Rev Dr Delany, was
so moved by Susannah Cibber's singing of 'He was despised' that

he was heard to say, 'Woman, for this thy sins be forgiven thee.'

The second performance of *Messiah* took place 'At the Particular Desire of several of the Nobility and Gentry' on 3 June 1742 at the same venue, again preceded by a public rehearsal. Because of the warm weather a pane of glass was removed from each of the Music Hall's windows 'to keep the Room as cool as possible ...' This was not a charity performance and tickets were sold at Handel's lodging in Abbey Street.

Handel sailed from Ireland on August 13th and never managed to return to what he called 'that generous and polite Nation'. During his stay he established 'the utmost degree of friendship and familiarity' with many noble families. His pleasant magnanimity as a successful artist enabled him to infer that he would gladly set aside all his fame for the joy of creating a melody as lovely as the Irish air 'Aileen Aroon'.[41]

Earlier in 1742, the governors asked the Rev Archdeacon Congreve to approach the Lord Primate with the request 'that if his Grace judgeth it not improper he'd apply to the Lord Lieutenant to remove the suspension imposed on Mr. Benjamin Johnson and to permit him to return to the Philharmonic Society.'[42] But in July 1742 Ben Johnson remained suspended from the band.

Two minor characters included in Brian Boydell's *Dublin Musical Calendar* deserve to be mentioned: Mr Cross 'copied music and "put it in order" for the annual benefit for Mercer's Hospital on 4 December 1755';[43] on the same occasion 'Crazy Crow' was paid a guinea for his work as porter to the musicians. 'Crazy Crow' (his actual name was George Hendrick) was a 'resurrectionist'. On his committal to Newgate for stealing bodies from graves in St Andrew's Churchyard in 1743 *Faulkner's Dublin Journal* had recalled that it was only a few years 'since one Johnny Bowwow was transported for the like villainy.'[44]

The governors made preliminary arrangements in November 1744 for a performance of Handel's *Grand Te Deum*, composed on the victory at Dettingen. This took place in St Michan's Church in the following February. Four years later, on 5 April 1749, the governors agreed to lend the Dean and Chapter of Christchurch Cathedral 'the Scores and Parts both Vocal and Instrumental of Mr. Handel's Te Deum Jubilate, and one Coronation Anthem to be performed before the government in their Cathedral on the 25th of this Instant April, being the Thanksgiving day for ye Peace'.[45]

Handel died on 20 April 1759. His association with Mercer's is recalled in James Joyce's *Ulysses*, when Leopold Bloom, on 16 June 1904, sees in Molesworth Street an advertisement for the Mirus Bazaar, 'in aid of funds for Mercer's Hospital. The Messiah was first given for that. Yes Handel. What about going out there. Ballsbridge'. Jenny Lind, 'the Swedish nightingale', was the chief attraction in an oratorio performed in Dublin in 1859, the centenary of Handel's death, and she visited Mercer's which shared the proceeds of the concert with the Charitable Musical Society for the Relief of Distressed Musicians.

Such were the highlights of Mercer's connection with music; lesser events include performances of T.R.G. Joze's two-act opera, 'Les Amourettes', in 1885 and concerts organised by Barton M'Gucken.

THE DAILY TASKS

What happened day by day within the walls of Mercer's? The febrile events and naked courage of such a place are largely irrecoverable but perusal of the minute-books enables the assembly of a mosaic going a little way to answer that intriguing question.[46] We soon learn that comforts nowadays demanded were undreamed of in the eighteenth century when it was required of the house-keeper that she have 'no Followers or Husband', be able to read and write and expected 'to see that the beds are filled with fresh straw every 2 months' and that each bed be provided with clean sheets every month or oftener if necessary. Frugality obtained and so as to reduce the risk of waste or dishonesty it was ordered in 1736 'That all Groceries and Spirituous Liquors be kept for the future by the Apothecary and Dispens'd as Medicaments.'

Dr Stephens issued regulations for the servants. The apothecary, steward and clerk were each allowed a pound of beef, a pound of bread and a quart of small beer daily. The apothecary, who was paid a yearly salary of £10 (to which a £5 bonus was generally added) lived in the hospital, supervised the nurses — 'to see that the Nurses doe their Duty in due Attendance upon the Sick' — dispensed medicines, and took charge of 'any Extraordinary Accident or any person's being brought in upon sudden Emergency such as Fractures, Dislocations, or the like' giving notice to 'The Surgeon in Waiting' of such accident. He was to give the clerk a daily list of patients and their diet.

The clerk was responsible for the quality and quantity of the supplies, keeping accounts, attending to storage and required 'to look very carefully that the Cook and Nurses deal faithfully in delivering the full allowances to each patient', attending at meal-times for that purpose. He was to avoid waste and ensure 'that no strong drink be brought into the House upon any pretence what-soever.'

The nurses were to keep their wards clean and sweet 'and to wash such cloaths, Bandages, Linnen and Bedding as you shall be directed from time to time by the Clerk and apothecary'. They were to give constant attention to the sick and attend the fluxing rooms in turn. 'You are not to suffer any patient to have a lighted candle within their Bed & you are to take a Special care of your fire and Candle that no damage come thereby.'

Mrs Elizabeth White, the housekeeper (the 'Matron' of more recent times) was paid £8 per annum. She, too, kept a close eye on the nurses who were to return to her 'the foul sheets ... for the Number of Clean sheets deliver'd.' She supervised their care of 'the Sick and Maimed' so as to keep them clean 'from vomiting etc' and to see that the pots were emptied every morning. The nurses, as we have seen, washed the bandages 'and other cloaths made use of to each patient' having them dry and ready by the time of the surgeons' arrival. The nurses must not leave the hospital without the housekeeper's permission. They were to have the patients in bed by nine pm and after the doors were locked at ten the keys were given to Mrs White. A certain Nurse Belton was dismissed per-emptorily in 1737 for acting contrary to the surgeons' directions. Nurse Humphreys was granted bail when accused of stealing coal.

Many complaints, which he denied, were levelled against the clerk, Robert Donnelly in 1738, leading to his resignation in August and his replacement by Isaac Steell who gave excellent service for many years. Donnelly compounded his faults by absconding without settling his account. Mrs White, as we have seen, was replaced by Mrs Jane Dover whose successors in due course included Mrs Freeman (1757), Mrs Boyd and Mrs Ann Fisher (1770). Porters were paid £3 10s per annum and supplied with blue surtouts.

The hard winter of 1739 necessitated a readjustment of the price of meat. The butcher was allowed 2$\frac{1}{2}$d per pound for the early months, fulfilling his bargain for the rest of the year.

Candle flames presented a constant risk and it was decreed in March 1741 that in the future no straw should be kept within the hospital. The housekeeper's purchase of 250 yards of linen caused comment but the purchase of four lancets required no more than a modest outlay.

'Ordered That a Shour be made to carry off the filth from the necessary Houses of the House ...' 1 September 1759.

'That the House be whitewashed and that the outside of the Windows in the front and rear and also the Iron Rails be painted, together with the Doors Window shuts and Chimney Piece in the Hall and Board Room.' 2 May 1767

'Resolved that from the 25th Day of June last the Wages of the Nursekeepers and Porters be raised from Three Pound ten Shillings to four pounds yearly — at the Recommendation of the Physician and Surgeon then present.' 6 July 1771

The comparatively sordid conditions in the hospital were a stimulus rather than a deterrent to the socially-conscious governors who constantly cultivated the aristocracy whose example prompted others to become contributors. Lord Mountjoy, Lord Tullamore and other noblemen were called upon to thank the Lord Justices for attending the musical performances.

A thousand tickets were printed for a play staged for the hospital's benefit in the Aungier Street Playhouse in 1736. At his death in the following year, Mr Robert Adair left the hospital £30; Marmaduke Coghill left £100. 'Dr Anderson paid Mr Steell Five Pounds from a Lady unknown, and Dean Hutchinson paid Mr Steell one guinea from a Person unknown.' Large sums were received from time to time but legacies sometimes required legal pressure to gain settlement. 'Agreed, That eight Guineas & one Moydore be given to Mr Ennis to fee Lawyers for the hearing against Mr Powels Executors.' A decree for £500 was granted. A Mrs Phipps left three houses in Back Lane and Nicholas Street for the equal benefit of the hospital and the Incorporated Society for the Promoting of English Protestant Schools in Ireland.

The Rev Mr Darby, Mr Hussey and Mr Howard came from the Charitable Infirmary on the Inns Quay on 3 September 1748 to say 'that several Hospitals intended to have a lottery' in 1749 and that 'the Governors of Mercer's Hospital may join in such a Lottery if they think proper.'

A favourable balance of £2,380 1s 10½d was reported on 24 June 1751. Money on hand was sometimes lent at 2½ or 3 per cent taking debentures or bankers' notes as security. Donations were occasionally made to such charities as the Society for the Support of decay'd Musicians.

Investments in ground rents augmented the hospital's income. The lease of 'a Concern in Great Britain Street' was bequeathed by a Mr Philip Ramsey. Lands in County Kildare known as Mason's Farm were purchased in 1758 and the board also expressed an interest in acquiring lands in County Longford and bought a tenement in Red Cow Lane.

Mrs Frances Ussher was requested to visit Mercer's Hospital in January 1768 and to report on 'the Oeconomy and Management of the House.'

THE EARLY SURGEONS
The impressively-named Hannibal Hall and many of his immediate medical and surgical colleagues rest securely in the impenetrable past and nothing is known of them save their regular attendance at Mercer's Hospital in their professional capacity and as governors. But George Daunt — 'Dauntless Daunt', the inventor of a lithotome — can be clothed with the identity bestowed on him by Gilborne's *Medical Review*:

> Undaunted Daunt in Rank is foremost still,
> His Operations nice our Annals fill;
> His well-contriv'd discoveries, of Note
> Improve the Art and Mankind's Good promote.

Born in August 1730, Gustavus Hume was thirty when he joined the staff as surgeon. He was then living in Longford Street and had a large practice displaying special attention to the treatment of sick children. He was also an ambitious builder responsible for erecting Ely Place and Hume Street. His dual interests merited Gilborne's eulogy:

> Gustavus Hume in Surgery excells
> Yet Pride of Merit ne'er his Bosom swells;
> He adds to Dublin, ev'ry year, a Street,
> Where Citizens converse and friendly meet.

The Act for Erecting and Establishing Public Infirmaries (1766) decreed that candidates for posts in County Hospitals should be examined and certified by a competent board of surgeons comprised of the Surgeon-General and the surgeons to Dr Steevens' and Mercer's Hospitals. The first meeting of this board was held in the

Music Hall, Fishamble Street, on 1 August 1766. Surgeon-General Nicholls was in the chair and Messers Daunt, Gibbons, Hume, Shrewbridge and Wittingham attended from Mercer's. Subsequent meetings were held in Mercer's board-room and were followed by a convivial dinner.

It was in Mercer's that Sylvester O'Halloran of Limerick and three other candidates were examined on 2 September 1766 and awarded their certificates. Mr Samuel Croker, destined to be the first president of the Royal College of Surgeons in Ireland was secretary to the examiners.

They continued to perform their task dutifully and found themselves 'obliged to hold regular and frequent Meetings, which, as Men of Profession, has greatly interfered with their Business, and made them great Sufferers by Loss of Time.' They petitioned parliament 'to order such Recompence to them, as in your great Wisdom shall seem meet.' [47]

A hundred and eight candidates were examined between September 1766 and March 1796. There were nineteen rejections, the commonest fault being inadequate apprenticeship. Percival Banks of County Clare presented himself in Mercer's on 6 June 1789 but was rejected for lack of indentures. Appearing again two days later he was again rejected as he had not been apprenticed to a 'regular bred surgeon'.

Henry Morris who, as we have seen, joined the staff at Mercer's in 1760 was president of the Dublin Society of Surgeons founded in 1780.

EIGHTEENTH CENTURY MEDICINE
How did William Stephens approach his professional tasks as he rode out to do his rounds and visit the hospitals? This is impossible to say. He did not, to be sure, carry the clinical thermometer or stethoscope that are among medicine's more recent symbols and beyond sharing with his present-day colleagues the anatomical verities of, say, Andreas Vesalius, and the revelations of William Harvey's treatise on the circulation of the blood, *De Motu Cordis* (1628), his concepts of health and disease must have differed totally from ours.

With commendable clarity of mind, Greek physicians had rejected the belief that diseases were the malign gift of angry gods and held that they had rational causes. The theories of the elements (fire, air, earth and water) and the four humours (blood, black bile, phlegm, yellow bile) provided an acceptable way of accounting for illness and was intelligible to Shakespeare who makes Ajax threaten, 'I'll let his humours blood.' We still use the words sanguine, melancholic, phlegmatic and choleric, useful fragments of discarded ideas but Paracelsus (1491–1541) burned the books of Galen and Avicenna publicly. He postulated an *archeus* which had a far-reaching influence and regarded matter as composed of three elements, 'salt', 'sulphur', and 'mercury'.

The presiding scientific genius of the earlier part of William Stephens' life was Isaac Newton (1642–1727). We do not know if Stephens read the *Principia Mathematica* but he would certainly have been directed towards Newton's thought by Herman Boerhaave (1668–1739). Stephens was fortunate in having known Boerhaave when the latter enjoyed the full vigour of his powers, an Olympian figure who taught medicine, botany and chemistry attracting many foreign students to Leyden.[48]

An eclectic, Boerhaave revered Hippocrates and took what he needed of his and later philosophies, espousing too the tenets of the iatro-mechanists, influenced by Descartes in this direction. Deeply Christian in his beliefs and behaviour he sometimes spoke of the body as a *machina nervosa*. He saw man as 'composed of a Body and *Mind, united* to each other; that the Nature of these are very different, and that therefore, each has a *Life, Actions* and Affections differing from the other; yet that there is such a reciprocal Connection and Consent between the particular Thoughts and Affections of the Mind and the Body, that a Change in one always produces a Change in the other, and the reverse.'[49]

The body, as Boerhaave saw it, has solid and fluid parts. The former 'are either membranous Pipes, or Vessels including the Fluids, or else *Instruments* made up of these, and more solid Fibres, so formed and connected, that each of them is capable of performing a particular Action by the Structure, whenever they shall be put in Motion; we find some of them resemble *Pillars, Props, Cross-Beams, Fences, Coverings,* some like *Axes, Wedges, Levers,* and *Pullies*; others like *Cords, Presses,* or *Bellows*; and others again like *Sieves, Strainers, Pipes, Conduits,* and *Receivers* ...' The body, then, is subject to mechanical laws attention to which should direct therapy.[50]

William Stephens, Boerhaave's pupil, is unlikely to have questioned the teachings of the master. The concepts of disease that directed him as he put gouty patients in Mercer's on a milk diet would have been those taught to him in Leyden. He emulated Boerhaave in the breadth of his scientific interests being the author of *Botanical Elements for the use of the Botany School in the University of Dublin* (1727) and from 1732 lecturer in chemistry. As already mentioned, he was one of a group which on 25 June 1731 assembled in the Philosophical Rooms in TCD and agreed to form the 'Dublin Society for improving Husbandry, Manufactures and other Useful Arts'. He took the chair on that occasion and on 4 December 1731 he and Thomas Prior were elected Secretaries for Home and Foreign affairs respectively.[51] Stephens' communications to the Society included a 'dissertation on Dyeing and the several materials made use of in dyeing' and a lecture on bees.[52]

He may have belonged to the complacent majority which in every age readily accepts the 'truths' enunciated by contemporary authorities. His little book on botany has been dismissed as lacking originality or critical faculty[53] but evidently he was not deaf to the pleas of others keen to search for new knowledge and when approached by Samuel Clossy he did what he could to help him.

Clossy who was born in Suffolk Street, Dublin, c 1724, obtained the MB degree in 1751. Most of the patients described in his *Observations on some of the Diseases of the Parts of the Human Body* (1763) were seen by him and submitted to autopsy either at Dr Steevens' Hospital or St George's Hospital, London, but it seems likely that his first allegiance was to Mercer's, so convenient to his home and with two of his teachers at Trinity College (Stephens in chemistry and George Whittingham in anatomy) able to sponsor him.[54]. Its closure for rebuilding was being contemplated when he commenced his research project and this would explain why Stephens 'invited' him to avail of the facilities offered by Dr Steevens' Hospital where he may have overstepped himself leading to the governors' resolution on 29 April 1756:

> Ordered that no dead body what so ever be opened or dissected in the Hospital but by special direction of the Visiting Physician and the Visiting Surgeon, and who so ever shall offend against this order be not permitted to attend or visit in the said Hospital, and be further prosecuted according to the law, and this order to be hung up in the surgery.[55]

Be that as it may, Clossy's communication to the Dublin Medical and Philosophical Society concerned 'a very neat man about forty' admitted to Mercer's in October 1761 and having been appointed officially to the staff in 1762 he was able to add the case of poor 'Elinor Proudfort, about twenty' to his monograph:

> ... she had an acute pain in her Hip, which propagated itself down the Thigh and Leg, even to the Ancle: we bled, purged, blistered, and applied the plaster in common use of Burgundy pitch and turpentine, with an eighth of euphorbium, to little purpose: In the beginning of October a large circumscribed swelling appeared in the Illiac region, which insensibly diffused itself toward the Spine, and the foregoing symptoms increased, even to a loss of the Limb, with a suppression of the intestinal and urinal Excretions. In November she left the Hospital for fear of being dissected.[56]

Clossy stands out from his colleagues at Mercer's as the prototype of the clinical scientist, less concerned, perhaps, with the fates of individuals than with general laws that he hoped to draw from their illnesses and thereby provide cures for wider application. His book was one of the earliest works on pathology in the English language. The classic in this *genre*, G. Morgani's *De Sedibus et Causis Morborum*, had appeared in 1761 but Clossy did not obtain a copy until he was settled in America.

On reaching New York in September 1763 he found that his friends were 'partly out of Favour' (one of them was posted 'to the wild Detroit') and realised that to succeed he 'must do something more than common'. He hired a disused store-house and began a lecture course on November 25th which he described in a letter to his friend George Cleghorn in Dublin:

> I procured first a female who had died of inflammation of the bowels, (a disorder very common in this country,) and began (because I had no bones to begin regularly) with the muscles of the lower belly, and in succession went through the contents of this cavity; the contents, then of the chest; and ended my first part with the encephalon and its membranes, explaining every evening the structure as fibrous, vascular, and nervous, and every succeeding evening their uses, motions, and diseases. Part the second, began with a black female, on which I went quite through the muscles, except those of the

uvula, which I could not find, partly from want of due experience, and partly from the foetor of the subject. Part the third, I could not complete, for want of a young subject, (for by this time myself and myrmidons were so known in the place, that we could not venture to meddle with a white subject, and a black or Mulatto I could not procure,) so that I ended in forty-four nights, speaking as freely as if I had been a lecturer for years.[57]

Later he dissected a black slave 'for the sake of the skeleton: he belonged to a friend of mine, and died of gripes and a jaundice.' Clossy noted that this negro was circumcised: '— a custom (as I am informed) of the natives of Angola.'

He was appointed tutor at King's College, New York, on 24 October 1765 with a salary of £144 and was to be allowed an additional £36 as professor of natural philosophy. When New York's first medical school was opened at King's College in 1767 Clossy was its professor of anatomy.[58]

His career was disrupted by the American Revolution, ill-health and a tendency 'to worship the Rosy God.' He sailed for England in November 1780 still retained by the military as a hospital mate, a post far below his capacity. His request, as a Loyalist, for compensation was disallowed as he was on the army payroll. When granted an annual pension of £80 in 1784 he returned to Dublin but died at his home in Suffolk Street on 22 August 1786.

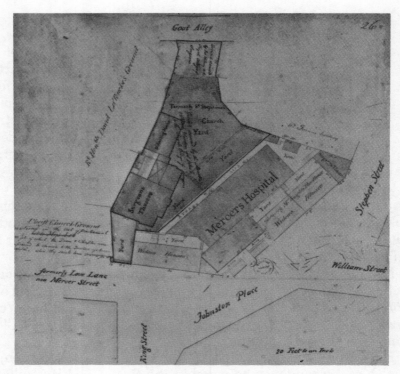

10.   *Plan of the RCSI's original premises to the rear of the hospital.*

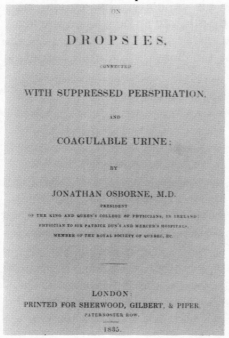

11.   *Title-page, 1835.*

12.　*Francis L'Estrange, Philip Bevan, Edward Ledwich.*

Chapter Two

1784–1834

CORRIDORS OF POWER

Mercer's is mentioned in *As I was Going down Sackville Street* by Oliver St John Gogarty, FRCSI. He would have seen it daily from his house in Ely Place — 'West against the sunset the roofs of Mercer's shone' — and explained in a letter to a Boston friend, Horace Reynolds[1] that the title of his book was taken from a ballad 'which Joyce found and rescued from oblivion and obloquy in "Faithful Place" ':

> As I was going down Sackville Street
> Hey, Ho me Randy O!
> Three bloody fine whores did I chance to meet
> With me gallopin', rearin' Randy O!

The predictable outcome of this encounter was a venereal infection:

> Then off to Mercer's I did go
> Hey, Ho me Randy O!

Elsewhere, Gogarty refers to 'Mercer's Hospital, contemporary with the time the floundering Faculty cut off the penis for Phagedena' but it was an awareness of their floundering that motivated the members of the Dublin Society of Surgeons to seek a Charter for a College of Surgeons.

When they achieved their object in 1784, Mercer's was fifty years old. The modest building which they acquired for their headquarters was situated in Mercer Street, so close to the hospital that when the College wished to expand, the governors were up in arms. Before giving details of this squabble, it is appropriate to record that the surgeons who obtained the charter included four from Mercer's — Daunt, Hume and Morris were three of the College's first six censors and in due course fourteen of the hospital's surgeons were to hold presidential office.

The Schools of Surgery in Mercer Street were opened towards the end of 1789 and the first meeting of the President and his colleagues in their own premises took place on 4 January 1790. The two storey building had a dissecting room and offices on the ground floor, a theatre, museum and preparation room on the upper. Within a few years the space was inadequate but a decision to build a larger dissecting room was resisted by the hospital.

The governors resolved on 17 October 1785 that their law agent should 'forthwith Lay a State of our Title to the Back Ground of Mercer's Hospital before Councillor Crofton whose opinion is to direct how to prevent Encroachments making by the College of Surgeons who are erecting a Building on said ground'.[2] Insufficient governors attended on 2 January 1796 to constitute a quorum but a week later it was ordered that their lawyer should follow counsel's instructions 'in conducting the suit to be Commenced against the College of Surgeons for encroaching upon the premises belonging to this Hospital'.

To deal with this perplexing situation, the College instructed its Court of Examiners to meet the governors 'relative to ascertaining the right of the Ground at the rear of the Hospital ...'[3] One of the censors, Francis McEvoy, reported to the College on 1 February 1796 that the governors had declined an offer of arbitration until they had taken 'the opinion of Counsel learned in the Law on that subject.' The governors at their meeting on 6 February 1796, were concerned in case further parley with College representatives might in some way 'Prejudice the Rights of the Hospital' and sought counsel's opinion.

This dispute was settled without litigation. The College extended the dissecting-room and in 1804 began to plan a move to a more commodious site on St Stephen's Green. The Committee appointed to supervise the new building and the disposal of the old premises recommended, in May 1809, that 'the College should offer to the Governors of Mercer's Hospital a portion of the Ground lying between Goat Alley (Digges Lane) and Mercer's Hospital which the College hold at a yearly rent of £3. 10 and for which they paid 100 guineas and should surrender to them a Building erected by the College on the Ground at the rear of Mercer's Hospital and contiguous to the aforesaid Holding in Goat Alley on the following conditions: That the Governors shall undertake to pay the rent of £3. 10 and shall join the College as equal sharers in the expense of separating their respective possessions by a sufficient Wall.'

The governors replied that the acquisition of 'the mere passage in Goat Alley' would be of little importance. They stressed how useful 'an established Chirurgical Hospital' could be for the College and suggested that 'the body of Chirurgeons should consider themselves naturally Guardians and individually promote the interests of such institutions, for these reasons and from the proposal of a highly and celebrated Member of the Royal College of Surgeons the Governors were led to hope that on the occupation of their new College the Chirurgeons intended to assist their Charitable Institution by a donation of the old College on the terms they hold it ...'.

At this stage the old quarrel erupted. A Member of the College, who was also a governor of Mercer's, maintained that the disputed ground belonged to the hospital and that 'the erection of a building thereon in the year 1796 and the quiet possession of the same were the result of a friendly acquiescence on the part of the Governors of Mercer's Hospital ...'. This prompted an enquiry by the College Committee and John Armstrong Garnett reported that the Committee possessed the deeds of conveyance of the College's holdings in Mercer Street and Digges Court; the boundaries in question were accurately described and showed 'that all the ground which has been occupied by the College since the year 1789 is their property, having been conveyed to them by Mr. Patrick Byrne in the year 1789 — who derived his Title from the Minister and Church Wardens of St. Peter's Parish'.

After a meeting between representatives of the two institutions, it was agreed that the lawyers of both parties should place the details of their respective claims 'relative to the Ground at the rear of the Theatre in Mercer Street' before counsel for his opinion. A further meeting of the committees was to be held in November 1810 but Abraham Colles informed the College that the Mercer's representatives failed to turn up. This apparent discourtesy actually resulted from a misunderstanding — the governors had dissolved their committee and formed another composed of Dr Hill, Charles Mulvany, Sir Henry Jebb, Robert Read and F. Collins but on the day of the meeting no effective committee existed.

The indignant College representatives felt that it was now

'expedient for the College of Surgeons to advertize their Holding in Mercer Street for sale' but wiser heads prevailed and insisted that the College should endeavour to settle the matter amicably. The president, John Armstrong Garnett, and Mr Colles were empowered to meet two representatives from Mercer's 'to decide on the sum of money to be paid by the Governors of Mercer's Hospital for the whole of the premises'. The College was pledged to abide by their decision and the governors agreed to do likewise.

Abraham Colles, on 4 February 1811, reported an agreement to sell the property for £300. The lawyers agreed to the following terms: 'That the Deed of the Premises to which the College can shew a good Title be executed forthwith in consideration of £200. The remaining one Hundred of the purchase money to be at the same time paid down to the College on their Receipt for it; and promising therein to execute a Deed for the other premises when tendered to them for that purpose by the Hospital.'

The College did not immediately leave Mercer Street. Not until January 1812 did Charles Hawkes Todd, the assistant secretary, arrange to transfer the books from the theatre and place them in the new library. On 4 January 1812, the hospital's treasurer produced the College's deed of assignment for the holding in Mercer Street and was authorised to pay £200. The late J.D.H. Widdess[4] was of the opinion that Mercer's never paid the remaining hundred pounds but it may well be that the College failed to produce sufficient evidence of title for the ground in Goat Alley to allow them to demand it.

Meanwhile, the feasibility of announcing another academic alliance was being explored. The 'Act for Establishing a Complete School of Physic' (1785), which had followed an investigation by the College of Physicians and Trinity College, recognised the importance of clinical lectures and directed that they should be given 'in the hospital or hospitals in the city of Dublin as shall be found most convenient for that purpose'. Mercer's was deemed to be more suitable than the Hospital for the Incurables, 'there being nothing there except bare walls'. The governors of Mercer's, when approached by representatives of the College of Physicians and Trinity College in 1786, agreed to set beds aside for clinical teaching but this arrangement fell through because a member of the staff, Dr Francis Hopkins, who had applied unsuccessfully for a post as King's professor, failed to co-operate.[5]

The College, instead, fitted up a house in Clarendon Street as a hospital but this was too costly and was closed after a few years. A house on Blind Quay (now Wellington Quay) was styled Sir Patrick Dun's Hospital in 1793 but it failed in 1798 and a new arrangement was arrived at with Mercer's which, from 1 January 1799, nominated thirty beds for teaching purposes.

Dublin's first professorial unit was short-lived. The irreconcilable viewpoints of Dr Edward Hill, professor of physic and physician to Mercer's, who favoured using available funds of Sir Patrick Dun's estate to purchase a botanical garden, and Dr Robert Perceval, professor of chemistry, who wished to build a new hospital, contributed to its failure but the records of Mercer's for 17 April 1800 show that there were additional reasons.

'Whereas a misunderstanding has arisen between the Surgeons of this House and the Professors of Sir Patrick Dun's Clynical Wards, Resolved that from this day no more patients shall be received into this hospital as Sir Patrick Dun's Wards, that these now here shall be attended to until Recovered or Discharged, and that no further communication between this hospital, and Sir Patrick Dun's shall exist'.[6]

Less than two months later, there was a change of mind and the governors considered the mutual advantages of maintaining a connection 'between this hospital and Sir Patrick Dun's Institution' and declared, 'That it is the opinion of this board that in such a junction there may be established one of the Compleatest schools in Europe for Physick, and surgery, that by erecting an additional Building to Mercer's Hospital there would be a saving of at least Cent per Cent to Sir Patrick Dun's Institution in providing an hospital for themselves ...'.

Certain irregularities of practice were to be avoided and 'the Surgeons of this Hospital shall be exclusively called on whenever surgical aid shall be wanted in Sir Patrick Dun's Wards'.

Eventually, however, Perceval's determination won the day and, through the School of Physic Act, the last act but one of the Irish Legislature, he arranged that the bulk of the income of Sir Patrick Dun's estate should be applied to the support of a hospital for clinical lectures. This, the present Sir Patrick Dun's Hospital, was opened in 1808. As late as the previous November, the College of Physicians was given the loan of two wards in Mercer's which it promised to support.

The conflicts in Mercer Street had rumbled on against the

distant background of the Napoleonic wars in which the
grande armée was accompanied by Dominique-Jean Larrey, its
surgeon-in-chief. Baron Larrey visited Dublin in 1826 and was
taken to the Foundlings' Hospital, the Fever Hospital and Dr
Steevens' Hospital, where he and Colles disagreed on a number
of points, though without acrimony, for neither could speak the
other's language.

Larrey then went on to the College of Surgeons and spent about
an hour in the library before examining the specimens in what
Erinensis, the *Lancet*'s waspish Irish correspondent, called 'that
sepulchre of useless curiosities, the Museum', which usually was
kept locked. 'What his reflections must have been', Erinensis
asked, 'at hearing the key revolve in the ever-closed door of this
Tartarus of morbid anatomy, I must leave the corporate Cerberus
which guards it to conjecture — well might he have said on passing
its gloomy threshold, "they order these things better in France".'[7]

The visitor proceeded to Mercer's where he demonstrated his
mode of cupping, which had the merit of being extremely simple.
Larrey first marked out the place of the operation by burning tow
under a glass; then, taking an instrument out of his pocket
resembling a horse phleme, he scarified the part within the circle,
with a lightness of touch and velocity of movement that indicated great manual dexterity. The blood, however, did not come
freely on the re-application of the ignited tow and receiver, and he
observed that the subject of the experiment was 'too fat'.

Larrey also favoured the use of moxa for a case of ascites in
Mercer's which led Erinensis to comment that it appeared that
moxa 'is one of his favourite remedies, though it has been almost
entirely abandoned in Ireland'. It may have been in Mercer's that
Larrey saw a case which he recalled later: 'In one of the hospitals
in the centre of the town we saw a number of individuals who
had been wounded in the risings which their state of misery
had provoked. One of these, a young man of seventeen, had a
remarkable head wound from a dragoon's sabre, which is a sort
of damascene blade like a Mameluke's. A heavy oblique blow on
the right side of the head had shorn through part of the parietal
bone and its coverings over an area of about six by eight centi-
metres'. The resulting depressed fracture was compressing the
dura mater and brain but free drainage was effected through the
upper part of the wound.

Larrey believed that it was too late to use the trephine. 'I recom-

mended my honourable colleague in charge of the surgical side
of the hospital to leave the case to nature ...'. The sequestrum or
piece of dead bone could be easily extracted when it became loose.
This prediction, Larrey subsequently learned from an Irish student who came to Paris, was accurately fulfilled, enabling removal
of the bone with the patient's recovery.[8]

THE PRESIDENTS
The surgeons who served the College of Surgeons as presidents
in its early phase were Gustavus Hume, Francis L'Estrange,
senior, Sir Henry Jebb, Gerard Macklin, Samuel Wilmot, Alexander Read and William Auchinleck. Hume was censor at the first
meeting of the College which was held in the board-room of the
Rotunda Hospital on 2 March 1734. He was State Surgeon from
1791 to 1806 and filled the office of president of the College from
January 1795 to May 4th, his early resignation possibly related
to involvement in a law case taken against the College by Mr
Frederick Drury who sued for reinstatement as a member having
been expelled for giving false and corrupt evidence in court.

Hume's partiality for oat-meal porridge as a nostrum led to his
being dubbed 'Stirabout Gusty' in a doggerel popular early in the
nineteenth century:

> 'H-me, twice as old as the College Charter
> Scours death with Stir-a-bout from every quarter.'[9]

His *Observations on the Origin and Treatment of Internal and
External Diseases, and Management of Treatment* was published
in Dublin in 1802; *Observations on the Angina Pectoris, Gout and
Cow-Pox* followed two years later. He favoured breast-feeding
not only because 'the mother's suck is certainly the most proper
nourishment' but for its additional advantages:

> When the upper classes of women undertake suckling, they
> become more domestic, consequently less likely to enter into
> the incorrectness of the present age, finding themselves more
> closely attached to both husband and infant: besides after the
> period of weaning, the constitution experiences all the
> sensations of a new marriage. And they who nurse seldom
> miscarry.[10]

Hume uses the term 'acrimony' to denote 'that state of the solids and fluids produced by constitutional defect, existing either from inheritance or early acquired, principally giving rise to, or in some degree connected with most of the diseases which I shall here after treat of.'

The operation of trepanning after head-injury was one which required the most careful consideration and Hume pointed out correctly that depressed fractures and extravasations between the skull and membranes were the principal indications for its employment. 'The State Physician of Dublin, who attended the hospital for lunatics, conceiving that lunacy was curable by trepanning, ordered the operations to be carefully performed on two patients, the one a male, the other a female: the first died on the first day, from fever, and inflammation of the dura matter, the other barely escaped, but without receiving the smallest benefit.'[11]

Fevers were the commonplace illness of the time with such attendant mysteries that for Hume 'The successful conduct of most fevers, is like the guidance of a blind man through an unexplored labyrinth, where if hurried on, or suddenly checked, the benevolent leader may unintentionally throw him down.'[12]

Hume died at his residence, 63 Dawson Street, on 7 February 1812, an event referred to in the Minute Book on March 21st:

> The Treasurer reported that he had received from Arthur Hume, Esq. in addition to his donation of Twenty Guineas, the sum of three Hundred Pounds at the request of our late highly esteemed friend Gustavus Hume Esq.

It was agreed that a new ward should be opened and 'stiled Humes Ward, as a small tribute of respect to the memory of the late Gustavus Hume Esq. who for the period of nearly sixty Years, exercised his professional skill, and gave unremitting and unwearied attention for the benefit of this Institution.' Arthur Hume was made a life governor and his permission was sought 'to permit a drawing to be taken from a Portrait in his possession of our late friend Mr Hume, in order that a print may be engraved from it.'

Francis L'Estrange (1756–1836) lived close to the hospital in William Street. He was president of the College in 1796 and had additional attachments to the House of Industry Hospitals and the Marine School. He retains a footnote in history as accoucheur at the birth of the poet, Thomas Moore, which took place in Aungier Street on 28 May 1779.[13]

Sir Henry Jebb, president in 1800, was a native of Boyle, County Roscommon, where his father, Richard Jeeb, practised as an apothecary. When the latter's two sons (Frederick was Master of the Rotunda Hospital in 1773) came to Dublin they replaced the second 'e' in their name by 'b', influenced by the current success in London of Sir Richard Jebb, MD, physician to the king.

Like his brother, Henry Jebb favoured obstetrics and it was for services in this sphere rendered at Dublin Castle that he was granted a knighthood in 1782. He lived in William Street and later in Grafton Street. He was twice married with three sons and two daughters. He died in 1911.[14]

Sir Henry Jebb rivalled his colleague, Hume, as a builder. He named a street of new houses North Frederick Street for his son. This young man joined his father in Mercer's as assistant surgeon. Then, taking a commission in the 18th Dragoons in 1809, he served in the Peninsula and at Waterloo, settling finally in Oporto where he was killed by a fall from a horse.

Gerard Macklin (1767–1848) came to Mercer's as assistant surgeon in 1796 and was later promoted to be surgeon. He lived in York Street moving with his wife and large family to Harcourt Place. He had a reputation for treatment of bladder stones and Cameron has quoted lines by the author of the *Metropolis*.

> Young (Macklin) spurns the name of modern fool,
> Antique his shoes that round the instep close,
> Antique his galligaskins, hat, and hose,
> Himself antique, all day in chariot lolling,
> Unlike those younkers that have legs for strolling;
> Yet kindliest manners grace his reputation,
> He seeks our love, and wins our estimation;
> Report allows that he's no small lithotomist,
> And in opakest cataracts suffers *not a mist*.
> But vain his garb, his grave composure vain,
> Without a reverend Busby and a Cane.[15]

Macklin was president of the College in 1806 in which year he was appointed State Surgeon. On 25 January 1815 he gave notice of motion of his proposal 'that Humes Ward be fitted with 8 Beds for the exclusive reception of Patients labouring under diseases of the Eyes.' This was a counter-proposal to Dr Hill's request that one or two wards be used for medical cases — medical patients having been excluded sometime previously as an economy measure. The matter was referred for the medical board's report and on February 25th the governors agreed to what was a rather drastic modification of Hill's demand for medical accommodation. 'Resolved — That whenever a patient in the Surgical Wards of the Hospital shall become affected with contagious Fever after his Admission so as to render his continuance among the other Patients dangerous to their safety it is highly expedient that such Patients not being a fit object for any Surgical Hospital should be removed to a separate Ward. Resolved that it be recommended to the Medical Governors for that purpose to open two Wards and transfer two beds to each.'[16]

Macklin retired from his post as surgeon in July 1830 and the governors resolved 'That the cordial thanks of this Board are due and hereby given to Mr Macklin for his unremitting and Efficient exertions to promote the Interests and support the Character of the Hospital for a period exceeding Forty years.' He continued to attend the governors' meetings and in 1831 presented his books and a valuable set of instruments and bandages to the hospital.

When Samuel Wilmot (1772–1848) announced his intention of entering the medical profession his father, a man of independent means and with an aversion to surgery, insisted that he should confine himself to medicine. He agreed to do so but after his father's death he extended his studied, becoming a Licentiate and later a Member of the College of Surgeons.

Wilmot joined the Mercer's staff in 1807; in 1826 he was elected professor of anatomy and surgery in the College of Surgeons which he served as president in 1815 and 1832. John Brennan, author of the *Milesian Magazine*, called him 'A man first in merit and modesty's scroll.' His son, Samuel George Wilmot, surgeon to Dr Steevens' Hospital, was president of the College of Surgeons in 1865.[17]

Alexander Read (1786–1870) was president in 1825 and 1835. Having been himself indentured to Sir Henry Jebb he took his teacher's youngest son as apprentice in 1822. Read was given permission by the governors to avail of 'the House in Stephen's Street commonly called the Straw-Loft' for the use of his pupils, paying an annual sum of £20 for this privilege.[18]

William Auchinleck (1787–1848), president in 1829, had been Gerard Macklin's apprentice.[19]

GOVERNORS' BUSINESS

On 5 September 1807 the governors realised that 'some Extra-ordinary Effort seems to be absolutely necessary to rescue this useful Charity from total Destitution ...' But ten days later when the treasurer reported the receipt of £500 'from Miss Daunt and Mrs Pleasants for the purpose of opening a new Ward in the Hospital for the relief of Patients ...', the situation looked brighter.

The College of Physicians, as already mentioned, sought accommodation for teaching in November 1807, requesting 'the loan of two wards which at present contain 12 beds, and are the flux Wards which the Surgeons present at a board held the 4th of November 1786 are willing to resign', for four months beginning the 1st of January. The College of Physicians undertook to support the beds placed in those wards 'at their own Expence, during the time of the loan — and they will make compensation for Every Expence which may be incurred in Consequence of the loan.'[20]

Early in January 1808, Dr Hill, Mr Hume, Sir Henry Jebb, Mr J. Rogers and Mr C. Mulvany were appointed to a house committee to meet on Mondays at 2 pm and deal with the affairs of the hospital. They soon realised 'that many and great abuses have long existed in this Charitable Foundation.' They ordered the door leading from the kitchen into Mercer Street to be kept locked and decided 'that the maintenance of a regular Table for the officers of this Hospital has been destructive of its funds, and very injurious in many respects — 'For the future the apothecary should be paid £50 per annum with lodging, coals and candle only.' Before long the use of medicines had been reduced and 'a most profuse consumption of Spirits' stopped without loss of benefit or comfort to the patients. The supply of aprons to pupils and apprentices was discontinued.

Powel's ward was to be opened for female accident cases, the same nurse to attend the two female wards, her wages increased from four pounds to six pounds. It was recommended 'to have always ready in the Hall a Bed, upon wheels or casters, upon which those that come in consequence of accidents, may be laid, and easily conveyed from thence in to the Ward ...' and onlookers should be prevented from entering the hospital. The custom of strewing sand in the galleries and wards militated against cleanliness and was to be discontinued. Coal was to be stored in some vault within the hospital to prevent waste and mismanagement.

Because of the low state of the funds an appeal was made by the governors to the Post-Master General of Ireland pointing out that many drivers, guards and attendants of the mail coaches received treatment in the hospital and requesting 'some annual Donation from the funds of the Post Office, to enable them to keep a Ward always ready for the accommodation of those, concerned with Mail Coaches, who are liable to accidents ...'

The receipt of a legacy of £1,000 bequeathed by Mrs Ann Keon with added interest of £149 7s. 7½d was acknowledged. A petition was sent to the Chancellor of the Exchequer, the Rt Hon John Foster, to be laid before parliament. It requested an annual grant of £500 stating that a debt of nearly £800 had necessitated closure of half the wards 'which occasioned the severest distress to those miserable objects who were accustomed to find ready relief in this Hospital.' The petition was returned: inadvertently it had been left unsigned and furthermore, as the Chancellor pointed out, it could not be submitted if unaccompanied by an official government recommendation.

The housekeeper, Mrs Watts, was dismissed in May 1808. Mr Leonard Parke was engaged as apothecary in February 1809 to be paid a salary of £100 if he also fulfilled the duties of the steward and housekeeper. Complaints received in February 1810 that bodies were being brought into the hospital for dissection were investigated and declared to be 'gross misrepresentations, artfully founded on circumstances themselves free of impropriety; And the falsehoods industriously propagated for malicious and sinister purposes.' A reactionary proposal that no pupils other than 'the Apprentices bound to the Medical Gentlemen of the Hospital' should receive tuition at Mercer's was rejected by the casting vote of the chairman, Sir Hugh Crofton.

The apothecary, inspired perhaps by envy of the medical students, was suspected as the originator of the damaging rumours. He left without notice in January 1811 and his accounts were found to be 'very deficient'.

On 23 February 1811 it was resolved 'That the relief afforded by this Hospital, shall in future, be confined as much as possible to surgical Cases, and that no medicines be distributed, but what are necessary to the Patients labouring under accidents, and other cases that require Surgical assistance.'

Entering a more optimistic phase, the architect was asked to value the Widows Houses on behalf of the governors and the

Archdeacon of Dublin (28 May 1814) but in 1815 the provision of an operating room was postponed until a legal dispute over house property was resolved. Planning to convert the upper rooms of the hospital into an operating area was resumed in August 1815. Subscriptions were canvassed and 'a Donation of complete Furniture for three beds for the Operation Wards' was received from Lady Hutchinson, a governor's widow, in 1816.

Fourteen years later the 'utterly inappropriate' situation of this upper-storey operating-room had been fully realised and a plan was accepted to build at ground level an operating-room with two wards adjacent. A contract was given to Mr George Patterson who undertook to complete the building by 20 October 1831 for £555 0s 0d.

The duties of the resident apothecary were reviewed in 1816 and included both professional and secretarial work. He was to send out notices of meetings to governors and committee members, to keep records, accounts and a register of patients including names, diseases, dates of admissions and discharges and by whom recommended. He was to send notices of accident cases treated to the newspapers twice a week.

The apothecary must not leave the hospital at the same time as the housekeeper; he should ensure that no disputes arose between nurses and patients and should there by such an occurrence he should report it to the attending surgeon or visiting governor. He should report from time to time on the state of the house and furniture, keeping an inventory of the latter. He was to lay before the management committee or governors at their meetings the required books and be responsible for their custody. He must co-operate with the house-keeper in seeing that the hospital's rules and regulations are observed.

The three old leaden bath-tubs were sent to the plumber and replaced by an increased number of new pewter baths. The house-keeper drew the governors' attention in 1824 to the 'want of air, order and cleanliness arising from so small and in every other respect inconvenient Kitchen, for a Public Institution not to mention the total departure from all idea of tidiness and order being occupied with a bed.' She recommended that a new laundry should be built, the existing laundry used to extend the kitchen and that a part of it should be adapted to provide a bedroom for the cook.

The management committee's plans for additional servants

and improvements in 1822 were postponed by the governors. They, the landlords, were responsible for the renewal of leases, e.g. in March 1824 the lands of Lismoy, County Longford, and concerned for the state of their properties. One of their houses in Back Lane having been deserted by a tenant was condemned by the Grand Jury as a nuisance and a ruin.

Salaries inevitably increased. From July 1826 the apothecary and the registrar were paid £75 annually, the house-keeper £50. The porter in 1828 received £7 per annum and 'is to be Clothed at the expence of the House.' A gratuity of one pound was given to Nurses Foley and Sweeney but 'in consequence of want of attention' Nurses Caffrey and Devoy wee reprimanded and given no bonus.

To expedite the provision of the ground-floor operating-room the medical board donated £100 and agreed to pay interest of five per cent out of fees from pupils on whatever sum the governors advanced from existing funds pending the accumulation of the required amount through subscriptions. The availability of the new amenity towards the end of 1831 enabled plans to be made for the utilisation of the vacated space. The medical board proposed 'admitting as in other Institutions Subscription Patients', using Daunt's ward for this purpose to accommodate men paying one guinea per month, and using the former, airy operation-room as an isolation ward. At the time the hospital had fifty beds but was capable of containing eighty and there was a pressing need for the increased number.

A peremptory letter from Dublin Castle on 14 January 1833, inspired by the Treasury, suggested that 'Monies outstanding on private Security for the benefit of Mercer's Hospital, should be called in, and invested in the Public Funds.' Having confirmed that there was no legal obligation to do so, the governors resisted the Lord Lieutenant's wishes being 'unanimously of Opinion that it would not be for the benefit of the Hospital that any change should be made in the manner in which the Funds of the Hospital are now invested.[21]

DR EDWARD HILL

Dr Edward Hill held Francis Hopkins (1752–1819) accountable for the breakdown of talks between the governors and the Trinity dons in 1786 — 'in a fit of the spleen he frustrated the negotiations.'[22] Be that as it may, Dr Hopkins, physician to Mercer's from

1786 to 1811, was more concerned with obstetrics than medicine. He was Assistant Master at the Rotunda Hospital (1789–1792) and in October 1803 was given permission to lecture on midwifery at Trinity College. During his Mastership (1807–1814) there were 18,127 deliveries in the Rotunda Hospital with 217 maternal deaths, a mortality rate of 1.1 per cent.[23]

Hopkins, a native of County Meath, lived at 83 St Stephen's Green and was six times president of the College of Physicians. Dr Hill also served the College as president on several occasions (1782, 1789, 1795, 1801, 1808, 1813) and spent his time lavishly on its administration. His survey of the estates of Sir Patrick Dun in County Waterford in 1811 was of particular benefit, or would have been had his proposals been followed. He drew up a bill for establishing a School of Physic in Dublin and sent a copy of it to Robert Peel, the Secretary of State for Ireland, in 1814. The offer of a ten guinea gratuity for his efforts to arrange and preserve the library was rejected by him in a letter characteristic of his testy temperament.

Edward Hill was born on 14 May 1741 near Ballyporeen, County Tipperary, the eldest of Thomas and Mrs Hill's seven children. He was tutored by a local clergyman until his father's early death, when the family moved close to Cashel where he attended a classical school daily until ready to go as a boarder to the Diocesan School of Clonmel.

He entered Trinity College, Dublin, in 1760, was elected scholar in 1763 and graduated BA in 1765. His intellectual brilliance was crowned by exceptional calligraphy; the task of writing out a testimonium for the Duke of Bedford was deputed to him by the Board, his reward five guineas. Instead of seeking a fellowship, a distinction thought to be well within his intellectual powers, he next turned to medicine. He took the MB in 1771, proceeded MD in 1773 and was elected a Fellow of the College of Physicians two years later.

Little is known of his medical practice but like Hume he was interested in sick children. Honours came to him swiftly, a lectureship in botany, the regius professorship of physic which he was to retain for forty-nine years, and the post of physician to Mercer's Hospital. Directly and indirectly he was involved with botany, the importance of which in medical treatment at that time cannot be over-rated. Just then, for instance, a Birmingham practitioner, Dr William Withering, having expertly selected foxglove as the active ingredient of a folk-cure, was about to introduce digitalis, a remedy still in daily use.

He was dissatisfied with the narrow strip of rat-infested ground available for him as a physic garden and went to endless trouble to improve the situation, finally, with the provost's approval, leasing a six-acre field at Harold's Cross. This venture, however, did not prosper and Hill went to law with the provost and fellows to recover his money.[24]

One presumes that although he never studied in Scotland, Hill would have favoured William Cullen's *Synopsis nosologiae methodicae* (1769) which divided diseases into fevers, neurosis, cachexias and local disorders.[25] But Hill is most interesting in his avocations: he was a prodigious bibliophile, a devoted student of John Milton's *Paradise Lost* and actively committed to printing.

Hill was given the use of the Printing House by the Board of Trinity College for five years on 12 March 1774. The period was extended and he was joined by Joseph Hill (the relationship, if any, is unknown) who in 1779 printed Anthony Vieyra's *Animadversiones Philogicae*. This was the first of a series of scholarly works printed by Joseph Hill, including the first work in Italian printed in Ireland[26] (Boiardo's *Orlando Innamorato*, 1784), but by printing tracts of a seditious nature he put the Board in an embarrassing position and Dr Hill was requested to vacate the Printing House.

Hill's library which he sold by auction in 1816, contained more than 1,800 volumes. These included eighteen incunabula and 101 books printed in the first half of the sixteenth century. The wide range covered the Greek and Latin classics, Greek testaments, Hebrew bibles, and French and Italian literature.[27]

From his youth, John Milton's writings had, as Hill put it, 'obtained a preference' in his mind. 'When chearful and devoid of care, I have resorted to them for amusement and instruction, and they have contributed often to console me in the hour of sorrow.' Having read many editions of the poetical works closely he became increasingly concerned by the number of ill-conceived alterations he noticed, particularly in *Paradise Lost*. He finally decided to republish the second edition of *Paradise Lost* printed in 1674 and embodying corrections made by Milton; to this end he collated it with several of the later editions.

He was twenty-eight when he embarked on this undertaking in which he planned to include an index to the great poem. He finished it forty-five years later in 1813. The dull task of transcribing in his fine meticulous hand a fair copy of the enormous index was completed on 29 July 1824.

The beautifully-written manuscript comprises five copy-books. These contain a prolegomena, the word-index to *Paradise Lost*, a discussion on French translation and criticism, accounts of the engraved portraits of Milton and of the plates used in the several editions.[28] He claims to have indulged in no hypothesis, to have removed nothing from the text and to have spared no labour in the endeavour to provide a standard for all future editions. He registers a plea (entailing the apotheosis of Milton) that *Paradise Lost* 'the boast and glory of the English language' merits the care the Jews and Muslims lavish on their holy books.

Hill was unable to secure a publisher for this venture. The manuscript of another of his unpublished works, *The History of Physic*, was presented to the College of Surgeons on 11 March 1843 by his nephew, Thomas Hill, a licentiate of the College. It contains 344 pages in which Hill gives an account of the medicine of antiquity up to the time of Celsus (first century BC). 'The first Man was in a certain sense ye first Physician; the Antediluvian Patriarchs invented some Arts, among which Physic has been ranked.'

'Erinensis' encountered Dr Hill at a social occasion at Mercer's where in the 1820s the octogenarian doctor retained his position as physician and governor.

> By accident he was dressed in the fashion; his coat, to the cut of which he has inviolably adhered for sixty years, presenting then as great a space between the hip buttons, as the most 'exquisite' of his neighbours. He talked of the Greek and Arabian lights of medicine, of Rhazes and Avicenna ... and on entering the room, I thought that one of the figures of Hogarth's 'Examination at Surgeon's Hall' had descended from the wall, to converse with us on the topics of his day.[29]

Hill appeared to enjoy himself and Erinensis felt it must be a consolation to the physician's juniors, with the prospect of old age still remote, 'to behold successive cargoes of everything on the board descend into the hold of an octogenarian vessel that had sailed in safety across the quicksands of all the climacterics, and whose timbers still promised to withstand the assaults of many another gale.'

Edward Hill attended his last governors' meeting on 28 August 1830; he died on 31 October 1830. Meanwhile Professor John W. Boyton who held the chair of the Institutes of Medicine and was appointed physician to Mercer's in 1812, had resigned for health reasons in 1826, dying soon afterwards. He was succeeded by Charles Lendrick who was president of the College of Physicians in 1828 and became King's Professor of the Practice of Medicine in 1832.

Realising, like others, that Ireland could not escape the ravages of the current pandemic, Lendrick lectured on Asiatic Cholera in the theatre of Mercer's Hospital on 15 December 1831. 'Gentlemen: I am aware of the difficulty attendant on giving instruction as to the nature and treatment of a disease, the precise form of which I have not witnessed ...'[30] His *Supplementary Observations on the Epidemic Cholera* was delivered in April 1832 by which time he had had ample opportunity to study the disease. It had been said of cholera 'that *it* begins where other diseases end — with death.'[31] According to the clergy it was a visitation of providence for the sins of the human race, a doctrine which Lendrick believed should not be hastily rejected. He was a man of strongly religious tempera-ment and his publications include an article on demonical possession.[32]

The first cases of cholera in Ireland in the 1832 epidemic occurred in Belfast early in March. Later in the month Dr William Stokes and Mr Lumley were sent to Kingstown (now Dun Laoghaire) to enquire into an obscure death in the port. Having completed their examination they pronounced the deceased to have died from cholera. After a momentary silence the crowd outside the house awaiting their verdict reacted violently with a torrent of verbal abuse followed by stones and mud. With difficulty the doctors entered their carriage and urged the postilion to whip up the horses. Before the year was out 18,317 cases were recorded in Dublin with 5,632 deaths.

A notice was posted on the door of Mercer's Hospital:

> This Hospital being principally Instituted for Surgical Cases, No person affected with contagious Disease, particularly with Symptoms of Cholera can, at any time be admitted. By Order.[33]

This decision was legitimate and wise; the authorities at Dr Steevens' Hospital acted similarly.[34] Most of the cholera cases were cared for in improvised hospitals or in their wretched homes and it was in the appalling circumstances of this epidemic that a new social force emerged when the nursing nuns of Mother Catherine McAuley and Mother Aikenhead accepted their mission.

> In the course of last summer, [the latter recalled in 1833], the cholera morbus broke out in the villages of Sandymount, Irishtown, Ballsbridge and Ringsend, and raged for five weeks with violence. We found some in the agonies of death, without the means even of procuring a drink; many perished without medical aid ... Excessive poverty produces a want of cleanliness which aggravates their misery. The lanes and streets are filled with filth in Ringsend and Irishtown; there are no sewers; no attention is paid to the ventilation of the houses, and the poor are obliged to buy even the water which they drink; it is of the worst description,and tends to promote disease as much by its scarcity as by its quality. The poor have no bed-clothes; we have often seen them expire on dirty straw, and are frequently obliged to furnish them with covering before we can approach to administer to their wants.[35]

Early in April, Grangegorman Penitentiary was converted into a hospital and the Sisters of Charity made their services available. A hospital for the city's south side was established at the Depot at Townsend Street and was served by sisters of the Order of Mercy.

Erinensis, to return to that acerbic critic, remarked that Mercer's 'instead of being bounded by four right angles, as most Christian dwellings are', was distorted by 'eight or ten wrong ones' to fashion a picturesque edifice indescribable in all but its more tangible peculiarities.

> First, then, there are four stories, and two fronts, one pro- truding in cut stone, the other receding to some distance behind, as if shy of its humble pebble-dashing, while four gables, I believe, tapered out into long chimneys [sic], crown the brows of this monstrous creation. Descending from these lofty outrages on taste, to others of a more lowly station, we find economy and convenience once more violated by a terrace, which renders this mansion of broken legs accessible to those persons only who possess the perfect use of their limbs. For what other purpose than as a type of the difficulty of obtain-

ing the benefits of charity, this architectural stratagem of admission was erected, I could never learn, except it might have been the intention of the builder to imitate the hall-doors on the round towers of Ireland, never less than fifteen or twenty feet from the ground, and which induced Swift to remark, in his inimitable irony, that they were built for the sole end of puzzling future antiquarians.[36]

His vignette of Alexander Read, 'the Autocrat of Mercer's', unkindly contrasts that worthy's present plight with his reputation for youthful athleticism:

> I learned with some surprise, that a man of his stoical deportment was at once time a 'first rate swell'; set the fashion to half the professional 'bloods' on town; could bound over any church-yard-wall in a case of surprise; and pommel half a dozen of 'charleys' to his own suit in a resurrection spree. But of the elastic limb, light heart, and fashionable addictions, the rheumatism and official cares have left us but the shell, if I may say so, in which these juvenile attributes once effervesced. At present a stick supports his painful steps; his manner of address, to one unacquainted with him, might seem to border on the condescension of misanthropy than the mere reserve of polite civility; and his dress might now be described as negligently elegant, if the Gordian convolutions of muslin into which his neck-cloth folds across his breast did not betray some lingering devotion to the goddess of *bon ton*.[37]

Erinensis portrays William Auchinleck's 'brows corrugated into a habitual frown. The pitted cicatrizations of his visage indicated an era in the history of beauty anterior to the discovery of Jenner, and the aristocratic inflation of his air would lead one to believe that the days of "Feudalism" had not yet expired.[38] He also sounded a note of disapproval, to be taken up by others more vociferously in the future, with the way the medical board controlled staff appointments. 'It is in this species of the elective system that we generally find fathers retiring in favour of their sons, uncles predestinating their little nephews to office before they cut their teeth; and friends "doing a kind turn" for each other, by adding another worthy neophyte, or "sound member", as Dr Harty has it, to the little confraternity of jobbers.'[39]

13.   *Richard Butcher. (Cartoon by Spex.)*

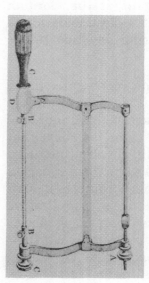

14.   *Butcher's saw.*

15.   *Sir Joseph Napier, Bart.*

16. *Address to Mr O'Grady, 1889.*

17. *Programme of the Mirus Bazaar, 1904.*

Chapter Three

1834–1884

CENTENARY

Mercer's Hospital attained its centenary on 11 August 1834. The event passed without mention in the *Governors' Book 1834–1870*, the guardians of the bethel preoccupied with such matters as the dismissal of a drunken porter. The new porter, incidentally, encountered misfortune and on 4 April 1835 the governors had before them 'The memorial of Jane Kelly Widow of the late Porter who lost his life in the service of the Hospital under peculiar circumstances ...' They allowed her a gratuity of two guineas and placed an advertisement in *Saunders Newsletter* for a successor: 'Wanted a person to act as Porter to the Hospital none need apply whose character will not bear the strictest investigation and who have not been accustomed to Act as Porter to a public Establishment.' The governors at this period included five members of the Digges La Touche family. William Tagert, surgeon, and Dr Jonathan Osborne joined the staff in 1835.

'Barrington's Act' had recently introduced a provision whereby the governors of hospitals and infirmaries could have buildings in their immediate vicinity valued to facilitate their purchase with a view to gaining space and improved ventilation. From Mercer's, acquisitive eyes were turned towards the adjoining Widows Houses which constituted 'a nuisance' the removal of which was desired.

Other matters of import during the 1830s included the Grand Jury's attempt to withhold its customary grant of £200 because the medical staff charged fees for attending inquests, and the introduction of a bill for regulating hospitals. The medical board suggested that 'a respectful remonstrance' should be sent to the Grand Jury requesting reconsideration of their resolution 'which is calculated to lower the Medical profession in public estimation by underrating their important services in forwarding the ends of public justice.'[1]

The bill for the better regulation of hospitals, dispensaries and other medical charities in Ireland proposed to place the hospitals and medical charities under the direction of four medical inspectors who would supersede the existing managements. 'Resolved, That a Petition be prepared and presented to both Houses of Parliament against said Bill ...'[2]

Hospitals, in those days, expected to balance their books and the realisation in 1838 that Mercer's 'was in Debt upwards of £300' led to an examination of 'the Accounts and affairs of the Hospital generally and the present system of Expenditure, to ascertain whether any alteration would be advisable therein.' This scrutiny revealed that an unreasonable increase of expenditure had occurred especially on 'Oil, Candles, Tow, Medicines, Stationery and Milk; that proper checks had been lacking and there had been a neglect of the standing rules. The oil and tow 'have for some time back been placed under the care of the Porter ... the Nurses have been in the habit of making use of said Articles for lighting the Fires in the Hospital and that the Porter has otherwise permitted same to be wasted.' The housekeeper had not kept control of the coals and candles. The apothecary's wife and their servant were living in the hospital and when taxed with the excessive increase of supplies obtained from the druggist the apothecary admitted that the porters and others had free access to his key which was hung up in the surgery. 'It is much to be regretted that our Apothecary has for some time past ceased to require the Signature or order of a Medical Governor in his pass book for Medicines or necessaries.'[3]

The first volume of Charles Lendrick's *Elements of the Practice of Medicine* (1840) was described by a reviewer as 'the production of a man capable of thinking and arranging his ideas, and therefore calculated to lead the student to exercise his mind in a similar way, a process from which he has been diverted in this city for several years, by false guides leading him into desultory scamperings over the field of medical science, or setting him to seek mares' nests in the thickets of theory.'[4] Lendrick died suddenly at Ashford, County Wicklow, in June 1841 and the *Elements* remained uncompleted.[5]

For Lendrick disease consisted of 'detrimental changes produced in the vital powers, and involving the functions, organs, or both.'[6] These changes were brought about by *morbid actions* of four kinds, irritation, inflammation, specific inflammation, and congestion. Irritability could be healthy or morbid and was influenced by *temperaments*—the nervous, the intemperate, the sthenic — and *reaction* which could be deficient or excessive.

Fevers were symptomatic or idiopathic with external causes *accessary* and *peculiar*. The former included cold, vicissitudes of weather, fatigue etc; the peculiar causes were malaria, pestilential agency, or infection.

> *Malaria*, is the name assigned to the vapours, especially those from marshy grounds ... *Pestilential agency*, consists in a property of unknown origin possessed by the atmosphere, and probably otherwise propagated, whereby disease is generated ... *Infection*, is the property of disease, by which it is transmitted from the sick to the healthy. Contagion is generally used as a synonymous term, although meaning, in its strictest acceptation, propagation by means of contact.[7]

Lendrick prescribed Cinchona or Peruvian bark, *liquor arsenicalis* combined with tincture of opium and senna, James's powder, wine etc. He advocated the use of leeches, cupping, puncture of the temporal artery, enemeta and other therapeutic measures.

Francis L'Estrange, son of the former president of the College of Surgeons, demonstrated a new type of truss for inguinal hernia to the Surgical Society of Ireland in February 1844. He mentioned, as perhaps a doubtful instance of its utility, that it had been used successfully to render a convict with a large hernia fit for transportation to Botany Bay. L'Estrange also invented an apparatus for the reduction of dislocations, a sound for locating bladder stones, and a calculofractor or screw lithotrite for which he was awarded a gold medal by the Royal Dublin Society.

Dr James Duncan (PKQCPI in 1873–1874), assistant physician to Mercer's in the mid-1840s, published *Clinical Lectures Delivered in the Theatre of Mercer's Hospital* which presents a summary of his views on ten important disorders. By way of introduction, Duncan referred to the pre-scientific era when anatomy, 'the basis of all real knowledge', was hardly known and conjecture was rife. 'Hence, whensoever physicians were at a loss to explain the phenomena of a disease, they drew upon their imagination, and spoke of the animal spirits and peccant humours with a familiarity and freedom that nothing but the most accurate acquaintance with their existence and nature could at all warrant.'[8]

He urged students to devote time to personal observations, noting the evolution of symptoms and their response to remedies; they should listen attentively to the patients in the wards — 'a different kind of cough attends the various affections of the lungs' — and recognise the short, suppressed cough of pleurisy, the paroxysms of whooping-cough, the 'full and open cough' of bronchitis, etc. He discussed with evident pride (after the confirmatory autopsy) the case of James Doran, a middle-aged labourer in whom a deeply-seated lung abscess had been diagnosed during life, the diagnosis 'written down the next day on the patient's chart — a circumstance particularly fortunate, as these happy hits are so often made or mended after the revelations of the dissecting-table ...' He described the plight of twenty-two-year-old Bridget Conolly, admitted to Mercer's on 19 January 1848 to be cupped, leeched and blistered for a pleural effusion:

> Her history is simply this: She was dismissed convalescent from the Kilmainham Fever Sheds about the commencement of the present month, and having, like too many of the unfortunate inmates of this charity, no friends or shelter to repair to, she slept for two nights in the open field and got cold.[9]

Duncan also published *Medical Statistics; their Force and Fallacies* (1847) and *God in Disease* (1851). He regarded disease as being 'due to the direct appointment of God Himself' and argued that this belief 'far from being reprehensible and derogatory to the character of the Divine Being, is in the highest degree proper to be entertained.' Sickness is a unifying force; pain is a warning and a directive. Milder indispositions afford leisure for serious reflection; serious illness reminds the afflicted of the uncertainty of life and prompts them 'to make suitable preparation for the great change that awaits them.'[10]

Robert Scraggs accepted the joint duties of registrar and apothecary in July 1841 with a salary of £70. He resigned two years later and was replaced by Alexander Duke whose successors in due course included A.G. Power (1846), M. O'Grady (1850), and James Shaw (1859). William Jameson (1843), Philip Bevan (1849), and Richard Butcher (1851) joined the surgical staff. The term 'Matron' was introduced when Mrs Murray was appointed to that situation on 8 September 1852. 'Mrs Murray to give Security of two persons

in the Sum of one hundred pounds to be approved of by the Board.'
Her guarantors were Dr Murray of Trinity College and Henry
Murray of the Westmoreland Lock Hospital.

An enquiry in October 1848 from the Central Board of Health
as to how many cholera patients might be accommodated led the
governors to say that they 'do not think they would be justified in
admitting Cholera patients into the Hospital, in as much as they
are of opinion that their doing so would deter those Patients for
whose relief the Hospital has been established from seeking relief
therein.'[11]

During the year ending 31 March 1853 there were 586 admissions and 16,000 extern patients. Expenditure for the year was
£913 9s 8½d; the income was £866 12s 11d.

When asked by the Lord Mayor on 24 February 1855 what
accommodation the hospital could provide for the sick and wounded
from the Crimean War, the governors offered 'to accommodate 40
of the wounded Soldiers and Sailors from the Crimea on the
Government providing the necessary expences.'[12]

The Lord Lieutenant's round of hospital visits on August 4th
took in Mercer's where Lord and Lady Cloncurry were received
at 4 pm by Mr Tagert, Mr Butcher, Dr Bevan, Dr Jameson, a number of lay-governors and Mr M. O'Grady, the apothecary. They
visited the wards, the operating-room, and the lecture-room.
Butcher showed them some cases of surgical instruments.

Tagert explained that election to the medical staff was the
prerogative of the medical board and gave his reasons for believing
that this was the most successful system. In France, surgeons and
physicians were appointed after sitting examinations in Paris but
'many a skilful man may be a profligate character'; when lay-
governors made the appointment their selection was often
determined on religious or political grounds; family or aristocratic
influence affected government appointments.

The medical board continued to guard the right to make medical
appointments, a prerogative held since 1734 but eventually challenged as a privilege susceptible to abuse especially when linked
to a system whereby an incoming doctor actually paid for the post
— the so-called 're-coup money' being shared by his future
colleagues. Mercer's was not unique in imposing a pecuniary
obligation on new recruits. The vacancy at the Meath Hospital
filled by the celebrated Robert J. Graves in 1821 occurred after an
interchange of money.

The failure of the Dublin Hospital Commission to make a grant to Mercer's as a teaching hospital in 1856 prompted an appeal to the Lord Lieutenant in which claims for recognition were made. For years the hospital had had an average of 100 to 120 pupils annually and 'was the first Hospital in this City in which clinical lectures were delivered.'

> Its locality is the best in the city, for an Hospital being in an impoverished and thickly inhabited district near the great thoroughfares at the same time it possesses a Considerable open space to the rere with a Southern aspect and has never been visited by any serious epidemic so Common in other Institutions.
>
> It is in the immediate vicinity within five minutes walk of the five principal Schools of Dublin. The Royal College of Surgeons, Trinity College, the two Peter Street and the Cecilia Street Schools the pupils can therefore be Summoned to operations or Cases of interest — and attend the public lectures, Library, Museums etc at the Colleges with the least possible loss of time.[13]

Economically-run and in existence for over a century, Mercer's had an active accident service and a large dispensary at which a great many patients were relieved annually. On these facts the claim for public support was based; a small sum would enable the addition to the hospital of a moderate number of Lock and Fever wards. His Excellency the Lord Lieutenant did not, however, see his way to ask the Commissioners to alter their decision.

The first Ladies Visiting Committee—Mrs Shaw, Mrs Osborne, Mrs La Touche and Mrs Longfield — was established in April 1858. The ladies issued recommendations for the supervision and purchase of linen and blankets and their report in this area caused the matron to be reprimanded. They also helped to organise bazaars held from time to time to raise funds.

The death in October 1860 of Mrs Peter Digges La Touche deprived the hospital of a friend 'whose unwearied exertions in its behalf were attended with so much advantage to the institution' that the board of governors adjourned in respect to her memory.

Dr William Moore and Mr Edward Ledwich joined the staff as physician and surgeon respectively and were elected governors in September 1861. Benjamin Lee Guinness declined the honour of governorship, pleading pressure of business. Because of failing vision Peter Digges La Touche resigned his position as treasurer and wrote on December 26th to Lord William Fitzgerald:

> I cannot say how gratified I feel for the kind letter you sent me by my son and I would feel much obliged to you if you would convey my acknowledgements to the Governors of the handsome terms in which they speak of my resignation. I always hope to continue a Governor and shall never cease to feel an interest in Mercer's and to further its welfare as much as lies in my power.[14]

A meeting was convened on 19 March 1862 'To consider the advisability of making arrangements to meet the present insufficient accommodation for the relief of the Extern patients.' An 'Improvement Committee' discussed the problem further and after consultation with an architect building was commenced by Mr Walter Doolin.[15] Meanwhile fund-raising had continued and the Dean of Ardagh preached a charity sermon.

> University Club
> 73 Stephen's Green
> 2nd June 1863

> My dear Sir,
>   I will have much pleasure in advocating the cause of Mercer's Hospital in St Anne's Church on the 14th Inst. I trust with the Divine blessing the claims of that Important institution will make up for my deficiency, please furnish me with particulars

> and Believe me yours very truly
> Augustus Wm West[16]

To Dr Moore, MD.

Mercer's did not escape the petty crimes that plague every institution:

> The Governors having investigated the charge preferred by Messers Waterhouse that a man in their employment named Daly was robbed of the sum of 8 shillings in the Hospital on

the 25th of December 1863 and having examined the Morning and Night Nurses the Resident Pupil the Porter Daly, and his wife and having regard to the circumstances of the case to the number of persons by whom Daly was accompanied to the Hospital, and the character of the Nurses are of opinion, there is no reason to Suspect any person in their employment of any impropriety in respect of the foregoing charge.[17]

But Nurse Maria Lynch was reported for having received cutlery and soap from a patient and was dismissed. Other nurses brought before the board were 'cautioned to be civil and obliging'. The night-nurse was scolded for disobedience to the matron in connection with dressing a wound. An occasional charwoman was employed to assist so that the wards might be washed twice weekly.

The long drawn-out attempt to gain possession of the Widows Alms Houses gained momentum. The sum of £150 was offered and when raised to £200 was accepted by the Archdeacon of Dublin but only then was it realised that the title to the property was missing.

The exemplary record of the La Touches was tarnished just a little when the honorary treasurer was admonished for not attending meetings and instructed either to attend or to resign. Edward Digges La Touche duly attended on 13 December 1865 to explain his absence. He submitted his resignation and was asked to withdraw it, which he did. He resigned eventually on 17 April 1867.

Early in 1866, in recognition of the difficulty 'in procuring proper nurses', the nurses were given a modest pay rise — those getting £1 8s per quarter were to be given £2 per quarter; the nurse already receiving £1 15s was to be given £2 7s per quarter. Following a complaint from the matron, Mrs Murray, the porter was instructed that he must rise and open the door when required for the admission of patients and that no stranger other than a patient should remain in the hospital at night. It was agreed in December 1866 that two additional wards be opened for patients with fevers and other acute diseases.

Dr Thomas P. Mason and Mr Edward Stamer O'Grady, recently appointed as physician and surgeon, were elected to the board of governors in February 1867. The matron, to judge from the following resolution of the board, was no longer coping with her responsibilities:

The Governors taking into consideration the amount of fresh work likely to be imposed upon the Matron of the Hospital by reason of the additions thereto and her own weak state of health are prepared to accept her proposal now to resign her post on the 1st of July 1867.

The Governors in consideration of her long services will give her a half year's Salary as a gratuity on her leaving.[18]

She was replaced by Mrs E.M. Boon, a thirty-six-year-old widow.

John Morgan joined the surgical staff in 1867 and was elected a governor in August. It was agreed that gas should be installed in the new pharmacy and that the porter should have an assistant. A new physician, Dr Henry Eames, was elected to the board of governors in February 1869 in which year it was agreed that Sisters of Mercy could visit patients of their own persuasion. Gas lighting was fitted in the fever wards in 1870 and the hospital provided with water-closets.

DR JONATHAN OSBORNE

Though less well-known than many of his Dublin colleagues, the stars of the golden age of Irish medicine, Jonathan Osborne is truly representative of a generation featured frequently in dictionaries of eponyms and it is just possible that Bright's disease might have been called Osborne's disease.[19] Acceding recognition of 'Renal Dropsy' to Richard Bright of Guy's Hospital in his monograph *On Dropsies Connected with Suppressed Perspiration and Coagulable Urine* (1835) Osborne confessed his initial scepticism towards Bright's (1827) discovery but he had become a convert 'by virtue of a long series of observations, many of which were instituted in the expectation of overthrowing it.'[20]

Osborne had studied thirty-six patients with dropsy establishing post-mortem findings whenever possible: he confirmed the presence of renal disease in nine autopsies but in those cases where dropsy was attributable to liver disease or 'impediments of the circulation' the kidneys were normal. This was the method by which Addison and Hodgkin and other nineteenth century clinicians made important advances, the very method pioneered by Samuel Clossy.

Ten of the series of dropsical patients studied by Osborne were 'confessed drinkers of ardent spirits'. One of these 'was able to follow his trade, until the circumstances attending the fire at the Custom-house afforded him an opportunity for indulging his passion for liquor. After drinking whiskey out of his hat to an extent which he was unable to define, he lay on the ground in a state of insensibility till late on the following day ...'[21]

Urine-testing was carefully performed. 'The urine should be that which is passed in the morning before breakfast ... On heating this urine, in a spoon, over the flame of a candle, white coagula are formed in those portions of the fluid next the metal, long before the heat has advanced to the boiling point: and when the heat is continued afterwards, the coagula becomes more firm and distinct.'[22]

One feels that a hospital doctor of the 1990s who would have found it difficult to talk shop with Charles Lendrick and impossible to communicate with William Stephens (had they all been summoned to some extra-terrestrial conference) could have chatted freely with Osborne. They would have been almost on the same wave-length (a puzzling metaphor for Osborne), both accustomed to methods of examination that included the stethoscope and percussion of the chest. Osborne used two circular pieces of sole-leather when percussing, striking with the edge of one perpendicular to the surface of the other. He still favoured bleeding and for ascites he recommended 'the repeated application of leeches to the rectum ...' The leeches were introduced into the rectum by attaching them with silk threads to grooves in a specially designed instrument.[23]

Leeches were widely favoured for blood-letting. As already mentioned, Lendrick prescribed them in his *Elements*. In typhus fever, for instance, 'Leeches, to the number of from six to twelve, should be placed behind the ears or at the temples, and mustard added to the fomentations applied to the feet.'[24] An apothecary of William Stokes' acquaintance recalled that a week rarely passed in his apprenticeship that he was not called to take a large number of leeches off a dead body.[25] The number of leeches used by St Bartholomew's Hospital in 1837 was estimated at 96,300. Their cultivation was a commercial matter and in the 1850s Lord Desart set forty acres of marshland near Callan to a group of Frenchmen who irrigated it from an adjoining stream and proceeded to raise a leech crop, a venture which caught the imagination of the *Wexford Independent*. '"The seed,", if we can so express it, was contained in sacks, each sack holding 15,000 leeches, which were scattered from the hand, just as corn is sown. What will be said to this new race of Gallo-Irish Bloodsuckers!'[26] Incidentally, there has been a recent return to the use of leeches (*Hirudo medicinalis*) to treat local congestion in skin-grafts and replants.[27]

Jonathan Osborne was born at Cullenswood House, County Dublin, in 1794. He was thus about a year older than Robert Graves (1795–1853) and senior to Sir Dominic Corrigan (1802–1880) and Dr William Stokes (1804–1878) by some eight and ten years respectively. Educated first by the Moravians and then at Trinity College, Dublin, which he entered in December 1810, he also spent some time at the University of Bologna. He commenced MB in 1818, proceeding MD in 1837; he was admitted a licentiate of the College of Physicians in 1819 and was president of the College in 1834–1835. He was a member of the Royal Irish Academy and held a chair of *materia medica* in the School of Physic from 1840 until his death on 22 January 1864.[28]

Before joining the staffs of Dun's and Mercer's, Osborne was physician to the Dublin General Dispensary and Humane Society in Fleet Street. A list of his publications compiled by Kirkpatrick included forty-eight items dealing with a wide range of subjects. His book *On Dropsies* was republished in a second, enlarged edition, *On the Nature and Treatment of Dropsical Diseases* (1837), which was translated into German.[29]

He was an excellent lecturer with useful and elegant prescriptions to offer. A cheerful, happy man with a quirky sense of humour, he is reported to have sat one morning sheltering under an umbrella from a drip falling from a window in the roof of the university lecture-hall. 'This, gentlemen,' he addressed the students, 'is the accommodation which the board thinks good enough for its professors.'[30]

Additional to his scientific attainments was Osborne's interest in literary aspects of medicine. He spoke Latin fluently and was well versed in Greek. He identified the poison given to Socrates in Athens as hemlock and suggested that the philosopher's puzzling last words, 'we owe a cock to Aesculapius', were uttered in a delirium.[31] He discussed the plague as described by Thucydides and offered scurvy as its cause, a theory untenable in the light of modern knowledge. Referring to the autobiographies of prominent physicians, Osborne cited Dr Stephen Dickson (fl. c. 1790) as the source on an unverified statement that Haller, Linnaeus and Albinus were candidates for a professorship of physic in Dublin but withdrew on learning that the post was to be divided into three.[32]

He made no attempt to conceal his increasing deafness. 'Speak up, sir,' he would bark at a muttering student, '*surdus sum.*' Because of progressive osteo-arthritis of the hips, he was eventually obliged to use two sticks. He made light of this disability insisting that it was much more natural for humans to walk with two sticks. But as he did not wish to be at a disadvantage at the Resurrection, he decreed that he should be buried standing erect. After his death his instructions were obeyed and his coffin was placed upright in the family vault in St Michan's Church.

Osborne had lived through a burgeoning time for medicine. In the year of his birth Lavosier, who gave oxygen its name, was guillotined in France; in the year preceding his death another Frenchman, Louis Pasteur, had commenced his investigation of the silkworm disease, *pébrine.* He was four when Edward Jenner published his *Inquiry into the Causes and Effects of the Variolae Vaccinae* and fourteen when Charles Badham coined the word 'bronchitis'. Rene Laennec introduced the stethoscope in 1816; the Anatomy Act (1832) regularised the supply of bodies for the dissecting-rooms; the Medical Registration Act (1858) controlled medical education and initiated the *Medical Register.*

Jenner's vaccination was introduced to Ireland by John Creighton in 1800; Abraham Colles described the fracture of the lower end of the radius now named for him in 1814; Dominic Corrigan provided the classic account of incompetence of the aortic valve in 1832; Robert Graves described exophthalmic goitre in 1835; Francis Rynd introduced hypodermic medication at the Meath Hospital in 1845.

Osborne's account of aortic valve disease in the second edition of his book on renal dropsy does not allude to Corrigan's fine description. Charles Lendrick in his *Elements* refers to Osborne in a complimentary way without specifically mentioning his contribution to renal pathology. This lack of punctiliousness is less likely to reflect professional envy than to indicate standards obtaining when there were few medical journals and editorial discipline was lax. *The Lancet* was first issued in 1823; *The Dublin Journal of Chemical and Medical Science* (re-named *Dublin Journal of Medical Science*) was founded by Dr (later Sir Robert) Kane in 1832 and carried contributions from Mercer's by Osborne, Lendrick, L'Estrange and Butcher. An earlier short-lived periodical, *Transactions of the Association of Fellows and Licentiates of the King and Queen's College of Physicians*, contains papers by

Osborne and Lendrick.

Competitiveness in medical education during Osborne's time is illustrated by the inauguration of a chair of surgery in Trinity College in 1849. The Catholic University Medical School was opened in Cecilia Street in 1855 and a small number of its students was attracted to Mercer's.[33]

The Dublin Pathological Society was inaugurated in 1838 and appears to have been a vigorous and well-attended assembly for the discussion of the emerging clinical science. Its early members included a trans-Atlantic post-graduate student, James Bovell, who later was Sir William Osler's mentor.[34] One is surprised, however, to find Osborne's name missing from the list of members.

Schleiden and Schwann's cell theory was formulated in 1839. John Houston in the early 1840s was Dublin's first enthusiast for microscopic studies; Robert Dyer Lyons gave the first course on microscopic anatomy at the Peter Street (later Ledwich) Medical School — his introductory lecture, *An Apology for the Microscope*, was published in 1851. Books of revolutionary importance which appeared in Osborne's lifetime included Virchow's *Cellularpathologie* (1858), Darwin's *Origin of Species* (1859) and Florence Nightingale's *Notes on Nursing* (1859).

Osborne's wish to secure further funds for Mercer's prompted him to display a list of donations in the hall which the board ordered to be removed as 'some additions and interpolations had been made by students and others'. He had prepared the list from the treasurer's books and from a series of *Faulkner's Journal* and urged that a sub-committee should prepare a revised list 'to be placed in a permanent form and in a conspicuous place.'

> The sums of money received appear large but it will be recollected that from them was defrayed the expense of rebuilding the hospital in 1757 also the purchase of stocks and rent constituting our present income and that with the exception of the proceeds of the annual Oratorios (as long as they lasted) the small annual subscriptions and the grant from the public funds they have been the main support of the Hospital for above a century.[35]

An address was presented to Madame Goldschmidt (Jenny Lind) when she visited the hospital accompanied by the Lord Lieutenant on 28 October 1859 after the performance to mark the centenary of Handel's death which gained £430 10s 6d for the hospital. The board-room floor was covered with cocoa-nut matting and a plain hearth-rug was purchased. The address was read by a lay-governor, Mr Horatio Townsend, author, as already mentioned, of *Handel's Visit to Dublin:*

> The interest of your good action [he said] will be increased to yourself by the reflection that the Hospital which you have so generously befriended was one of the early charities of this City for whose benefit the Illustrious Handel gave the first performance of the Sublime Oratorio in which you have taken so distinguished a part. That grand monument of Handel's piety and genius was inaugurated in the cause of suffering humanity. And afterwards during his life and since his death (of which the present year is the centenary) it has in frequent performances contributed more to the relief of human suffering than any other production of genius.[36]

ANAESTHESIA

Setting off for the Richmond Hospital on New Year's Day 1847, John McDonnell may have experienced the nervous excitement that accompanies a venture into the unknown. There was an eighteen-year-old country girl, Mary Kane, from near Drogheda in the surgical ward. As the result of a puncture wound from a thorn she had a septic elbow-joint, ulcerated and life-threatening. Amputation of the arm was the only cure and after consultation he had decided to carry out this drastic procedure, however mutilating and agonising. A morning had been appointed for the operation but, encountering a colleague on the previous evening, he was given a copy of the *British and Foreign Medical Review* which described how an operation had been performed painlessly in Boston on 16 October 1846 on a patient rendered unconscious by inhaling the vapours of rectified sulphuric ether.

McDonnell postponed the operation for two days to obtain the necessary apparatus and subject himself to a few brief spells of insensibility. And then he determined to put this astonishing new discovery to the test. At the hospital he was joined by Mr Carmichael, Dr Hutton who had drawn his attention to the miracle performed in Boston, Dr Adams, Mr Tufnell and others. The initial attempt to administer the ether was not successful but soon all went smoothly; Mary Kane lost consciousness and the amputation was performed speedily and painlessly. Mr Carmichael watched the girl's face as McDonnell made the incision and saw that it did not stir. When asked on regaining consciousness if she had been aware of the sawing of the bone she said she had felt nothing.

This was the greatest moment of John McDonnell's career. The ether vapour had fulfilled its purpose without affecting the function of the heart or vital brain centres. He anticipated that by skilfully altering the inspiration of ether and air prolonged operations could be carried out but experiments on animals should first be done.

On his return to his home, 4 Gardiner's Row, he wrote to the editors of the *Dublin Medical Press*:

> I regard this discovery as one of the most important of this century. It will rank with vaccination, and other of the greatest benefits that medical science has bestowed on man. It adds to the long list of those benefits, and establishes another claim, in favour of that science, upon the respect and gratitude of man. It offers, in my opinion, an occasion, beyond measure more worthy, for *Te Deums* in Christian cathedrals, and for thanksgiving to the Author and Giver of all good, than all the victories that fire and sword have ever achieved.[37]

McDonnell's innovative operation was watched by the Richmond's students and by many leading surgeons from other hospitals who came to see it. Straightaway, Jolliffe Tufnell borrowed the apparatus and watched by Mr O'Bryen Bellingham of St Vincent's Hospital, he gave ether to four soldiers — dental extractions were performed for two, the administration being experimental in the others. Confusion and violent behaviour were prominent and one of the soldiers thought he was dancing in a public house.[38]

At the Meath Hospital, Mr Collis removed a toe-nail on January 6th under anaesthesia — the term was introduced by Oliver Wendell Holmes. Some days later, J.A. Orr removed a lipoma of the testicle under ether at the City of Dublin Hospital, Baggot Street. Mr L'Estrange used ether in his home for a dental extraction which was so successful that the patient insisted on having a second tooth removed — 'She described her sensation to have been as if travelling on a railroad.'[39]

Mr Cusack removed a deeply-imbedded needle from a girl's foot under ether in Steevens' Hospital and said he 'might as well have cut a piece of board, so complete was the insensibility.' Mr O'Bryen Bellingham amputated a foot through the ankle-joint at St Vincent's.

William Jameson was probably the first to administer an anaesthetic in Mercer's Hospital. He gave ether to an adolescent with an ocular disorder for its pain-killing effects and mentioning this case at the Surgical Society of Ireland on January 9th, he said he planned to use it fully for an amputation in a day or two.[40]

At the Surgical Society on January 23rd, Richard Butcher, then a young surgeon recently co-opted to the Fellowship of the College of Surgeons, displayed his instinctively conservative nature when he reminded his senior colleagues of ether's side-effects—delirium, convulsions, prolonged stupor. 'In *lithotomy*, how often have I seen Mr Cusack extract the stone in a few seconds. Would it be for this momentary pain, then, desirable to subject the patients to so *dangerous a remedy*?' Butcher questioned the effects anaesthesia might have on surgical technique 'when all the parts lie dead and flaccid before the knife'. He said that to use ether for dental extraction or minor matters was 'a kind of sporting with life beneath the sagacity of a medical practitioner.' He approved of its use for patients so terrified of the knife that fear actually endangered their lives and predicted that otherwise the supposed advantages of ether 'will, I am convinced, evaporate as quickly as the fluid employed ...'[41]

This reactionary attitude cannot have persisted. Butcher was to gain considerable renown in surgery which had now entered a new phase and he is one of the shining lights in the history of Mercer's. William Tagert was then too old to adapt easily to the new challenge and he became increasingly disabled by illness; Jameson (president of the College of Surgeons in 1861) had divided interests, practising both midwifery and surgery; the courteous and retiring Bevan held a chair in anatomy and spent hours in the dissecting-room; Butcher sprang into fame and soon ruled the roost.

RICHARD BUTCHER

Born on 19 April 1819 at Danesfort, a house overlooking the lakes of Killarney, Richard George Herbert Butcher was one of the sons of Admiral Samuel Butcher, a native of Copple, Bedfordshire, who after his marriage to Elizabeth Townsend Herbert of Cahirnane settled in County Kerry. Educated in Cork, the boy moved from John Woodroffe's school of anatomy to the Peter Street School in Dublin and finally to Guy's Hospital where his teachers included Sir Astley Cooper.

He took the diploma of the English College of Surgeons in 1838 adding the Letters Testimonial of the Irish College three years later becoming a Fellow in 1844.

Sir Charles Cameron described Butcher as dark-complexioned with well-oiled, jet-black hair and handsome features. He was strongly-built, liked to show-off his muscles to the students when he rolled up his sleeves before operating, and was an ideal subject for cartoonists.[42]

He introduced a modification of the common surgical saw and despite the instrument's fearsome appellation, 'Butcher's saw', he was a deeply conservative operator keen to achieve minimal blood loss and to save all that was possible of man's 'precious porcelain'. He gave details of the saw in the *Dublin Journal of Medical Science* (1851) and described two amputations, the first a below-knee amputation done for the unfortunate youth on whom O'Bryen Bellingham had performed Syme's operation. 'Two months after having been dismissed cured from St Vincent's Hospital', wrote Butcher, 'he presented himself for admission at Mercer's Hospital.' Butcher had operated under chloroform. 'The saw which I have used for this operation', he wrote, 'and which I most strongly recommend now, for the first time, to the profession, is a modification of the bow-saw used by cabinet-makers for cutting out fine work when curves are to be executed.' It cuts evenly, rapidly and without splintering the bone, '... it readily cuts in a curve, if required; and from its slender proportions it can be easily slipped under the flaps and used without bruising them, or catching in the retractor.'[43]

The second patient came to Mercer's on 27 June 1851 with (in modern terminology) an advanced pyogenic infection of an elbow-joint requiring amputation as a life-saving measure. 'In consultation, it was not considered advisable to place the patient under the influence of chloroform, owing to his enfeebled condition. In a few seconds the limb was removed ...'

A dramatic incident is recalled in Butcher's 'Reports in Operative Surgery'. John Lynch, aged twenty-eight, came to Mercer's in 1854 with a grossly swollen septic knee with multiple sinuses and abscesses. Amputation was refused and the man remained in hospital in wretched health. One afternoon when Butcher was exam-

ining a patient in the next ward the nurse screamed out that Lynch
was bleeding to death. Butcher rushed into the ward and saw that
a student had compressed the femoral artery controlling the tor-
rential haemorrhage. The popliteal artery had ruptured and must
be tied.

> It was a difficult task: the patient was never taken from the
> bed in which he lay; he was rolled over gently upon his left
> side, and the inner and posterior surface of the limb exposed
> by an incision fully six inches in length, along the inner side
> of the femur in its lower part; the vessel was reached. I
> grasped it at the rent, and freed it extensively from the parts
> around it; and, having done so, applied a ligature above and
> below the opening ... All bleeding ceased immediately after
> this proceeding ...[44]

The patient 'rallied wonderfully after the great loss' and had blood
transfusion been feasible would have survived but the improvement
was 'only like the brilliant transitory flickering of a lamp before it
finally goes out.' Poor Lynch died some hours later.

Butcher's books included *On wounds of arteries and their treatment* (1851), *On excision of the elbow and wrist joints and the
preservative surgery of the hand* (1855), *Essays and reports on
operative and conservative surgery* (1865). His professional success
was not paralleled in his home life. His childless marriage to Dr
Evory Carmichael's daughter, Julia, was unhappy and they separ-
ated. Butcher presented a life-boat costing £1,000 to his native
county in June 1879 in memory of his father. The National Life-
boat Institution erected a boat house for 'The Admiral Butcher' in
Tralee. He died at Towerville, Sandymount on 21 March 1891.

At the spring commencements held in Trinity College on Shrove
Tuesday 1863 the honorary degree of MD was conferred on Arthur
Jacob, Richard Butcher, and Thomas Mackesy of Waterford, the
first provincial president of the College of Surgeons. By an odd
coincidence Dr (later Sir William) Stokes received his primary
medical degree on the same occasion. Some years later *The Irishman* compared Butcher's and Stokes's management of cases
harmed by shooting incidents to the latter's disadvantage.

Constable Patrick Kenna and Sergeant Stephen Kelly of the
DMP were admitted to Mercer's with gunshot wounds on 31 October 1867 having been shot in the dark by a prowler whom they had

stopped to interrogate. Kenna was dying when Butcher saw him and the autopsy showed lethal injuries to the right kidney, liver and vena cava. The bullet which struck Kelly glanced off a coat-button before lodging in the chest. Butcher attended to his general condition before worrying about the bullet's precise location. Many days later, after repeated examinations, he detected a little puffiness in the angle between the spine and the seventh inter-costal space. Cutting down on it he extracted the ball with a small piece of the button adhering to it in less than a minute. Sergeant Kelly left hospital on December 23rd.

Head Constable Talbot, a police spy, was admitted to the Rich-mond Hospital on 11 July 1871 with a gunshot wound in the neck. Coming to the hospital in the small hours, Surgeon Stokes deemed it necessary to remove the missile immediately. He operated with the aid of a poor and flickering light and failed to locate the bullet either then or when he made a further attempt to remove it later in the day. Talbot died in a delirium on July 16th and when Robert Kelly was charged with his murder he pleaded that death had resulted from the ill-advised operation. Isaac Butt, counsel for the defence, said 'It was what Mr Butcher ... had called "meddlesome surgery".' According to *The Irishman*, Talbot 'did not die of the bullet — but of the probe, knife and forceps.' Found not guilty of murder, Kelly was remanded on a charge of shooting at the police-man and sentenced to fifteen years imprisonment.[45]

Butcher's presidency of the College of Surgeons in 1865 and his class of more than a hundred and seventy pupils had added further lustre to his hospital but in 1868, when he was at the height of his prowess, the Rev Samuel Haughton, MD, registrar of Trinity College's medical school, attracted him to Sir Patrick Dun's Hos-pital, the carrot being a newly-created lectureship in surgery.

Founded as a medical service, Dun's had lacked a surgical department until through Haughton's intervention it was pro-posed on 27 December 1864 that the permanent staff should con-sist of three physicians and three surgeons. The surgical posts were to be held by the professor of anatomy and chirurgery, Benjamin George M'Dowel; the professor of surgery, Robert W. Smith; and the university anatomist, Edward Hallaran Bennett. But in July 1867 M'Dowel was reported by the governors to the Board of Trinity College. His absences were so conspicuous that a student writing a series of verses picturing the staff made a pertinent comment:

Where is the next chirurgen? For my pen
Waits to portray the gay and gallant Ben.
Alas! he's salmon fishing far away,
Dr M'Dowel can't attend today.[46]

Appointed lecturer in surgery, Butcher transferred his entire
practice to Dun's Hospital to the delight of Haughton who said
subsequently at a public function: 'Since the day I entered Trinity
College, I do not believe that a greater benefit was conferred on it
than on the day on which I induced Mr Butcher to undertake the
teaching of operative surgery in the School of Medicine.'[47] Dun's
gain entailed a corresponding loss for Mercer's but this was mitigated by the endeavours of John Morgan and Edward Stamer
O'Grady.

JOHN MORGAN

John Morgan was born in Dublin's Temple Street on 21 December
1829. His father, Thomas, a Baptist clergyman, obtained a position
with the Bank of Ireland; his mother was elder sister to Arthur
Jacob, professor of anatomy in the RCSI and a pioneer ophthalmologist. Thomas Morgan's post in the Bank necessitated an oath
of allegiance which he refused to take, being opposed on principle
to oaths of any kind. When he lost his job Mrs Morgan opened a
school in order to support their six children.

John, the second son, entered Trinity College at the early age of
thirteen but took no degrees until 1859 when he became BA and
MA, taking the MD in 1871. Meanwhile he had graduated LRCSI
in 1850 and embarked on a career in surgery and anatomy. He
became FRCSI in 1857.

He married Marianne Dopping of County Meath; they had one
son and lived at 23 St Stephen's Green, North. Like his uncle he
was keenly interested in comparative anatomy and was appointed
to the chair of descriptive anatomy in the RCSI in 1861. His
appointment as surgeon to the Adelaide Hospital was followed by
similar appointments at Mercer's and the Lock Hospital. He was
closely associated with the management of the Irish Medical
Association.[48]

John Morgan died on 4 March 1876 from what was called 'rapid
enteric fever' after a short illness. Being particularly interested
in syphilis he had been to Spike Island a few weeks previously to
visit William Burke Kirwan, a convict who had formerly been
William Wallace's illustrator.[49]

EDWARD S. O'GRADY

Edward Stamer O'Grady was born in Baggot Street, Dublin, into a well-to-do family. He was the son of Edward O'Grady, an officer in the 4th Dragoon Guards, and his wife Wilhelmina Rose; the grandson of Edward O'Grady, third son of Viscount Guillamore, by his wife Mary Stamer. After education at the Academic Institute, Harcourt Street, Dr Wall's School, Hume Street, and Trinity College (where he graduated in medicine and surgery in 1859), he was able to afford an extensive tour of continental medical centres and also visited hospitals in New York, Boston and Philadelphia. He studied under Chassagnaic in Paris, under Langenbeck in Vienna, and in America was impressed by the lectures of Yandell and Marion Sims. On his return to Ireland he took the diplomas of the Colleges of Surgeons and Physicians; he became FRCSI in 1861 and MKQCPI in 1883.[50]

O'Grady lectured at the Carmichael School and joined the staff at Mercer's. The possession of a private income reduced his need to acquire a large private practice without diminishing his interest in his profession; rather to the contrary, indeed, for he was able to subscribe to foreign journals and accumulate a great polyglot library in which the standard works in English, French and German were included. A contemporary described him as 'Genial, learned, indefatigable ...' with a deeply sympathetic nature and recalled the 'bright halcyon days in Mercer's where on the crowded benches of the operating theatre students in every hospital in Dublin gathered to see O'Grady operate.'[51]

He was the first in Dublin to perform intestinal resection and he contributed articles to the *Dublin Journal of Medical Science* and the *Medical Press*. Accidents were his forté. The story was told of his encounter in Bray with an accident in which a man was bleeding to death and how he brought him safely to Mercer's, controlling the bleeding points with his fingers throughout the journey. And on an occasion when a fire had caused an overhanging wall in Trinity Street to fall imprisoning a fireman, O'Grady freed him by cutting a heavy beam across with his surgical saw. He then spent the night in the hospital attending to other casualties.

A TIME OF UNREST

Richard Butcher gave his first lecture at Dun's Hospital on 2 April 1868. He spoke on excision of the knee-joint and introduced to his audience John Game, a shoemaker, on whom he first performed the operation fourteen years previously. Mr Game strutted about the lecture-room displaying the limb's useful movements and showed how admirably suited the stiff knee was to his trade for he used it for hammering shoes on.[52]

Butcher's departure from Mercer's initiated a disruptive struggle for power the first stirrings of which may have been already evident when the medical board's plans for alterations in the dispensary were discussed by the governors on 23 October 1867 the required funds (£12) being guaranteed by Mr Samuel Close, a lay-governor, Dr Moore, Mr O'Grady and Mr Morgan. An 'Improvement Committee' with five members, three medical and two lay, was set up and issued a report which was read on 18 February 1868 but has not been preserved. On February 27th Dr Moore proposed and Mr O'Grady seconded a proposal that 500 copies of an appeal stating that the hospital had a debt of £400 be circulated without delay.

A letter in *Saunder's Newsletter* on 12 March 1868 from 'One of the Governors of Mercer's Hospital' ventilated problems generally reserved for private discussion. These included 'the rotatory system of duty'; the custom whereby each medical officer paid for his post; the retention of the pupils' fees by the medical staff without deduction for the hospital. The letter was almost certainly written by Edward Stamer O'Grady who would have found the duty rota intolerable — two surgeons were on duty for a month at the end of which their patients were discharged or taken over by their successors on duty, the 'right of reservation' limited to one bed.

> So long as some of the medical officers were aged men, and the others busily occupied by extensive school or private engagements, the too numerous surgical staff (however injurious to those patients whose lot it was to be thus transferred from one surgeon to another) were content. As younger members got into the hospital they felt that the above system required alteration and some months ago the junior surgeons essayed, unsuccessfully, to effect a change.

When it was not possible to change the system it was proposed to leave the vacancy unfilled but this, too, had not been practicable for staff-members would lose their expected 'recoup money'.

From precedent the gentleman now about to retire calculates on a large sum — £1,250 — for his place; and it was proposed in order to prevent his being a loser by the sinking of the surgeoncy, that, inasmuch as his own very large proportion of pupils' fees would be divided among his remaining colleagues, that, they should each either pay him a sum in hand or let such share of fees lie by till the amount agreed on was paid off.[53]

This was unacceptable to the senior members of the board. They did not wish to face immediate loss and looking to the future each wished to retain the right to sell his post to his nominee. In the event Mr Benjamin F. M'Dowell was appointed when Butcher departed.

The special meeting called to consider the unauthorised letter in the newspaper referred the matter to the medical board. The deliberations of that body for this period are not available but its curious conclusion was that taking into account the state of the exterior of the hospital 'it would be advisable to endeavour to assist its funds by a Voluntary donation or the resignation of each of its officers.'

Before long the sacrosanct method of making medical appointments in Mercer's came under full scrutiny. Counsel's opinion as to its legality was sought. Mr La Touche and Surgeon Brenan proposed and seconded the motion 'That the Board of Governors of Mercer's Hospital do proceed by way of information in the Court of Chancery against the Members of the Medical Board to ascertain if the present practice of electing the Medical Officers is an illegal one in such manner as they may be advised.' But their motion was defeated.

Next to be queried was the right and propriety of the medical staffs' individual election as governors, a custom dating back to 1734 and gradually accepted as an entitlement. The availability of medical knowledge had obvious advantages at governors' meetings but a situation might evolve when medical governors could dominate allowing the medical board to become the hospital's veritable ruler. Marshal N. Clarke, a lay-governor, may have shrewdly suspected that this was actually happening when he proposed on 26 June 1868 'That the Physicians and Surgeons attending the Hospital be called upon to resign their Governorships and divest themselves of the character of Trustees.' After some discussion the unseconded motion was withdrawn.[54]

Towards the end of the following month the secretary read a letter from Mr Hayes, solicitor, intimating that he had been instructed by Mr Edward Stamer O'Grady 'to take legal proceedings relative to the last appointment of Medical Officer' to the hospital and asking if the governors as a whole wished to become plaintiffs. This matter eventually was settled amicably. O'Grady withdrew his suit but immediately introduced demands at board level to alter the arrangements whereby beds were allotted and the method in which medical duties were discharged. He also requested an investigation into the system requiring payment of 'recoup money'.

When O'Grady deplored the 'rotatory system of Duty' on 9 December 1868 he was supported by his colleagues and by February 1869 the offending system had been dropped. The medical staff continued to press for improvements — 'The Sanitary arrangements are most defective the atmospheric cubic space insufficient for the number of beds in the house and the dispensary accommodation very inconvenient.' At least £1,500 would be needed and as this could not be provided out of the hospital's current income the doctors decided to offer financial aid.

> We the undersigned Members of the Medical Staff do hereby promise to pay annually to the funds of the Charity during our connexion with the Hospital a sum of £50 sterling to be levied out of the fees of pupils attending the Hospital in consideration of £1500 sterling expended on the improvement of the Hospital.[55]

The undertaking was signed by Drs T.P. Mason and Henry Eames, the physicians; and by three surgeons, Edward Ledwich, John Morgan and Benjamin F. M'Dowell. O'Grady was the odd man out. An independent spirit, perhaps? Certainly a force for change in the hospital and unafraid of incurring unpopularity in its attainment. He challenged next the policy of having fever wards in the hospital. After discussion the governors decided not to alter a rule which decreed acceptance in the fever wards of 'Cases arising in the Hospital or such occasional cases as could not be refused without extreme danger to the patient.'

The governors also proposed a modification of the existing method of appointment of medical officers and suggested that applications should be sent in response to advertisement by the honorary secretary who should pass them to the medical board for selection of an appointee. The board of governors would then make the appointment and the honorary secretary should insert the result in three newspapers giving the names of all the applicants and that of the successful candidate. This was not acceptable to the medical board.

THE LEDWICH SCHOOL
Dr Thomas Peter Mason (1817–1900), a member of the Society of Friends, graduated LRCSI in 1842 and MB London in 1846. Although he became FRCSI in 1852 and was for a time Assistant Master of the Coombe Lying-in Hospital, he followed a career in medicine with appointments as physician to Mercer's and Cork Street Fever Hospital and lecturer in anatomy at the Ledwich School of Medicine in Peter Street.

William Moore (1827–1901) graduated MB from Trinity College, Dublin, in 1850 and practised briefly in his native place, Ballymoney, County Antrim, but returned to the capital where he was elected FKQCPI in 1859 and proceeded MD in 1860. He obtained appointments at Mercer's and the Pitt Street Hospital for Diseases of Children, lectured in medicine at the Ledwich School and was president of the College of Physicians in 1882.[56]

Henry Eames (1841–1873), the youngest son of the rector of Tyrrellspass, County Westmeath, showed an early flair for languages. He learned French in Rouen where he spent two years and having failed to gain a place in the Indian Civil Service, entered Trinity College. He took prizes in Arabic, classics, and modern languages and graduated BA in 1864. Three years later he took the MB, proceeding MD in 1870. He had a lectureship in medicine at the Ledwich School and was regarded as the chief promoter of the 'Hospital Sunday' institution. He contributed papers to the *Dublin Journal of Medical Science*[57] and was acquiring a growing practice when he contracted fever with fatal consequences at an early age.

Edward Ledwich (1817–1879) appears to have been a doubtful acquisition for the hospital. According to Cameron, 'he had an aversion to performing the major operations in surgery' and lacked flair as a clinical teacher. He excelled, nevertheless, as a grinder at the Ledwich School and with Thomas, his younger brother, he published a successful textbook of anatomy which went into many editions.

Benjamin F. M'Dowell (1840–1879), a native of Carlow, took the LAH in 1861 and while holding the post of resident apothecary to the Lock Hospital continued his education at Trinity College, passing the MB examination with first-place in 1867. He was lecturer in *materia medica* at the Ledwich School.[58]

One of the most prominent of Dublin's private medical schools, 'the Ledwich' claimed to be the successor of the 'Theatre of Anatomy' established in 1809 by John Timothy Kirby and Alexander Read at the back of a laundry in Stephen's Street near Mercer's. The laundress's notice advised 'Mangling Done Here' and the wags inferred that it did duty, too, for the anatomy school. This moved in 1810 to 28 Peter Street where Kirby was sole proprietor of a 'Theatre of Anatomy and School of Surgery' which flourished until its closure in 1832 when Kirby became professor of medicine in the Schools of the College of Surgeons.[59]

Kirby's school was re-opened as the 'Original School of Medicine' by G.T. Hayden in 1836 but it suffered in the 1840s from the rivalry of the 'Dublin School' which had moved from Digges Street to become an unwelcome neighbour. Then in 1849 two former pupils of the 'Original School', Dr T.P. Mason and Mr Thomas H. Ledwich, returned as lecturers and re-vitalised the place. Before long, Mason and the Ledwich brothers were the school's chief proprietors. After Thomas Ledwich's death in 1858 the students requested that the school be re-named the Ledwich School of Medicine.

Being so convenient to Mercer's it was natural that a close connection should have developed between the hospital and the school in Peter Street. Jonathan Osborne, William Tagert and Samuel Wilmot had lectured there in the 1840s but in 1877 a scandal sullied the association. It was alleged that a director of the school had improperly issued to a pupil a certificate of attendance at Mercer's. The board of Trinity College refused temporarily to recognise the certificates of the Ledwich School.

ANTISEPSIS

If, as Wilfrid Trotter held, the names of patients whose involuntary participation has advanced surgery deserve to be remembered, then it is proper to recall that a County Down labourer, Eugenius Miskeley, is the first person on record to have benefited from the use in Ireland of the antiseptic measures advocated by Mr Joseph (later Lord) Lister. He was operated on at the County Down Infirmary by Mr John Maconchy who (using Butcher's saw) performed an excision of the knee-joint following the 'clear, accurate, and detailed description given in Mr Butcher's work *Operative and Conservative Surgery.*' Maconchy had been told of Lister's antiseptic fervour by his junior colleague, Dr Edwin Nelson, who had seen Lister himself apply carbolic acid dressings in the Glasgow Infirmary. Nelson, the assistant surgeon, had already followed the method but did not publish his results.[60] The first Dubliner to proclaim support for 'Listerism' was Henry Gray Croly, surgeon to the Royal City of Dublin Hospital, Baggot Street.

Joseph Lister was born into a Quaker family at Upton, Essex, in 1827. He graduated from University College Hospital, London, in 1852 and in the following year went to Edinburgh to work with James Symes, a leading surgeon who was reputed 'never to have wasted a word, a drop of ink, or a drop of blood.' He became assistant surgeon to the Royal Infirmary in 1856 and professor of surgery at Glasgow University in 1860. In the course of fundamental investigations into the nature of inflammation, his attention was drawn to the work of Louis Pasteur who had proved that putrefaction resulted from the presence in the air of living germs. Lister realised that wound suppuration, too, was caused by those germs and set about devising ways to exclude them using carbolic acid as a disinfectant.

Lister described his 'New Method' in the *Lancet* in 1867 and spoke 'On the Antiseptic Principle in the Practice of Surgery' when the British Medical Association met in Dublin in August of that year. His operative results had improved immeasurably; his patients rejoiced but contemporary colleagues bridled in disagreement. Many surgeons failed to grasp the underlying principle and ridiculed the carbolic spray that became a symbol of antisepsis.

Slowly, and despite a tenacious opposition, 'Listerism' gained credence. An honorary MD was conferred upon Lister by Dublin University on 26 June 1879 and next day he gave a demonstration in the Richmond Hospital. The swan-song of Lister's critics is said to have been sung by Professor William Savory of St Bartholomew's Hospital at the British Medical Association's meeting in Cork in 1879 but full acceptance was delayed and from time to time antisepsis was discussed by the Surgical Society of Ireland.

Addressing that body on 27 February 1880, William Stokes, FRCSI, described two uneventful ovariotomies and asked, 'Did not antisepsis, or I should say "Listerism", play a chief role in bringing about the result? He would be, I think, a hardened and hopeless sceptic who would answer the query in the negative.' But Edward Mapother, the president of the RCSI, expressed his disbelief in the practice which he never used in St Vincent's Hospital.

The younger men assented more readily. Rawdon Macnamara, junior, who had worked under one of Lister's pupils in the North of England, favoured Listerism. His father challenged the validity of Pasteur's experiments and believed that Charlton Bastian, the last serious upholder of spontaneous generation, had disproved them. He conceded that because of the attention given to Listerism they had become more alive to all that was summed-up in the word 'hygiene'.

Samuel Haughton, the accomplished cleric who held doctorates in divinity, medicine and science, poured scorn on Listerism, dismissing it as a new-fangled notion and a perfect humbug. He had seen the antiseptic system practised in Edinburgh, Newcastle-on-Tyne and London. 'To assist in an operation it was necessary to be a believer for the success of the operation. I have no objection whatever to attending religious worship of a form I did not quite agree in myself; but antiseptic treatment is occult, beyond all religious belief, the presence even of an unbeliever being detrimental.' He did not pretend to be able to discuss authoritatively the statistics produced for or against the carbolic acid system but he felt authorised to speak on the question of germs. 'As a scientific man,' Haughton said, 'and not merely as a medical man, I believe that there never was a more miserable idea brought before the world of science than that expressed in the words, *omne vivum ex ovo*.'

Haughton asserted that to postulate for any living thing in the world a previous living thing was nonsense. 'It might arise from the obscure complex conditions of a festering wound; but to say all external germs must be excluded from it was downright nonsense.' As a man of science he could not believe it.[61]

Sensing that they were getting into deep water, Mr Stokes said it was a pity the theoretical aspect of the subject was entered into at all ... Edward Hallaran Bennett and Henry Gray Croly proclaimed their support for antiseptic methods. The latter said that in the past few weeks he had learned more of Listerism from Lister himself than he had known before.

Mr Wheeler's paper, 'A Record of Cases Treated Antiseptically and of Cases According to Lister's Method' read before the Society on 21 January 1881 exemplified a common tendency to equate Lister's teaching with certain details of his method and to deny him the essentials of his contribution.

'I am not', Wheeler said, 'a believer in the spray and gauze, but I do believe in that system which I have termed antiseptic surgery.'

Mr Thornley Stoker crossed swords with him at once pointing out that in terming one system 'Listerism' and the other 'antisepticism' he implied that Lister's method was not antiseptic at all, whereas antisepticism and Listerism should really be convertible terms. Mr William Thomson said that many surgeons imitated Lister but were unconsciously prejudiced against him, disbelieving in the method and disregarding the small details on which so much depended.[62]

Mr O'Grady of Mercer's is not cited in the reports of the Surgical Society's debates nor does he, in the 'Clinical Records' for this period which he published in the *Medical Press*, allude specifically to the antiseptic method. He does, however, mention using chloride of zinc, carbolised cat-gut sutures and making provision for adequate drainage which suggests a modified Listerian approach, a not uncommon compromise.

The wranglings of a reactionary rear-guard gradually abated and on 18 May 1881 the *Medical Press and Circular* expressed the general conviction by hailing Lister's discovery as 'epoch-making', predicting that it would mark 'the starting point of a new era in modern surgery.' The scope of surgery was, indeed, increased immediately as surgeons dared more frequently to invade the body cavities, the abdomen, the chest, the skull, and eventually operations in all those areas were performed in Mercer's Hospital. Such interventions were facilitated in the nervous system by increased knowledge of the localisation of function; in the abdomen by the recognition of specific disease patterns. The term 'appendicitis', for instance, was introduced by Reginald Fitz of Boston in 1886 and the possibility of performing a life-saving operation to remove a diseased appendix became an attractive goal.

NURSING

The Matron, Mrs Boon, was given leave of absence for a month in August 1873 'subject to her visiting the Hospital from time to time same as last year.' Her son may have kicked over the traces while she was away for Dr Mason proposed 'that Mrs Boon's son be not permitted to sleep in the Hospital in consequence of irregularities in the house.'[63]

Internal management was just then a matter of concern to the governors who believed it would be helpful if 'a Registrar and Matron be appointed who shall be husband and wife, if possible, the husband to act as Registrar and House Steward and the wife as Matron. Salary for both £105 with rooms fire and light the Registrar to have £5 per cent on all increase above the present annual income of the Hospital which he may be the means of obtaining.' This did not prove possible. Mr Anthony McGucken became registrar in September 1873 and held the post for many years. Mrs Boon was questioned in October about articles supplied by Messers Pim and she was sacked in December. She was replaced by Mrs Jane Smyth.

The venturesome antiseptic surgery was already creating an increased demand for skilled nursing the lack of which was exercising the minds of members of the Ladies Committee. They had reported Nurse Campbell in February 1874 to the governors who deputed the secretary 'to caution her against taking any Liquor, which can affect her fitness for attending to her duties.' The mild rebuke did not satisfy Mr John Morgan who recommended her dismissal.[64]

Nurse Quirke was admonished in December 1874 for being drunk. The house committee was empowered to dismiss 'any of the Nurses or Servants of the Institution' and it was decreed that the registrar 'may give in charge to the Police and prosecute at once' any nurse found intoxicated on duty. The feasibility of improving the system of nursing 'by a Contract entered into with one responsible person, as at Guy's and King's College Hospitals' was discussed but a special board meeting held on 6 January 1875 decided that 'the proposed system of "Lady nursing" is inadvisable.'

Early in 1878 discussion was established with the Dublin Nurses' Training Institution, Holles Street, which offered to supply a Lady Superintendent of Nurses and to pay her salary, board and lodging to be provided by the hospital. She would be responsible for the discipline of the nurses and should have power to engage and dismiss them. Her duties would be separate from those of the matron, the latter to deal with stores and housekeeping. The committee of the Nurses' Training Institution 'should have power to send probationers during the daytime, to the Hospital to be trained under the Lady Superintendent. These would assist in the work of the Hospital.' When this offer had been mulled over the collective wisdom of the board decreed 'that the question of appointing a Lady Superintendent to the Hospital be postponed for the present.'[65]

Representatives from the Dublin Hospital Sunday Fund who visited hospitals receiving its aid issued a report on nursing early in 1879. They noted that at the City of Dublin Hospital, the Meath, Mercer's, Orthopaedic, Steevens' and Whitworth Hospitals 'the nurses are merely under the supervision of a matron who has not received any special training in the management of the sick, and who is charged with the onerous duties of housekeeping etc.' At Dun's Hospital, however, the nursing was supervised by the Superintendent of the Nurses' Training Institution who had been trained at St Thomas's Hospital, London. The Lady Superintendent of Cork Street Hospital had trained at the Children's Hospital, Edinburgh, and Inverness Infirmary. The Superintendent of Nurses at St Mark's also acted as matron; she had been trained at St John's House, London, and Charing Cross Hospital.[66]

Nurses were required to be of good character, able to read and write. On average they were paid £12 per annum with food and uniforms. Their working conditions varied from place to place. At Mercer's they took their meals in the main kitchen, and slept in rooms opening off the wards without separate entrances. They were overworked, with no regular recreation periods other than a few hours in the afternoons or evenings once or twice a week. They were allowed three weeks holidays and a vacation gratuity of £1.

The recommendations in the Sunday Fund's report included the following: the employment of a trained Lady Superintendent whose sole duty should be to teach the nurses; wards should be grouped to facilitate nursing, each group having a responsible head nurse; nurses should be trained and properly qualified — assistant nurses not to act as wardmaids and scrubbers; meals should be taken in a special room at fixed hours; better sleeping-accommodation, daily recreation and regular holidays were desirable.

This report embarrassed many of the governors. They were not yet convinced that the nursing services needed such radical change but the hospital was indebted to the Hospital Sunday Fund for generous donations: £236 (1875); £287 (1876); £208 (1877); £355 (1878). They had no intention of antagonising such an important source of help and their reply reflected diplomatic agreement.

> Resolved, That the Governors of Mercer's Hospital having carefully considered the Report on the nursing arrangements in the Hospital, receiving aid from the Dublin Hospital Sunday fund, and having conferred with their medical officers do Authorize the Registrar to communicate to the Hon Secretaries of the fund that the Governors concur in the substance of the recommendation made in the Report and that they will endeavour to Carry out their suggestions, as well as the finances of the Hospital will permit.[67]

The report from the Ladies Committee in the spring of 1880 made constructive suggestions as to how at little cost the nurses' dresses could be improved but the board decided that 'the pecuniary circumstances of the Hospital' did not permit the expense. In the following year the report from the same committee led the governors to observe that they 'would feel obliged if the Ladies would kindly favour them with particulars of the duties of the Matron and say in what respect the Ladies consider them excessive.'[68]

The Ladies Committee issued an unequivocal recommendation in April 1882 that a Lady Superintendent be appointed to supervise the nursing. Dr Duffey, one of the honorary secretaries of the Sunday Fund, was their spokesman when the governors met. His proposals were accepted by nine votes to one and a committee was formed to define the respective duties of the Lady Superintendent and the matron. At the next board-meeting, however, it was clear that many governors had had second thoughts. Dr Duffey's proposal to ratify the earlier agreement was countered by an amendment which required an appointment of an assistant to the matron rather than an independent Lady Superintendent. Dr Mason wished to have the matter adjourned until November but on July 12th it was finally agreed to appoint an assistant matron.

The successful candidate, Mrs Ferguson, was to be paid £15 per annum with a furnished bedroom, fire, light and rations. A letter of protest at the change of plan was forwarded by a lay-governor who in November proposed unsuccessfully that the appointment be rescinded. It was then proposed and agreed that the question of the appointment of a superintendent of nurses should be adjourned *sine die*.

The response of the Ladies Committee was dignified and, for those times, courageous: the ladies resigned *en masse*. Mrs J.J. La Touche proposed and Mrs O'Donel seconded the resolution:

> That the Ladies Committee having made many attempts to improve the nursing of Mercer's Hospital and being thoroughly dissatisfied with the system ('if any') of nursing hitherto carried on, and the Board having practically refused to carry out the recommendation made to them by this Committee, feel that in the interest of the Hospital itself, it is their duty to resign—hereby resign their office as a Ladies Committee.[69]

Whatever discomfiture the governors may have experienced is hidden by the conventional phrasing of their acceptance of the resignation 'with regret' and with 'our best thanks for their past Services'. Two governors, Mr H.A. Cowper and Mr James Bessonnet, as a gesture of loyalty to their wives also resigned.

The resignation of the matron, Mrs Smyth, was accepted with regret in October 1883; her successor, Mrs Canning, was appointed Matron and Superintendent of Nurses on 2 January 1884.

THE NAPIER AND LEDWICH WINGS
James Shaw, apothecary and registrar was granted an increase of salary in April 1872 at which time the hospital records showed:

Patients in hospital last day of February:	39
Admitted during month of March:	93
	132
Dismissed during same month including two deaths:	97
Remaining in hospital last day of March:	48

The accounts were audited for the months of April and May and cheques were signed for:

	£	s	d
Alliance Gas Co. Coke	4	4	0
Sir A. Guinness & Co. Porter	12	19	0
Messers P.A. Leslie & Co. Drugs	15	4	8
Messers Pim Brothers, Goods	54	11	6
Messers P.A. Leslie & Co. Drugs 2nd Acct.	18	1	4

| Mrs Boon House expenses | 12 | 0 | 0 |
| Wm D. La Touche Esq., Rent | 5 | 0 | 0 |

Further details of hospital statistics are obtained from the reports of the Dublin Hospital Sunday Fund.

Average number of in-patients in years 1879, 1880, 1881: 879 (Dun's 964, City of Dublin Hospital 889)

Number of accident cases treated annually as out-patients: 2,741 (Dun's 1,192, City of Dublin Hospital, 348)

Total number of beds maintained: 79 (Dun's 80, City of Dublin Hospital, 94)

Average length of stay in days: 21.4 (Dun's 22.2, City of Dublin Hospital, 29.85)

Total income 1880: £2,4876 1s 0d.
Expenditure: £2,613 6s 11d.

Annual cost of each bed: £151 7s 7d.

Cost of 'provisions' per bed per day in pence: 8.6

Annual costs per bed:			
Drugs	5	16	11
Surgical and medical appliances	1	6	3
Provisions	13	1	10
Porter and ale	0	11	8
Wines and spirits	1	7	11
Clothing	0	2	8

Annual wages of servants per bed: £3 9s 11d.

Servant's food: annual cost per bed: £3 5s 8d.

The number of accident-cases seen as out-patients was far higher at Mercer's than at any of the other hospitals drawing aid from the Sunday Fund.

The unexpected death of a lay-governor, William J. Napier, on 3 December 1874, at the early age of thirty-seven, deprived the hospital of an enthusiastic honorary secretary and member of the Dublin Hospital Sunday Fund. Some years previously while on an annual fishing holiday in Scotland this bachelor angler had fallen into a pool in the Spey and the subsequent emergence of spinal disease was attributed to the accident.[70] The death certificate (erysipelas complicating progresive locomotor ataxia) indicates an independent cause.

A month later Willy Napier's parents, Sir Joseph Napier, Bart, and Lady Napier, offered to found a ward in commemoration of their elder son. Then a stroke of good-fortune in the form of the long-delayed sale to the hospital of the Widows Almshouses (despite some uncertainty regarding title) enabled the Napier benefaction to provide a new wing.

Sir Joseph Napier, whom Daniel O'Connell nicknamed 'Holy Joe', was a brilliantly successful lawyer. Born in Belfast in 1804, he was educated at 'the Inst' in that city and at TCD where he revived the Historical Society. He opposed Catholic emancipation actively in 1828. Later he campaigned against the disestablishment bill and when it became law he worked towards the reconstruction of the Church of Ireland. He represented Dublin University in parliament and held office as attorney-general and lord chancellor of Ireland. He was vice-chancellor of Dublin University from 1867 until his death in 1882.

The sale of the widows Houses was agreed on the understanding that the governors would build a new almshouse close by in St Stephen's Street to be vested when completed 'to the uses and for the Charitable purposes for which the two old ones, have hitherto been devoted' and in the ownership of the Archdeacon of Dublin and Sir John Foster, Bart.[71] The transfer of this property was not completed without some 'hiccups' and the representatives of St Peter's Vestry complained that the widows had been removed 'to rooms not first submitted to our approval.'[72] Finally the purchase was completed to the satisfaction of all and the tender of Mr Samuel Robinson, builder, was accepted. Mrs Eames, in April 1875, signified her intention of making a donation of £250 on condition 'that a Bed be placed in perpetuity in the New Napier Wing in memoriam of her late Husband Dr. Eames.'[73]

By April 1877, Sir Joseph and Lady Napier had expended £2,000 on the building project. The new almshouses were ready for occupation in September and possession was given to the original owners. The Napier Wing was completed towards the end of 1878. Mr O'Grady pressed for its immediate use but on December 18th this was postponed for lack of funds. The need for emergency wards was urged in May 1879 and the ladies wished to have a children's ward.[74]

At his death in 1879, Edward Ledwich left £1,150 to the hospital. This formed the nucleus of the Ledwich Building Fund to provide a new wing facing King Street and it was agreed in March 1884 'to proceed at once with the new building.'

Dr Benjamin F. McDowell died in 1879 and was succeeded by Surgeon Ward. Dr Duffey resigned in October 1882 and was replaced as physician by Dr Charles F. Knight who according to custom was elected governor in January 1883. On February 2nd Knight attended his first board-meeting; he became an active and contentious member but his career was to end in disgrace and bankruptcy.

A special meeting of the board on 15 October 1883 appealed against a recommendation of Dublin Corporation's Committee on City Hospitals to reduce Mercer's grant by a third. The Corporation's wishes had been followed in such matters as installing a telephone and employing a resident surgeon. It was pointed out that *all* elections were made irrespective of the religion of the candidates and twice out of three times the resident surgeon had been a Roman Catholic. Over 95 per cent of the patients were Catholics and almost all the hospital's servants professed that religion. The rooms for extern patients 'accommodate on an average fifty a day of the poorest and dirtiest inhabitants of the city (many of whom state that they never had a bath in their lives); experience has shown us that it is almost impossible to keep them as your Committee and we ourselves would wish, or as they may perhaps be found in other institutions which do not do so much of this class of work.'[75]

18. Female medical ward, 1808.

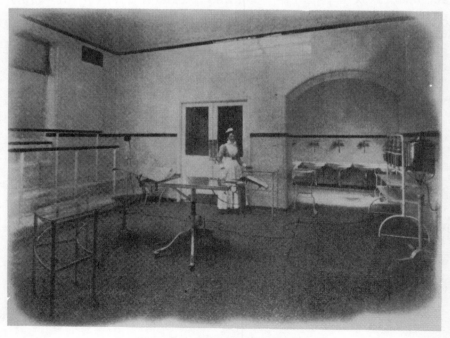

19. Operating theatre, 1908.

20.   *Sir John Lumsden.*

21.   *Mr Charles Maunsell.*   22.   *Mr Seton Pringle.*

Chapter 4

1884–1934

THE AUGEAN STABLE

By August 1884 a contract had been signed for clearing the site of the proposed extension fronting King Street. The Ledwich Wing planned by the architect, Mr Brett, would provide a new surgery, theatre and pharmacy; apartments for the matron, resident medical officer and resident pupils and a new waiting-room for extern patients. A 'pay-ward' was also mooted, a development which the *Medical Press* did not altogether welcome. 'Pay-wards are, generally speaking, nothing better than mouse-traps, and are inevitably abused by the admission to them of persons who are perfectly well able to remain out of hospital and pay for advice.'[1]

Having passed its 150th anniversary, an assured future seemed to lie ahead for Mercer's but those privy to happenings behind the scenes knew that dissension was rampant and that the hospital's very existence was threatened. The figure looming largest in the centre of the storm was Mr Edward Stamer O'Grady. Since his arrival in the hospital in 1866 he had quarrelled with most, if not all, of his colleagues and if their testimony is to be trusted he had become intolerably outspoken and autocratic. He upset the matron, Mrs Jane Smyth, by humiliating her before the nurses, students and patients. He spoke abusively to nurses and ridiculed and insulted his professional colleagues. When a majority of the medical board selected Dr John H. Griffin as RMO on 3 February 1884, in preference to a candidate supported by O'Grady, he flew into a rage denouncing the appointment as jobbery and nepotism. Subsequently he lost no opportunity to criticise and reprimand the young doctor.

William Collins, a patient admitted by order of Mr O'Grady, died of typhus fever on November 5th whereupon the surgeon hinted to the grieving widow that the RMO had neglected her husband. He urged her to report the matter to the coroner but an inquest cleared Dr Griffin of the surgeon's malicious charges. Other complaints about the RMO and the matron were also investigated by the board of governors and found not proven.

O'Grady's own infringements of the rules, by having more patients in the house than he was entitled to, and by insisting that an unrecommended country patient be admitted, were discussed and deplored. Dr Knight's proposal, seconded by Dr T.P. Mason and carried unanimously on 25 February 1885 recorded the board's 'strong and unqualified disapproval of the line of conduct pursued by Mr O'Grady as an Officer of this Institution and also in his capacity as Governor of this Hospital.' A less serious breach of discipline was O'Grady's use of the board-room for examination of extern patients.

An altercation between the disgrunted relatives of a patient, Farrell, and the matron and RMO, Dr Kennedy, was highlighted by the *Medical Press* in January 1887. Taken away from the hospital, Farrell died and his widow laid charges against Mrs Canning and the doctor. It was alleged that the latter was guilty of manslaughter and the governors asked Dublin Corporation to set up a committee of inquiry.

Dr Kennedy was exonerated by a judge and jury from the charge of inhumanity to a dying patient and assured that he should never have been submitted to trial. Dublin Corporation cleared the hospital executive of neglect but the editor of the *Medical Press* inferred that this was an elaborate 'whitewashing of the hospital administration and administrators' and without mincing words, referred to 'the decadence of the institution within the last three years'[2] evoking an indignant letter from Dr Knight, who pointed out that during the years in question the Board of Management had been enlarged, patients had been admitted in increasing numbers and in a proper manner, the hospital freed from debt and the building fund increased.[3]

The rejected charges concerning the unfortunate Farrell made it clear that the widow had been advised from within the hospital. At a special board-meeting on February 18th it was proposed that each of the MOs be asked to state in writing 'did he or not directly or indirectly instigate promote or encourage the charges ...' The motion was carried, O'Grady dissenting. He alone of the medical officers refused to state that he had played no part in the accusations. Dr C.F. Knight, by now O'Grady's most bitter opponent, elaborated his reply to provide evidence of the surgeon's complicity.

O'Grady responded by inferring that the hospital's minute-books had been altered. He also alleged that Mr Jameson, a lay-governor and the son of a former surgeon to Mercer's, had committed 'an indecent outrage on the modesty of a female patient' and proposed 'that in future no lay-governor shall persistently dally in the female wards at unreasonable hours.'[4] When this unlikely accusation was examined it transpired that Jameson, in the course of his duties as a member of the house-committee, had entered a ward where a female patient's wound was being dressed in an unscreened bed and left immediately when spoken to by O'Grady's student. The governors condemned the offensive nature of O'Grady's innuendo but the latter produced a letter from the student involved in the incident who complained that the governor was standing a mere foot or so from the partially-clothed woman while speaking to the nurse in attendance and was in no hurry to move when asked to do so.

O'Grady threatened legal action for damage to his professional reputation by governors acting in concert against him. Giving injurious evidence to the Dublin Hospitals Commission, he said: 'When I spoke to the Matron about one of the nurses, not very long ago, she said, "Oh, she's well enough when she's not mad."' He disparaged Mercer's in the College of Surgeons where he was an examiner. When the venue for Fellowship candidates was discussed he said, 'Oh, not to Mercer's please. There are no surgical cases there.'[5]

On 8 March 1887 the board of governors asked the other MOs to state in writing 'whether they have found the difficulty in working with Mr O'Grady (or with each other) that Dr Knight has, and stating the specific facts on which they reply.' Without exception, the physicians and surgeons related their difficulties in working with O'Grady. Dr Ward referred to his defiant hostility and wrote: 'It is a matter of history that Mr O'Grady has fought with his former Colleagues the late Doctors Jameson, Morgan, Ledwich, McDowell and Eames and with Dr William Moore and Surgeon Butcher who are still alive.' Mr Nixon recalled how he had been challenged by O'Grady to strike him and how the surgeon had called two of the lay-governors 'Puppets'. Dr Mason said that he had 'not sought the privilege of professional intercourse with Mr O'Grady since the period of the inquest in which the name of Mr Griffin your late Resident Medical Officer was introduced ...' When invited to comment, O'Grady said that 'the letters appear to me to refer almost entirely to a period long since passed'; he then moved to the attack and complained of the lack of cleanliness in the hospital.[6]

The Dublin Hospitals Commission's adverse criticism in June 1887 did not deter the administration from 'actively stirring the unclosed cloaca', to use the *Medical Press*'s indelicate metaphor.[7] The governors were determined to rid the hospital of the obnoxious surgeon who promptly sought an injunction against them. This was not granted but the judge indicated that if the governors acted capriciously O'Grady could seek legal redress.

On Monday October 24th a special board-meeting was held in one of the hospital's wards, the contestants legally represented 'by a complete bar of lawyers and solicitors', and Dr Knight moved for O'Grady's dismissal. He was not charged with neglect or incompetence but was declared to be personally and socially disagreeable to his colleagues who could not 'pull' with him. The consequent lack of harmony was ruining the hospital. A short-hand writer was provided to record evidence and Sergeant Dodson Madden, QC, was present as assessor.

Mr O'Grady's defence, as reported by the *Medical Press*, was 'that his colleagues are a family party who have had other interests than the good working of the hospital and the treatment of the sick poor, that he, therefore, was not content with their management of the hospital ...' His appeals to the board of governors had been snubbed but he was not prepared to countenance the method of administration.[8]

The proceedings continued throughout the week and on November 2nd, possibly for the convenience of the lawyers, the contentious gathering reconvened at Number Two Arbitration Room, in the Four Courts, where further meetings were held in November and December. Finally an amendment moved by a lay-governor, Mr Thomas Hewson, BL, was voted on and carried before being put as a substantive resolution and carried:

> Whilst highly disapproving of the part taken by Mr O'Grady in Connection with 'Collins inquest' and the charge brought against Mr Jameson we are of opinion that the evidence brought before us fails to establish any charge of misconduct or offence against the duties of his office which would justify us in removing Mr O'Grady from the Office of Surgeon and Governor of this Hospital.[9]

On the proposal of Henry Vincent Jackson, seconded by Sir
George Moyers, the following was added:

> That this inquiry just concluded proves demonstratively,
> that there is an entire want of harmony amongst the Medical
> Staff and that it is the opinion of the Governors That any
> Medical Officer who does not use his best exertions to perform
> his duties to this Hospital in harmony with his Medical
> Colleagues, or who endeavours to bring the administration of
> the Hospital into disrepute will merit a reprimand from the
> Governors, and that three such reprimands will Subject the
> officer to instant dismissal from his position of Doctor or
> Surgeon to this Hospital.[10]

Nineteenth century medical journalism was characteristically
outspoken, a style set by the *Lancet*'s editor, Thomas Wakley and
emulated by Arthur Jacob who, with Henry Maunsell, founded the
Dublin Medical Press in 1839. Archibald Jacob was milder than
his father but despite his protests of objectivity one feels that his
sympathy was enlisted in O'Grady's support. The situation may,
of course, have had elements that justified this partisanship.

'With the complete evidence before us', the editor wrote, 'we
must declare Mr O'Grady unquestionably guilty of having broken
a cracked basin, pulled down a window blind, and reprimanded
the matron and nurses.' He had failed to fall in with the wishes of
his colleagues, had insisted on performing his duties at inconvenient times and had demanded more than his fair share of
beds. But the explanation of much of O'Grady's behaviour, according to the *Medical Press*, was that on joining the hospital he had
found himself 'part of a system to which no conscientious man
could lend himself'. When he remonstrated at the Medical Board
he was snubbed; on appeal to the lay-governors he found them 'a
mere knot of nominees of the Medical Board.'

> The time has, we think, come for plain speaking as a means
> to reform, and we state unhesitatingly that Mercer's Hospital
> has been for many years nothing better than an appanage of
> the Ledwich School, and a machine for manufacturing the
> hospital certificates requisite for the students of that School.
> Since the time — thirty years ago — when the proprietors of
> that School became the actual proprietors of Mercer's Hos-

pital, almost every appointment made in it — lay or medical — has been dominated by that clique. If a vacancy occurred in the medical staff the selection of a successor was practically dictated by that clique, and if report says true, the money arrangements of the purchase system, which, as the Hospital Commission said, existed in its worst form, were financed by that clique. If a Governor was wanted he was selected by that clique, and, as a natural consequence, voted on all occasions with his nominators. Everyone who conformed to the views of that clique was 'in the swim,' and no one else.[11]

Returning to the attack in its next issue, the *Medical Press* insisted that reform in Mercer's must begin with the governors. These were forty-eight in number of which fourteen never entered its doors from year to year; many of them were related to members of the staff either by blood or marriage; five were the hospital's MOs, another its solicitor. 'Finally, two of those governors are noted as never having contributed one shilling to the funds of the institution, one of them because, as he says, he did not care to throw his money away on such a mismanaged establishment.' The editor predicted correctly that the governors could not dismiss a medical officer without proving his incompetence or negligence.[12]

O'Grady retained his appointments as senior surgeon and governor and before long the vagaries of fate were to ordain that it was Dr Knight who should be in trouble. Meanwhile the board of governors' decision to pay the legal costs out of the charitable funds rather than out of their own pockets led to the withdrawal of grants from the Dublin Hospital Sunday Fund, while a movement was on foot to give public recognition to O'Grady's courage in opposing a hospital management of which he disapproved.

Hardly had Dr Charles F. Knight been charged in the recorder's court early in 1889 with misappropriating the funds of a student he had undertaken to tutor than he was declared bankrupt.[13] His examination led to further adverse publicity for Mercer's and exposure of the system whereby hospital posts were purchased.[14] Dr Knight had paid £1,400 for his succession to Dr Duffey. The maximum income he received from students was £40 and in one year his teaching fees had fallen to below £8.

Knight, who so recently had urged O'Grady's dismissal, now unsuccessfully disputed the right of the board of governors to dismiss himself. His legal advisers saw his post as an asset to be

sold to the highest acceptable bidder for the benefit of his credi-
tors. The solicitor for the assignees demanded the appointment of
a replacement. Dr Ephraim MacDowel Cosgrave was elected by
the medical board but the proceedings were declared irregular and
the board of governors having decided to assert its power to
appoint medical staff, discussed inconclusively how they should go
about it.

A testimonial arranged by the friends of Mr O'Grady took the
form of a handsome brougham and harness which were presented
to him in September with an additional gift for Mrs O'Grady, a gold
and emerald bracelet.

When the filling of the vacancy created by Knight's dismissal
and departure to England was again discussed, O'Grady was
opposed to further additions to the staff but the post was advertised and on 29 January 1890 the board of governors appointed Dr
Hugh Auchinleck who polled sixteen votes to eleven for McDowel
Cosgrave. Either would have been competent to fill the post but as
the medical board had selected Cosgrave and the governors
favoured Auchinleck a legal contest seemed likely. Fortified by
counsel's opinion, a member of the medical board applied for a writ
quo warranto to compel the lay board to show by what authority
it had elected Dr Auchinleck.

The washing of soiled linen in public continued when the entire
medical staff was subpoenaed to give evidence in the Bankruptcy
Court as to the amount of money usually paid for a post on the
hospital staff. The case between the medical and lay boards was
heard in March 1891 but it settled nothing. The court simply ruled
'that, as Mercer's Hospital is a private and not a public institution,
a writ *quo warranto* cannot issue against its executive, and therefore, Dr Auchinleck cannot be displaced by this method, if he is to
be displaced at all.'

The *Medical Press* did not attempt to conceal its exasperation.

Inscrutable, truly, are the ways of the law! Here is an open
hospital for the treatment of all comers, established and
endowed 150 years ago by a will which specially sets forth its
public character, and vests its funds and its trusts in a body
of Governors. It was then incorporated by a special Act of
Parliament, confirmed and enumerated as a 'public' institution
by a subsequent Act, and supported to some extent, by public
benefactions, and yet the aggregate wisdom of the full Court

of the Queen's Bench decides that it is a private establishment and that its administration cannot be touched by the
usual process of law. Thus the controversy rests.[15]

Auchinleck assumed the duties of physician though initially
unrecognised by the medical board. He was not elected to the
board of governors but complained to the board of the inadequate
nursing. Mrs Auchinleck presented twelve unbleached calico
night-shirts as a good-will gesture and promised to send night-
gowns for the women's medical wards.

Presumably genuine efforts were made to maintain a patched-
up peace and since it was now clear that dual membership of
medical and lay-boards gave disproportionate power, attempts
were made unsuccessfully to recommend that medical officers
should not be governors. The Ladies Committee was reconvened
towards the end of 1890 with the result of re-directing critical
attention to the quality of the nursing.

The governors considered the proposals submitted to them but
they declined to dismiss Mrs Canning and the ladies again resigned. When Mrs Canning eventually resigned after further complaints it was agreed to advertise for 'a thoroughly trained Matron
and qualified nurse.' Miss Parke took up duty as Matron and
Superintendent on 7 October 1891.

The Ladies Committee remained disbanded until May 1892.
Several ladies then agreed to re-join. Some of the doctors' wives
declined to do so but they participated with the others in arranging 'A Grand Ball' in aid of Mercer's to be held in the Pillar Room
of the Rotunda on December 16th.

Dr John Elliott was appointed RMO early in 1893 and re-elected
by the board of governors on 6 February 1894 when it was
'Resolved that the Account for Fowl, Oysters, ordered for the use
of our Resident Surgeon during his recent illness Contracted in
the Service of the Hospital be paid, £5. 3. 5.' This fortunate conva-
lescent, grown into power, was the man whom Sir John Lumsden[16]
remembered when he came to Mercer's as a newly-appointed physician. 'It was then a strange place: an autocrat ruled the Hospital
— Dr Elliott — popularly known as "Bull" Elliott.'

The Senate of the Royal University of Ireland intimated in 1894
that withdrawal of its recognition of Mercer's as a teaching-
hospital was being considered because there were too few beds. To
comply with the regulations it was agreed to open additional

wards and on 25 March 1895 Dr Elliott, who was undertaking the duties of Mr MacGucken absent on sick-leave, wrote to apprise the Senate that this had been done.

Miss Parke resigned on 1 November 1894. She was succeeded by Miss Law who in turn was replaced in November 1895 by Miss Edith Manifold. In the following March the Matron and Lady Superintendent complained to the house committee of Mr O'Grady's discourtesy to her and of his 'insulting familiarity' to the nurses — he had, indeed, put his arms around one of them. Whatever fragile peace had obtained in the hospital was shattered. O'Grady adopted a legalistic attitude demanding that Miss Manifold should cite dates and produce witnesses. He was also at odds with the RMO believing that Dr Elliott directed patients intended for him to his colleagues or kept them under his own care in the medical wards. The governors, on the other hand, expected Miss Manifold's indignation to subside and Elliott was in their good books for undertaking the registrar's duty and for achieving economies in the purchasing of drugs.

Mercer's appears to have remained in what the *Medical Press* called 'the cold shade of adversity' until in November 1896 the long-suffering or muddled governors 'in despair of compounding an emulsion out of incompatible ingredients have thrown the whole of the constituents of the prescription into the sink and mean to start again to compound a bland and effective mixture.' The governors, to the editor's astonishment, had taken the unprecedented step of asking the entire medical staff to resign or be dismissed. They reserved the right to re-elect one or other members of the staff should they seek re-instalment.[17]

The ensuing consternation within the hospital and abroad may be easily imagined. Many uninvolved outsiders approved of the drastic remedy; rumour had it that with one or two exceptions the doctors were ready to resign but no resignation was actually submitted pending a meeting between the lay-board and the medical staff on 12 January 1897. This turned out to be a protracted attack by O'Grady on the governors' alleged maladministration and was adjourned until February 16th when, after a lengthy discussion, Dr Mason proposed that the medical officers should resign their governorships but retain their positions on the staff. The doctors withdrew to permit freer discussion by the lay-governors. Mason's proposal proving acceptable, was ratified at the next board-meeting.

The MOs, with the exception of O'Grady, resigned as arranged from the board of governors. He was given a month to consider his position or face dismissal, a threat which he fended off with a logical reply:

> If I am unfit to remain on the Surgical Staff of the Hospital, the Board are bound in discharge of their duty, to remove me; and if, on the other hand, I now do, as I have done for thirty years, devote my time and skill to the interest of the patients, they have no power to dismiss me *because I refuse to resign my seat on the Board*, and insist in forcing the Governors to notice the abuses which are carried on in the Hospital, and which, in the interests of the Resident Medical Officer and the Matron certain Members of the Board refuse to see — or, as one of them stated to me, endeavoured 'to hush up'.[18]

O'Grady also complained that on a plea of modesty a nurse had hesitated or declined to attend a case devolving upon her; in April he submitted a letter which pointed out that it was proposed to dismiss him because he desired to do his duty and had protested when not permitted to perform it. He held that his complaints had been investigated by a biased committee to which he had no access. The *Medical Press* deplored the continued disorganisation. 'It is known that, properly officered and administrated, Mercer's would be one of the most valuable teaching centres in Ireland ... for the relief of the sick and the instruction of the profession.'[19]

With O'Grady still in their midst, a regular attender of meetings, a tireless purveyor of endless missives of complaint, the governors finally felt impelled to take the drastic step contemplated in November 1896. A proposal on May 4th to dismiss the staff was carried by eleven votes to six and advertisements for a new staff were inserted in the *Medical Press* and other journals. 'Whoever is so lucky (?) as to be inducted', the editor of the *Medical Press* remarked, 'will derive satisfaction from the fact that he will be liable to be shown the door by the hall porter if the Governors happen to be of opinion that his tie is not of the proper pattern.'[20]

There were nine candidates for two posts as physician: Drs Edward L'Estrange Ledwich and John Lumsden were selected. Nine surgeons applied including Dr Montgomery A. Ward from the old staff who was reinstated; the new appointees were Mr Henry Moore and Mr J.D. McFeely. Pending the arrival of the newcomers the 'dismissed staff' carried on and the agony of those with a genuine regard for Mercer's was exacerbated when a solicitor's letter demanded satisfaction in respect of a patient who, it was alleged, had been tied down in bed, his wife refused permission to see him, the whiskey and eggs prescribed by the doctor withheld and a certificate of death from *delirium tremens* issued when in fact he had died from pneumonia.

The new staff assembled in the board-room on July 14th (the symbolism of which may have passed unnoticed) to be addressed by the governors and sent to the wards to allocate the beds. But very soon they returned with the request that the governors should allocate them. Patients were given the option of accepting the services of the newly-elected staff or transferring to other hospitals. Some refused to do so and decided to remain under the care of their present doctors who visited them daily. Mr O'Grady came and went as usual.

Hoping to ease the situation during the transfer period, the governors decreed that only accident and emergency cases were to be admitted; those admitted must be attended by a member of the new staff; medicines were not to be dispensed for prescriptions issued by any person other than a member of the new staff. On 3 August 1897 a motion 'that the Board dispenses with the services of Mr O'Grady as Governor' was discussed without reaching a conclusion and postponed. The surgeon continued to attend his patients but hospital officials were instructed not to carry out his orders for medicines and nursing. The house committee then passed a resolution discharging O'Grady's patients from the hospital. Pending their departure they were left without food for twenty-four hours but when O'Grady saw what was happening he went out and purchased food which he brought back to his patients, provisioning them as for a siege.[21]

The powers of the house committee to clean the Augean Stable were questioned by the *Medical Press* which demanded the resignations of the governors. 'Who elected the Governors?' the editor asked. 'A coterie of themselves. Who works the Governors? Another coterie.'[22] An additional aggravation was a legal action taken by Dr Elliott against O'Grady for libel.

For more than a decade the affairs of the hospital had moved from crisis to crisis leading bodies such as the Sunday Hospital Fund, as we have seen, temporarily to withdraw support. Next to register a vote of no confidence was the Dublin Corporation which threatened to withhold its grant of £300 a year unless represented on the board.

Counsel's opinion was obtained as to the legality of ordering the porters to prevent O'Grady from entering the hospital, by force if necessary, and his dismissal was to be considered again on October 4th, the relevant resolution given the forefront of the notice paper:

> That having read the opinion of counsel and that, inasmuch as Mr O'Grady has insisted upon introducing a patient into the Hospital in direct opposition to the rules laid down by this Board, and has, otherwise, openly disobeyed and disregarded the orders recently made on the reconstruction of the medical staff, it is hereby resolved that Mr O'Grady be and is hereby removed from his office of Governor of this Hospital, and that we accordingly adopt the necessary steps to give effect to this resolution.[23]

In the event, however, discussion was deferred, ostensibly because of 'the lateness of the Hour' but probably from an unwillingness to grasp the nettle or perhaps because dawning sanity caused the board to realise that O'Grady's expulsion would have fresh legal repercussions. An impasse had been reached which was resolved unexpectedly, and one might say tragically, by O'Grady's death. He was taken ill with pneumonia on October 14th but refused to rest and was carried daily in a cab to the hospital to see his patients. His condition deteriorated on October 18th and he died at 5 pm.

THE O'GRADY MEMORIAL

Is it possible to apportion blame for the unedifying events of this discreditable period? Edward Stamer O'Grady did not lack admirers in Dublin medical circles and his pupils and others set up a committee to collect funds for an 'O'Grady Memorial'. This took the form of a marble drinking-fountain mounted on a base of Caen stone which was erected on Leinster Lawn in front of the premises of the Royal Dublin Society.[24]

O'Grady had been fortunate to have the support of the *Dublin Medical Press*, an organ accustomed to championing doctors' rights and regularly defending dispensary medical officers in their struggles against the Boards of Guardians. The argument that a

clash of personalities does not justify the removal of a surgeon
from office is convincing, up to a point, and the *Medical Press*
presented O'Grady as the hero of a struggle against a professional
clique motivated by gain and able to persuade or order the lay-
governors to do their bidding. There is, however, an alternative
role which may suit him better, that of the vocal bully, a not
uncommon figure in many hsopitals. His inability to get on with
three RMOs in succession suggests that he rather than they were
out of step.

Nevertheless, a governor, Mr G. de B. Ball, dissociated himself
publicly, in a letter to a newspaper, fromthe movement to dismiss
O'Grady. He asserted that the surgeon was 'the object of personal
malice' and that 'certain Governors have formed themselves into
a clique'.[25] A few other governors prudently extricated themselves
from the mess but the resignations did not include those of any of
the high dignitaries whose names seemed to guarantee the board's
integrity. The handling of the matter was curiously inept, prompt-
ing a correspondent in the *Medical Press* to ask: 'Why did they
dismiss the entire staff, on what charges and by whom preferred?
Have these accusations been substantiated, and are the whole
staff *proved* guilty? Lastly, have the Governors the power to so
peremptorily turn out a complete medical staff without a hearing?'[26]

Was the *Medical Press* thought to be so blinded by professional
prejudice that the governors could disregard its caustic com-
ments? The editor countered this suggestion by pointing to the
reponse of the lay press.

> From first to last, during this controversy not a single news-
> paper has had a word of apology to utter for the Governors,
> while many of them — the last being the Dublin *Figaro* —
> have denounced their arbitrary proceedings in terms more
> unmeasured than any used by us.[27]

Was Mr O'Grady a Don Quixote tilting a lance for professional
freedom, ethical values and surgical standards against the robber
barons of the Ledwich School? Or was he simply an over-bearing
and somewhat paranoid person extending his easy dominance of
wards and operating-theatre into the more contentious atmosphere
of board-room and hospital committees? One cannot answer those
questions with any assurance of veracity and it is a relief to pass
on to the period of resurgence in which Mercer's recovered its for-

mer reputation and regained public confidence. That this renais-
sance had bitter birth-pangs is indicated by Sir John Lumsden's
recollections of his early years in the hospital when there was
'constant friction between Governors and Staff.'

THE NEWCOMERS

Edward L'Estrange Ledwich, a former Mercer's pupil, was forty-
two and married with two children when appointed physician. The
grandson of Francis L'Estrange and nephew of Edward Ledwich,
he was the author of *Surgical and Descriptive Anatomy of the
Inguinal and Femoral Regions*. He lectured on anatomy at the
Ledwich School and after its amalgamation with the College of
Surgeons he was College Anatomist. Jack Lumsden (b. 1869), son
of the manager of the Provincial Bank, Drogheda, was younger
and relatively inexperienced but he had a good manner and
already held an appointment as MO to Guinness's Brewery. He
had graduated MB from TCD in 1894, proceeding MD in the
following year. By his marriage to Caro Fitzhardinge, daughter of
Major Fitzhardinge of Kingscote, County Galway, he was to have
six children. A graduate of just five years standing, Henry Moore
had worked in Basutoland. He was not destined to remain long in
Mercer's for he resigned in 1900 when appointed to the staff of the
Royal City of Dublin Hospital. Joseph D. McFeely, FRCSI, took
his primary degree in 1884 from the Catholic University Medical
School.

From his *Recollections of an Old and Observant Practitioner*
(1931) we learn that McFeely was once a coroner and dispensary
doctor in County Donegal and also a Peace Commissioner, an
office which brought him into conflict with local ruffians. As this
did not augur well for the success of his practice he moved to
Dublin and was appointed Assistant Master to the National
Maternity Hospital, Holles Street. An outbreak of puerperal
fever was laid to his account but he rejected the charge, pointing out that the infections predated his arrival.

He became FRCSI in 1896 and decided to practise surgery. His
appointment to Mercer's, he recalled, 'was in general looked upon
as a wonderful success. I was the first of my Persuasion who had
ever occupied a position on the staff— I was said to have made the
first breach in the battlements of sectarian prejudice — and so far,
the last.' The board of governors, he noted, had three clergymen,
a number of lawyers and several businessmen amongst whom

there were only three Catholics.[28]

'Bull' Elliott was soon in bad odour with the newcomers. Complaints against him were laid before the governors by McFeely, Lumsden and Ledwich and his long reign as RMO ended when he was replaced on 1 March 1898 by Dr Wentworth Taylor.[29] Meanwhile the sudden death of Montgomery A. Ward on 30 December 1897 created a vacancy filled by the election as surgeon of Mr R.C.B. Maunsell.

On the advice of the new medical board the post of gynaecologist was advertised. This was filled by Dr John Glenn, MD, FRCPI, who in due course was succeeded by Gibbon FitzGibbon (1909) and Bethel Solomons (1911). Glenn had been senior assistant physician and external assistant to the Rotunda Hospital where with Dr (later Sir William) Smylie he contributed a chapter on obstetrics and gynaecology to the *Medical Annual* (1893). His paper 'Treatment of Severe Haemorrhage by the Infusion of Normal Saline Solution' (*Transactions of the Obstetrical Section, Royal Irish Academy of Medicine*, 1895) reflected the grave need which existed before blood transfusion became possible.

In December 1897, Mr McFeely thoughtlessly charged a fee of £5 to a well-to-do gentleman brought to the hospital following an accident in Grafton Street. This patient, Mr C. Kearney of Vico Lodge, Dalkey, provides the first record of an x-ray examination in Mercer's. The fee of £2 10s charged by Mr Richard Lane-Joynt who was called to the hospital to perform the examination was not questioned by the governors in their subsequent investigation of the matter, but McFeely was brought before the board, severely reprimanded for the breach of his honorary status, and directed to return the fee.[30]

Robert Charles Butler Maunsell was elected to the staff on 1 February 1898. The son of Robert Maunsell of Ballinasloe, County Galway, he was born in November 1872 and educated in Dublin at the High School and Trinity College where he graduated in 1894. He had been house-surgeon at Dun's Hospital and became FRCSI in 1900. His manner was confident and he remained calm in emergencies. He had little small-talk and could remain disconcertingly silent.[31] Surgeon Moore was replaced by Henry Croly. The latter in turn was to be succeeded in 1903 by Seton Pringle whose family made generous benefactions to the hospital.

The proposal to open a children's ward was approved of by the board of governors in June 1898 but postponed with customary caution. A legacy of £5,000 enabled the project to go ahead in 1899, the desired amenity to be called 'the James Weir Ward'. The house committee was authorised 'to rearrange the beds to be sent to the Children's Ward so that the total number of beds in the Hospital be not increased, without the authority of the Board, until the annual income of the Hospital is sufficient for their maintenance.' As if to re-emphasise the need for stringency the medical staff was directed to reduce the number of occupied beds during the summer months 'except in the case of paying patients so that not more than twenty non-paying patients be admitted.'

One is surprised, from the modern vantage-point, to find the physicians recommending the admission of typhoid cases but strict isolation was by no means universally imposed in the 1890s. Quite a rumpus ensued, however, in September 1898 when, as Miss Manifold complained, 'by order of Dr Lumsden the Resident Medical Students entered the night nurses' bedroom they being only just got up and removed their beds to another room to make room for two patients admitted that day suspected of having Typhus fever.' Lumsden was hauled over the coals by the house committee.[32]

A demand from Dublin Corporation for direct representation by the appointment of three of its members as govenors — a demand contrary to both the letter and the spirit of the charter, amounting, indeed, to blackmail — was discussed in October 1898. After the customary notice of motion the following resolution was passed unanimously on November 1st:

That the Governors of Mercer's Hospital regret that the Dublin Municipal Council by withholding from the hospital the usual grant out of the Corporation funds have inflicted a serious injury upon the poor of this city. The Council have insisted that as a condition for receiving the grant the Governors should elect upon their board three gentlemen as representatives of the Council. The Board have fully explained to the Council that they have no power to comply with the Council's request, but, so far, to no purpose. There are at present upon the Board two members of the Council and the Board have always welcomed and acted on the advice of the Inspection Committee appointed by the Council. Under these circumstances the Governors feel bound on behalf of the poor to appeal from the Municipal Council to the Local Government electors of the City of Dublin and to urge every voter at the coming elections to vote for those only who are the friends of the poor and to press upon their representatives the duty of supporting the Dublin Hospitals as heretofore.[33]

When the Corporation remained unmoved a compromise was suggested — a visiting committee to be formed consisting of three representatives of the municipality and three governors, the former being free to attend meetings of the house committee and 'be duly summoned to the Monthly Board Meetings to make their Report.' Final agreement was not reached until January 1900 when the Corporation appointed Alderman Russell, Councillor Beattie and Councillor Murray as its representatives on the board of Mercer's Hospital.

The governors acknowledged the receipt of £153 3s from a concert organised by the Misses Ada and Eileen FitzGibbon, daughters of Henry FitzGibbon, the consulting surgeon. The directors of the Theatre Royal refused to make a donation. 'If anything in the way of a benefit performance could at any time be arranged we might settle the matter in that way.'

The proposal that a Ladies Visiting Committee be appointed was passed unanimously on 4 April 1899, governors and staff being invited to make nominations. The matter was postponed at the following monthly meeting.

When the governors met on 2 January 1900 the finance sub-committee's report lay before them, stating: 'We have carefully examined the accounts of the Hospital and we estimate that the income for the year 1900 will amount to £2,200, and the expenditure for the same year will be fully £3,000 unless we can diminish the present rate of expenditure.' The message was stark to minds unprepared for deficiency budgeting; the question was how to remedy the situation. The options were considered in detail. An increase in subscriptions might be achieved by energetic collectors. Outgoings could be reduced by more sparing use of coal, gas, nursing, medicines and stimulants.

There is a considerable expenditure upon Special nursing, and we have an ample staff of nurses and probationers, we think that in this Hospital which is intended for the relief of the poor the employment of special extra nurses is wholly unnecessary.

We find that under the head of Stimulants expensive wines are used and we think that the Stimulants should be of the class that the patients would use in their own homes.[34]

The Boer War presented a need and an opportunity. At a special meeting held on 12 January 1900 it was agreed to offer the military authority 'Forty three beds ... for the use of wounded soldiers (preferably of Irish Regiments) upon the usual terms given by the Military Authorities elsewhere.'[35]

Queen Victoria's visit to Dublin in April 1900 was acknowledged by an appropriate resolution proposed by R.H. Davis, Esq., JP, and seconded by Sir Rowland Fanning, JP:

> That the Board of Governors of Mercer's Hospital, the oldest hospital in Dublin [sic] for the relief of the sick of all denominations and in which upward of sixteen thousand patients are annually treated, offer to Her Gracious Majesty the Queen their warmest welcome on her arrival in Ireland and desire to express their feelings of loyalty and gratitude for the interest which she has always shown to this portion of her dominions and particularly to her poorest subjects.[36]

This loyal address was duly acknowledged in Whitehall and a letter send from Dublin Castle on May 23rd, headed 'The Queen's Gift to the Poor of Dublin', bore Her Majesty's donation.[37] The Queen-Empress, the governors learned, had left £1,000 to be distributed by the Viceroy for the benefit of the city's poor. Mercer's share of her bounty came to £25.

The registrar provided statistical data:

Patients admitted in February: 90
Average number of patients in the house: 58
Accident cases attended: 257
Dispensary cases: 1,003
Patients in the house on March 1st: 59

Dublin Corporation's sensible request, as summer approached, 'that the various Hospital Boards should communicate with each other ... and make arrangements as will obviate the closing of all the Hospitals at the same time of the year', was received and acknowledged but the matron's instructions were 'to close the

Medical Wards and remove the surplus beds from the Surgical
Wards and reduce the number of nurses and servants as usual.'[38]

Towards the end of 1900, a ceremonial opening of the children's
ward was planned. When Her Excellency the Countess Cadogan
was unable to officiate the committee turned hopefully to Her
Royal Highness the Duchess of Connaught but were again disappointed.

TWENTIETH CENTURY

Man's gentler illusions include the belief that division into centuries melts time's implacability, reducing the mystery of eternity
and fostering the promise of ameliorative progress. The agonised
indigents who tossed and turned throughout New Year's Eve in
Mercer's Hospital woke, nevertheless, to a bleak dawn, the first of
a new century. Dublin spun, it is true, towards a distant millennium and towards closer political liberty. On New Year's Day
1901, however, stark realities of hunger and pain shadowed the
existences of many, their frames twisted by rickets, their tissues
softened by scurvy, their innards despoiled by tuberculosis and
syphilis, their bodies ravaged by pyogenic infections.

Contemporaneous with civilisation, the healer has brewed his
herbs, even in the cave, and assembled his amulets. Aeons later
the better-organised bastions of medicine, for a variety of motives,
continue to offer more. With lambent clarity the people of Paris
call their great municipal hospital the *Hôtel Dieu*. The strongly-
evangelical voluntary hospital system which served Ireland from
the early 1700s still has nostalgic adherents hopeful that its vir-
tues shall not perish under state administration.

Staffed by unpaid surgeons and physicians, directed by honorary governors and offering its services free or at a pittance, the
voluntary hospital, as we have seen, relied on community support. This can be grudging and benefits intended for the poor were
not uncommonly availed of by other parsimonious sufferers.
Despite a star cast — their Graces of Dublin and Tuam, the Rt Hon
Lord Justice FitzGibbon, Sir Henry Cochrane, Rev G. Mahaffy,
Sir Rowland Fanning and others — the governors at Mercer's
found their funds ebbing. They were, perhaps, cautious to a fault,
though they were themselves competent men with access to the
best advice.

They certainly were earnest and well-intentioned. At Mercer's
it was business as usual on 1 January 1901. Ten governors turned

up for the first meeting of the century. Nothing sensational appears to have happened. They appointed Dr T. McKell, MB, as house-surgeon for a twelve-month period ... 'the appointment to be terminable for any cause that in their opinion may be sufficient.' The half-yearly tender for supplies was renewed ... 'except that the Matron was directed to get the vegetables where she could get them best and cheapest.'[39]

In February it was agreed to maintain seventy-one beds only forty of which would be free, paying patients to be charged 10 shillings weekly. The Duchess of Connaught's promise to open the children's ward could not be fulfilled because of the death of Queen Victoria. The assurance of 'our unswerving devotion' to King Edward VII was correctly, and no doubt sincerely, expressed.

Emil von Behering was awarded the Nobel Prize in 1901 for work on serum therapy which helped to control diphtheria; Paul Erlich introduced '606', an arsenical compound effective in the treatment of syphilis; these were first fruits peeping from a cornucopia that before long would overflow with therapeutic gifts which added disconcertingly to the cost of running a hospital.

The semblance of peace obtaining since the death of Mr O'Grady and the departure of Dr Elliott was soon to be riven by a series of events leading to resignations, expulsions and recriminations. What should probably have been no more than a romantic breeze was fanned into a full gale by denunciatory voices. It was, it should be remembered, a time when probationer nurses were exploited by harsh regimes and guarded with a vigilance elsewhere reserved for the seraglio.

The first intimation of dissent was the probationers' letter to Lord Justice FitzGibbon. This necessitated a special meeting which was attended on 8 April 1902 by sixteen governors, the full medical staff including the house-surgeon, Dr H. Knapp, Miss G. Powell the Lady Superintendent, Sister Merrins and several probationers. There is no record, alas! of the wordy statements and counterstatements that were made but the outcome was a compromise. 'The Governors through the Chairman impressed upon the Nurses and Probationers the duty of obedience to the Lady Superintendent and upon the Lady Superintendent the duty of maintaining discipline with consideration and kindness and expressed the hope for co-operation in future.'[40]

Dr Knapp who submitted his resignation on May 27th, appealed to the board that in failing to accept an order of a governor to facilitate a visitor at any time he was following the house-committee's ruling. His explanation was accepted but the night-nurse had made charges which he did not attempt to rebut.

Miss Powell also resigned. 'As I have already mentioned', she wrote, 'I have a high ideal of what nurses and nursing should be, and as to the discipline that should be maintained but the effects of my efforts have been greatly hindered by want of support on the part of the Board.'[41]

Before long, Lord Justice FitzGibbon was explaining why a special nurse had been sent back to the City of Dublin Nursing Institution and six probationers suspended. The relevant information given in the minute-book is tantalisingly incomplete but 'grave irregularities on the part of the Resident pupils of the Hospital' are referred to and there can be no doubt whatever that the cause of unrest was the proximity of opposite sexes, their youthful behaviour constrained by the dictates of narrow-minded elders determined to ensure that boy (medical student) should not meet girl (probationer nurse). It was Pierrot and Columbine in a clinical setting with reality tripping them up.

Whether there was more to it than blushes and furtive glances, whispered words and quickened pulses, cannot be said but seems unlikely. The Archbishop of Tuam was determined, nevertheless, to take immediate action. 'Not one of the young men', he insisted, 'who went into the Nurses' room ought to be left for one day in the Hospital. No one who screened them, whatever the rank, ought to remain.'[42]

The medical staff appear to have been in no great hurry to join the governors in painting a lurid scenario. When 'the alleged misconduct of Resident student Mr Richardson' was investigated it transpired that the lad's worst crime had been to intercept a letter addressed by a nurse to her brother, knowing that it was really intended for himself. Had she dared to write to him directly she would, it seems, have been in very hot water. Richardston was spoken to, censured and dismissed from the hospital.

The governors thanked the staff for their co-operation 'with respect to the recent alleged irregularities on the part of the Students' and ordered closure of the wards 'as usual for the purpose of the Annual cleaning and airing from 1st July to 1st October next.' Meanwhile, after discussions between the house-committee and the City of Dublin Nursing Institution, from which probationers were recruited, carpenters and masons were set to work to separate the area occupied by the nurses from the rest of the building. It was agreed that exits to the roofs be kept locked by the matron. She was to have full control of the probationers who must inform her of their comings and goings and should wear uniforms when going out.

Miss Powell was replaced by Miss C. Fullagar who was asked to take her meals with the probationers and treat them in a friendly way as if they were all members of a large family. The new RMO, Dr Moore, was to be responsible for the behaviour of the resident pupils and report them to the house-committee if necessary.

Probationer nurses were generally the daughters of strong farmers and others who could pay the entrance fee and buy uniforms. On two evenings a week they attended the Metropolitan School for Nursing established in the 1890s by matrons of the voluntary hospitals who drew up a nursing science course which included anatomy and physiology, nursing, hygiene, invalid cooking. Unpaid in the first year, the girls were given £6 and £12 in the second and third years of training. Hours of duty: 7 am to 8 pm; one half-day off per week. Holidays (three weeks) were taken in the summer with no days off at Christmas or Easter. A month's night-duty was followed by two months on day-duty.

Miss Fullagar resigned in November 1904 and was succeeded by Miss A. Butler who stayed until 1 August 1907. She was then replaced by Miss E.F. Beamish who, on arrival, presented a problem in that she owned a dog. She was obliged to keep her pet in the yard behind the Nurses' Home and it was not to be permitted to pass through the hospital 'by day or night, except under strict control ...' Miss Beamish left in 1908 and Miss Hanna was appointed.

A disagreement in 1909 over financial matters between the hospital and the City of Dublin Nursing Institution led the latter to decide to terminate the arrangements for training. At first the house-committee decided that Mercer's could 'go it alone' but finally the agreement with the Nursing Institution was amended and restored.

The numerous innovations of the twentieth century included rubber gloves and in 1903 the house-committee was empowered 'to add a set of five pairs of antiseptic gloves to the surgical Appliances supplied for use in the Theatre and Wards ... the gloves when supplied to be in charge of the Theatre Sister.'

Mr McFeely's retention in the hospital in March 1903 of a patient with an infectious illness led the house-committee to ask for his resignation. Called before the board, the surgeon said he did not intend to be either insolent or disrespectful but he believed the case was not infectious. His opinion was not questioned and the house-committee's resolution was withdrawn.

A year later, having claimed a fee of twenty-five guineas from the Admiralty for an operation on a coast-guard, a patient in a public ward, McFeely was again summoned to appear before the governors. His defence was unconvincing — 'I know it is the practice of the Admiralty to pay fees in such cases unless they can get out of it on some pretext, and I fail to see what claim they have either on the charity of this hospital, or on my professional services' — and the earlier misdemeanour was also held to his discredit. He faced an unsympathetic board and with a measure of grace tendered his resignation acknowledging 'the Courtesy and Consideration which I have received from the Governing body and my colleagues on the medical Staff.'

This incident is not mentioned by McFeely in his memoirs, nor does he register the least resentment towards the governors: 'There were many honourable men on the Board of Mercer's Hospital. One in particular, a retired K.C., was my greatest and most intimate friend, and he almost besought me not to resign. He belonged to the old school of crusted Tory.' Putting it in Milton's rather unsuitable phrase, McFeely decided to 'seek fresh woods and pastures new'. He left Dublin and settled in Shaw Street, Liverpool, as a general practitioner with a surgical attachment at the Mill Road Infirmary.[42a]

The vacancy created by his departure was filled by William Ireland de Courcy Wheeler, known to generations of students as 'Billy' Wheeler. He was twenty-five and inexperienced when appointed honorary surgeon (p. 140) but the governors' recruitment of a staff so youthful that Mercer's became known as 'the children's hospital' was justified by their appointees' excellent performance. Wheeler's reputation as an operator and teacher was soon established and when he resigned in 1932, Sir John Lumsden spoke of him as 'the man who made Mercer's.'

The major event of 1904 for Mercer's was the Mirus Bazaar and Fête, preparations for which had begun in April 1903 with the formation of an executive committee. The list of 'Patrons and Patronesses' promising support included their Excellencies the Lord Lieutenant and Countess Dudley, the Lord Mayor and more than seventy distinguished names. A general meeting in November to solicit popular support was presided over by the Duke and Duchess of Abercorn.

The Mirus Bazaar and Fête opened in the Royal Dublin Society's grounds at Ballsbridge on 31 May 1904 and closed on June 7th. The attractions included old favourites — clay pigeon shooting, golf contests, croquet tournaments — and a new and exciting novelty, motor-car rides in the jumping enclosure. The champion Japanese wrestler took on two at a time; a St Bernard dog ambled around drawing a little cart full of match-boxes for sale; a 'tramp-pianist' gave an exhibition of dancing while playing his own accompaniment; the Limerick Fair Green, a fair within a fair, represented an Irish country fair in miniature; the Bijou Theatre put on short comedies; the Irish Animated Photo Company held an exhibition of living pictures. The sale of raffle tickets was not permitted in the Dining Hall where cold luncheons were provided for 1s 6d, a four-course dinner for 3s 6d.

One of the daily papers described the Fête as 'a veritable fairy-land of colour and fancy spectacle.' It was generally conceded that in variety and excellence 'Mirus' surpassed any of the bazaars which had been almost an annual feature of the Dublin scene in the ten years since the first of the great bazaars, 'Araby', centre-piece of a story in James Joyce's *Dubliners*.

The weather was perfect. The total attendance was 54,565. The treasurers hoped to have about £7,000 after paying expenses but the sum eventually received by Mercer's Hospital was £4,399 3s 4d. This enabled the governors to provide a new operat-ing-theatre and anaesthetic-room, an x-ray department and six bedrooms for the sisters 'all of which will be electrically lighted.'

The close co-operation between governors and staff during the lengthy preparation for the bazaar, and the success of the venture, restored harmony to the hospital. With the hope of re-establishing a useful link with the medical board (and in the belief that Lumsden and Maunsell would be useful allies), Lord Justice Fitz-Gibbon proposed and R. Mitchell seconded a motion that the rule barring the election of members of the medical staff from mem-bership of the board of governors be rescinded. When the motion was discussed on November 1st there were seven supporters but many governors may have felt the ghost of Edward Stamer O'Grady invading the room and fourteen voted against it.

Having succeeded to the post of chief medical officer at Guin-ness's in 1899, Dr Lumsden was now in a position to engage the firm's good-will in the interest of the hospital. A donation of £300 in 1904 was followed by a cheque for £310 in 1905, and a grant of £344 in 1909 for attention given to employees of the brewery, including twenty-nine x-ray examinations. In 1903 Lumsden founded the St James's Gate division of the St John Ambulance Brigade and his name became inseparably associated with that organisation through which he was to make a major contribution to the transport and care of the wounded shipped to Ireland in hundreds during the first Great War. He opened a tuberculosis ward in Mercer's in 1907.

His publications which were not extensive, included a useful pamphlet on infant feeding intended for the wives of workers at the brewery and a report for the directors: *An investigation into the income and expenditure of seventeen brewery families and a study of their diets*. He was extern examiner in medicine to UCD and physician to the Viceroy during the term of office of Viscount Fitzalan. His flair, it seems, was for social work and administration rather than clinical medicine and he became medical adviser to the Commission of Irish Lights.[43]

Lumsden and the other members of the medical staff joined the governors on a building committee set up to effect the improvements made possible by the Mirus Bazaar. A further intimation of the governors' growing confidence in the merits of their staff was the formation in 1906 of a finance committee consisting of eight or more governors and the members of the medical board. The decision to keep the hospital open during August and September also indicated a better state of affairs.

The building plans were augmented when the family of John Pringle, a County Monaghan business-man who had died in 1905, decided to expend a large sum of money on the hospital in his memory. During his lifetime, Pringle had already endowed 'the Conrad and Muriel cot' in the children's ward. Now a vacant house, 3 Mercer Street, was purchased for use as a Sisters' Home; a laundry was built and equipped; the awkward steps in front of the hospital which Erinensis had ridiculed, were removed placing at street-level the main door which led through a granite porch to an imposing stairway.

Seton Sidney Pringle, the benefactor's son, was born in Clones on 6 July 1879, and educated in Coleraine and at TCD where he graduated in 1903. A strikingly handsome man, with a pleasant manner, a northern accent and an immense capacity for work, his success in surgery was assured following his appointment to the staff.

Students have a talent for nicknames but the shifting of vowels that created 'Satan' Pringle were mere punning unless, somehow, it evokes a whiff of a Dantesque inferno where, amid ether fumes, a dauntless operator, unprepared to countenance the word 'hopeless', essayed radical cures on advanced cancer cases. With Maunsell and Wheeler he formed a potent triumvirate at Mercer's and helped to bring it back into the forefront of Irish surgery. But he left the hospital in 1918 when appointed to the Royal City of Dublin Hospital.[44]

A ball held during the 'Castle season' provided £277 13s 3d which went to the 'x-ray-room account'. The hospital's first radiologist, Dr William Geoffrey Harvey, was appointed in November 1906 with carefully outlined terms of service. He was appointed initially for a year with the nominal salary of £1 and was thus excluded from the honorary staff and was not a member of the medical board. He was to examine only cases referred to him by members of the staff and would receive a percentage on x-rays which were paid for, such percentage 'to be fixed or altered by the Governors as they may see fit from time to time.' Dr Harvey's appointment was actually the dual one of 'pathologist and x-rayist'. When he resigned in January 1910 he was replaced by Dr H.W.Mason as 'x-rayist' and by Dr J.T. Wigham as pathologist.[45]

An epidemic of typhoid fever occurred in the children's ward in January 1908. A child contracted the disease by playing with the toys of an infected child. Two nurses were infected because the cramped condition of the lavatories made the disinfection and disposal of motions difficult. The City of Dublin Nursing Institution's allegation that defective feeding of the nursing staff was contributory was rejected.

The Ladies Committee was re-constituted but soon there were resignations and on the proposal of Colonel Courtnay it was agreed that appointees to the Ladies Committee should be elected by the board of governors. When Mrs Courtnay resigned on 1 February 1909 she expressed disbelief in the usefulness of the committee as then constituted. 'As I take a very great interest in the Hospital', she wrote, 'I shall with the consent of the governors be pleased to start a Guild to help to provide linen for the Hospital and so lessen the heavy expenses on the Hospital in providing linen ...' Her offer was accepted; rules were drawn up by her husband and on 4 May 1909 Mrs Arthur Courtnay of 19 Longford Terrace, Monkstown, was appointed first president of the Linen Guild which over the years, and in various forms, was to help the hospital in many ways.[46]

A second bazaar at Ballsbridge in 1909 for Mercer's and the Orthopaedic Hospital brought £948 6s 2d to the hospital's coffers but the governors remained constantly aware of financial constraints and the need for economy. Determined to avoid disproportionate occupation of free beds they watched bed numbers vigilantly and staff had to account for it when there were too many patients in the house. The admission of country patients, who, as the doctors pointed out, came to the hospital direct and without notice, also caused contention but the staff stressed that other Dublin hospitals were delighted to have patients from the country in their wards.

An attempt to impose increased charges on patients from Guinness's was rebuffed and Dr Lumsden, in his capacity as MO to the brewery, communicated with the registrar. 'I would point out', he wrote, 'that since 1900 Donations to the amount of £2,572 have been paid by the Company to the funds of Mercer's Hospital.'

Expenditure on rubber gloves worried the administration until in 1910 Seton Pringle arranged a special rate for them at Messers Fannin. 'It is now universally recognised by the profession and by the public that it is necessary to use gloves for aseptic surgery and should a case go wrong because gloves were not used it would be a very serious matter.'

Monies from the King Edward Memorial Cot Fund were used to buy a picture of the late monarch to be hung in the children's ward over a cot to be designated the King Edward Memorial Cot. The composition of the house-committee was re-arranged to include two members of the medical staff.

MEDICAL STAFF

A hospital's reputation depends on the quality of its nursing and the capacity of the medical staff. In the former sphere the benefits of 'Nightingale nursing' had been slowly acquired and the election of Miss R.J. Burkitt as Lady Superintendent in 1911 was a fortunate decision. At the bi-centenary, Sir John Lumsden was to say, 'For close on 25 years Miss Burkitt has been our Matron, and never was a hospital better served.'[47]

When Edward L'Estrange Ledwich retired in 1913, Frank Purser (p. 137) was elected physician and ushered in the modern phase; on leaving to take up a post at the Richmond Hospital in 1919 Purser was replaced by Rowlette who had been on the staff of the Charitable Infirmary in Jervis Street.

Robert J. Rowlette was born in Carnacash, County Sligo, in 1873 and took an honours degree in philosophy in TCD before graduating in medicine. He was lecturer in pathology at Queen's College, Galway, and then settled in Dublin. Apart from athletics (an excellent athlete in his youth, Rowlette was honourary MO to several Olympic teams) his interests, other than medicine, were literature and politics. A founder of *TCD* he became editor of the *Medical Press and Circular* and first editor of the forerunner of the *Irish Medical Journal*. He was returned unopposed to the Dail as university representative in 1933 and later represented Trinity College in the Senate. An obituarist described Rowlette, who died in 1944, as a 'sensitive stainless soul of widest sympathies' and it is regrettable that at his death a project dear to his heart, the amalgamation of two or more of the smaller Dublin hospitals, remained unfulfilled.[48]

Joining the staff as assistant physician and anaesthetist in 1920, Leonard Abrahamson was promoted visiting physician in 1927. The medical side was strengthened further by the appointment of additional assistant physicians, F.J. O'Donnell (1928), Joseph Lewis (1930) and Brian Pringle (1933).

Dublin's first electrocardiograph machine, according to W.F. O'Dwyer, was installed by Dr R.V. Murphy at Jervis Street Hospital where it occupied a room to itself, 'a massive prehistoric dinosaurus-like contraption' unlike to-day's neat instruments.[49] Be that as it may, Abrahamson was one of the pioneers of modern cardiology in Ireland.

The electrocardiograph, developed by A.D. Waller (1889), Willem Einthoven (1902) and others, was slow to become generally available. When Professor A. Lindsay of Belfast spoke to the Section of Medicine of the Royal Academy of Medicine in Ireland on electrocardiography in November 1915, James Little, regius professor of medicine in Trinity College, admitted that he had no knowledge of the subject. Lindsay's own experience at the time extended over little more than a year. 'I am very dependent', he said, 'upon the path hewed out and the landmarks erected by previous explorers.' Electrocardiography did not come before the Section again until 9 December 1921 when Leonard Abrahamson's paper, 'An introduction to electrocardiography' was read.[50]

The machine he used, as Sir John Lumsden explained, had been presented by the Red Cross and the Order of St John and installed in Mercer's Hospital as being a suitable central situation 'and the understanding was that it should be available free for the examination of cases from any of the hospitals.' In 1927, Abrahamson made the first report to the Academy of a case of coronary thrombosis in which the diagnosis was made during life and verified by autopsy. He left Mercer's in 1930 to practise at the Richmond Hospital. He held the chair of medicine at the College of Surgeons (1934–1961) and was known to generations of students as 'the Abe'.[51]

Gibbon FitzGibbon, son of the consulting surgeon to Mercer's, Henry FitzGibbon, was born in 1877 and graduated from TCD in 1900. He served as civil surgeon in the Boer War and was Assistant Master at the Rotunda Hospital before coming as gynaecologist to Mercer's from which in 1911 he was attracted to the larger opportunity at the Royal City of Dublin Hospital. His skilful successor, Arthur Holmes, was hampered by progressive deafness and retired in 1914 to devote himself to fishing and poetry. The vacancy created was filled in August by Bethel Solomons, the first Jewish doctor in Dublin to specialise.

An outstanding personality, Bethel Solomons, son of an optician, played rugby for Ireland and starred in the university dramatic society before revealing the clinical flair that made him a leader in his speciality. His autobiography, *One Doctor In His Time*, refers to his twelve happy years at Mercer's.

> I had a great deal to do as visiting gynaecologist, for, towards the end, Holmes had not bothered much. I threw my energy into the reorganization of the department. My first task was to clear the ground for myself. I found that some of the surgeons were tackling gynaecology and I had to insist, quite firmly, that I was there to do that work.
>
> At the time of my appointment, the staff at Mercer's was perhaps the best in Dublin. There were three surgeons of exceptional ability, Charles Maunsell, Seton Pringle, and William de Courcy Wheeler. Their work and technique was magnificent, but Wheeler and Maunsell disliked each other and their relations were in a constant state of ferment. Even if the atmosphere was somewhat explosive, this situation

made for interest. The amount and quality of the surgery was never better at any hospital, however.[52]

Dr Solomons was the nurses' 'guardian' dealing with whatever problems of conduct might arise. His annual party at his home in Fitzwilliam Square was one of the year's popular events for the probationers. He hired taxis to collect them and bring them back to the hospital.

In December 1922, Solomons mentioned to the governors that some friends of his wished to promote 'Sweepstakes' in aid of the hospital. At their January meeting the governors considered a proposal that a sweepstake on the Derby be organised. Rev E.G. Sullivan, MA, and others expressed their 'entire disapproval' of the scheme which was postponed indefinitely.

Solomons replaced Gibbon FitzGibbon as Master of the Rotunda in 1926; the latter then returned to Mercer's as gynaecologist while Solomons went from success to success, elected president of the RCPI and featured by Joyce in *Finnegans Wake*: 'in my bethyl of Solyman's I accouched their rotundaties.'

FitzGibbon's *Contracted Pelvis* was published in 1924. Sister Eileen Martin (now Mrs Dooley) recalls him in his later years when he was called 'Daddy' FitzGibbon. 'He was tall and thin and his language was not exactly "drawing-room".' The nurses were scared of him and he was sometimes brusque with students. A flustered young man attempting a vaginal examination was upset because the glove was not sterile. 'Is the penis sterile?' asked FitzGibbon. He was a pioneer in advocating early mobilisation and made his patients walk on the first post-operative day.

It was agreed in 1913 to advertise for 'an Anaesthetist unpaid'. Dr Jim Beckett, a notable athlete and uncle of the future Nobel-Prize-winner, Samuel Beckett, was appointed. He moved to the Adelaide Hospital in 1919 and was replaced by Dr J.P. Brennan[53] and Dr P.J. Gaffney. Dr Arthur B. Brooks was elected assistant surgeon in August 1927 but in December he opted to become assistant anaesthetist. Three years later he left Mercer's to devote himself to general practice; he retired not many years ago and now lives in Dun Laoghaire. T.J. Gilmartin became assistant anaesthetist in 1932.

Dr T. Garrett Hardman, appointed radiologist in 1914, was succeeded by F.G. Stewart in December 1932. Dr John Hackett Pollock who worked briefly as pathologist (1921–1923) before moving to the Richmond, published papers relevant to his speciality and under his pseudonym, *An Pilibín*, he wrote novels, verses and plays. He was the author of at least nineteen books including *The Lost Nightingale*, a romance based on the life of John Dowland, sixteenth-century lutanist and poet who is said to have been born in Dalkey. Dr Mary Connolly (1927) and Mr T.G. Wilson (1928) were elected ophthalmologist and laryngologist respectively.

The surgical department which Solomons legitimately eulogised recruited Thomas H. Croly (1922), James Owens (1928) and John H. Coolican (1931) as assistant surgeons. Maunsell's sudden and unexpected death in 1930 led to promotion for Owens. He was elected visiting surgeon on November 11th after two minutes silence had been observed for armistice day. Two years later when Sir William de Courcy Wheeler left Ireland, J.H. Coolican, a Catholic, was passed over and Seymour Heatly was elected surgeon. It may have been this decision to which Councillor Robert Briscoe, TD, (who represented the Corporation on the board) alluded at the governors' meeting on December 6th when he said he had heard adverse criticism of the governors' action. Briscoe spoke at some length but having been replied to by the chairman and others, including Father Roche, O Carm, he said he was satisfied there had been no collusion.[54]

Assistants had no beds and relied on the good-will of senior colleagues when they had patients to admit. To 'borrow' a bed or two was permitted but now and then an assistant was brought before the board to explain his abuse of this privilege. Apart from minor admonitions of this kind the relationship between staff and administration was now one of mutual respect. The election of Lumsden, Maunsell and Wheeler to the board was, indeed, proposed by J.F. Boydell and W.B. Brooks in December 1926 but their resolution was withdrawn when Lord Glenavy drew attention to the legal impediment: 'It is plain beyond question that these gentlemen are Officers of the Hospital and while they are not as such ineligible for election as Governors, they would if elected automatically forfeit under Rule 9 their position on the Staff and I think it fairly certain that none of them would accept election on these terms.'

VARIA

'The lamps are going out all over Europe,' Viscount Grey declared on the eve of war coining a phrase to end an era. 'We shall not see them lit again in our lifetime.' At Mercer's Miss Burkitt was the first to respond to the call of duty and on 11 August 1914 the board responded with an appropriate resolution: 'That this Board wish Miss Burkitt "God Speed" and look forward to her safe return to resume her duties as Matron.' On 3 November 1914 the house-surgeon, Dr McCullagh, submitted his resignation having been called up by the military authorities. His seniors in the hospital were given rank related to their eminence and many of them spent some time in France.

Large numbers of wounded reached Mercer's where the contribution of Miss Jordan, the acting-matron, was duly recognised.

> The Governors of Mercer's Hospital congratulate Miss Jordan on the honour conferred on her of the Medal of the Royal Red Cross. They feel the honour is no more than she merited by her whole-hearted devotion to the wounded Soldiers, and those who were the Victims of the Easter Week rising.[55]

Lumsden and Wheeler had both acted courageously in Easter Week. The former, leading an ambulance unit into the thick of bitter fighting in Baggot Street, went on alone to attend to the wounded of both sides. He was awarded the silver medal of the Order of St John for life-saving and the Red Cross special medal for gallantry. From 1917 to 1918 he had the rank of major in the RAMC attached to Number 83 General Hospital at Wimereux. He was knighted in 1918.

Wheeler was mentioned in despatches for treating wounded soldiers under fire during the Easter Rising. On Easter Monday, ignoring snipers, he made his way across St Stephen's Green to Mercer's to attend an officer with a chest-injury. Two days later he attended a soldier at the corner of Dawson Street in the small hours. He also administered to two officers of the Sherwood Foresters who were wounded in Fitzwilliam Street. Constance Heppell Marr, honorary secretary of the Dublin branch of the British Red Cross Society, expressed the Society's thanks and appreciation to Wheeler 'for the splendid services you rendered during the recent Rebellion.'

Another given leave to go to France, Sister Deery, was promised that her post would be kept open. Miss Burkitt was awarded the Mons Medal and returned to Dublin in 1918 replacing the acting-matron Miss Keane who married Sean Keating, the artist.

The Linen Guild which, as we have seen, was inaugurated in 1909 assisted in collecting 'a mile of pennies' in 1912. It was dissolved at the end of that year, reconstituted in 1914 to run out of steam again in 1922. The president, the Countess Dowager of Desart, then asked the governors to dissolve the Guild. 'The Registrar was instructed to inform her Ladyship that it would be preferable for the Guild to dissolve itself.'[56] This was done and in the following year the St John Ambulance Brigade formed a Linen Guild for the hospital 'endeavouring to retain the interest and support of the members of the old Guild', an arrangement that terminated on 31 December 1926.

The provision of accommodation for resident women students was discussed in January 1920 and deferred but in March 1921 Miss Lena Walsh undertook to pay for maintenance as a resident. The names of two women were included in a list of prospective governors but it was pointed out 'that the Board had no power to elect ladies. The Board would however be glad to consider any nominees of the two ladies.'

When Alan Gregg, who was making a survey of Irish medical education for the Rockefeller Foundation, visited Mercer's in 1925 he found it 'very poorly adapted as regards architecture for modern hospitalisation; the wards are comfortable in appearance and well-kept but the flooring is very old and means constant work to keep up ...' Gregg found 'great signs of overcrowding, especially in the men's medical ward where extra low beds were being used in between the standard beds.'[57]

Over the years the hospital has received many letters effusive in praise of what has been done for patients, but there have also been letters of complaint such as that of a widower who in 1925 informed the governors that when the nurses were settling his late wife's bed, thinking her asleep, she had overheard one of them say, 'They're going to operate on her again to-night for gallstones. The divil won't kill that oul' wan. Poison she should get.'[58] During the 1920s the generosity of Lady Ardilaun helped to make Christmas a happy occasion. Her Ladyship visited the wards on Christmas Day and she provided a festive dinner for the patients and nurses and a similar meal for the servants on New Year's Day. Miss Lumsden and her friends put on a concert for the patients on St Stephen's Day.

Labour relations were hardly yet a serious issue for managements in areas where the majority of the workers were women but the low level of laundresses' wages was brought to the governors' attention in 1921. When Miss Louie Bennett, Secretary of the Irish Women Workers Union, requested pay at the rate of 30s 0d per week and 11½d per hour overtime for laundry workers in 1927 the demand was rejected. A deputation was received on 13 September 1921; the matron interviewed the workers and in due course an increase of 2s 6d per week was conceded.

Plans for the future included a new nurses' home and with this in mind the governors negotiated to buy the adjoining houses in Mercer Street. O'Connor and Bailey's yard was acquired in 1932 and the hospital was decorated for the Eucharistic Congress. Sister O'Carroll, the hospital's first sister tutor was appointed and nurses came from the Skin and Cancer Hospital, Hume Street, and Our Lady's Hospital, Rochestown Avenue, Dun Laoghaire, to complete their training at Mercer's.

The St Helen's Fête, a raffle for a black pig, Mrs Maunsell's ball in Horse Show Week and Lady Wheeler's 'mile of half-crowns' were some of the stratagems by which Mercer's hard-pressed supporters raised funds. Aid from the Hospitals Sweepstakes was at first declined. The draw for Ireland's first hospital sweepstake, the so-called 'Iodine Sweep', took place in the board-room of Jervis Street Hospital in 1925. The Public Charitable Hospitals Act (1930) legalised sweepstakes and six hospitals participated in the first official Irish sweepstake on the Manchester November Handicap, 1930, sharing almost £132,000.

When the governors discussed 'the Lottery Bill' on 4 March 1930 they decided that should the bill become law they would not avail themselves of the Act under any circumstances. Mr George L. O'Connor dissented and by April 1931 others were of similar mind. At a special meeting, with the Archbishop of Dublin in the chair, Captain Gordon Ferrier proposed 'That the Hospital do take part in the Sweepstakes organised by the Irish Hospitals Trust Limited', and G.L. O'Connor seconded the motion. The meeting was adjourned to enable the board to have the opinion of the medical staff. The staff strongly favoured participation but at the reconvened meeting Captain Ferrier was persuaded to withdraw his motion after a long discussion.[59]

The moral arguments had rather lost their force by August 1930 when notice of motion was given of a proposal that 'in view of an excess expenditure of £1800 for the first seven months of this year a proportionate number of Beds shall be closed, to enable the

Hospital to maintain patients out of income.' The futility of the situation with its interminable penny-pinching was evident to many of the governors and notice was given of a motion to rescind the decision of March 4th and to make immediate application for inclusion in future sweepstakes.

Facts and figures were discussed at a meeting held on September 8th, the last day for handing in applications, and it was clear that while certain grants and subscriptions would be forfeited, the hospital stood to gain enormously from the sweepstakes. The chairman, Reginald Keatinge, OBE, insisted, nevertheless, that the principle was wrong and he must therefore oppose it. Taking the contrary viewpoint, another governor said that the private views on morality of those opposed to the sweepstakes had already lost the hospital £70,000 whereupon a clergyman stressed that he looked at the question not from a private but from a public point of view: each governor had a duty to see that the Irish people were not demoralised and in his opinion sweepstakes would have, and were having, a demoralising influence — a high view of life was being cast to the winds. But the reactionary voices no longer carried conviction and the resolution to accept the bread of mammon, or the windfalls of lady luck, was passed by eight votes to six.[60]

The governors agreed on 5 September 1933 (Rev E.J. Sullivan, MA, dissenting) to hold sweepstakes in 1934, together with other hospitals, on the Grand National, Derby and Cambridgeshire, and indulging in their newly-acquired prosperity they proposed to spend £350 on the department of electrocardiography and also to buy a portable ECG machine at a cost of £250.

The Hospitals Commission made a grant of £3,658 in respect of a deficit for 1933 and on 3 July 1934, as the hospital approached the bi-centenary, its bank account showed a credit balance of £4, 487 3s 1d. The governors prudently arranged to place £4,000 on deposit. Their relatively comfortably situation had entailed a surrender of autonomy and a greater loss of independence was inherent in a resolution passed unanimously at a special meeting of the board on 17 July 1934: 'That the Governors of this Hospital are in favour of Amalgamation with one or more Dublin Hospitals provided that such Amalgamation can be adequately financed and that the ultimate detailed scheme of Amalgamation meets with the approval of the governors.'[61]

DR FRANK PURSER

Francis Carmichael Purser was born in 1877 in India where his father held office in the Civil Service. From Galway Grammar School he went to TCD where academic success (MB, 1899, MD, 1901, FRCPI) was paralleled by prowess on the rugby field. He was capped for Trinity and Ireland and held the chair of medicine at the College of Surgeons (1917–1926). He was a nephew of John Mallett Purser and of Sarah Purser, RHA, who held her famous salon at Mespil House.

His interest in diseases of the nervous system made him authoritative in that area though basically a general physician. His publications included papers on amyotonia congenita and peripheral nerve injuries. In collaboration with William Boxwell he wrote *An Introduction to the Practice of Medicine*.

During the first World War, Purser held the rank of Major in the RAMC and was consulting neurologist to the Forces in Ireland. His services were rewarded with an OBE. He was appointed professor of neurology in Dublin University in 1926 the chair created 'for the present holder only.'

Frank Purser married a daughter of Dean O'Brien of Limerick. They had a son and two daughters both of whom graduated in medicine. A man of powerful physique and strong character, Purser disliked publicity but from a sense of duty accepted important offices such as the presidency of the Irish Medical Association. An avid reader, with a particular regard for Conrad, he would have relished more than many George Borrow's reference in *Lavengro* to the wind on the heath.

He loved the outdoor life and when he could afford it bought a small-holding at Calary devoting what leisure he could spare to his hobby, re-afforestation. His friend, Boxwell, who thought him 'modest beyond understanding, sensitive and shy', conceded that at times he was dour and uncommunicative. A change of mood made him an ideal companion, a master of word-pictures.

'His descriptions', Boxwell recalled, 'of his climbs among the Reeks, of being lost in a fog in the crater of Carrauntoohil, of being caught in a storm fishing for sharks in an open boat off Achill, or of herons keeping their twilight watch like grey ghosts by a stream in Galway — these are things to remember.'[62]

In the Michaelmas term of 1933, Frank Purser was appointed unopposed as King's Professor of Medicine to Dublin University; on 18 October, St Luke's Day, he donned the ornate robe of the president of the Royal College of Physicians of Ireland. 'Life is sweet, brother; who would want to die?'

Robust and vigorous, fifty-seven years old and at the summit of his career it may never have occurred to him to ponder Borrow's question but he was to be the first PRCPI to die in office for more than two hundred years.

On Wednesday, 28 February 1934, Purser lectured at the university and in the afternoon saw patients in his home, 32 Fitzwilliam Place. Walking from his consulting-room to the front-door with his last patient he experienced chest pain which he analysed with clinical detachment — certainly it was cardiac, *dolor cordis*; yet the sense of impending dissolution that may accompany angina pectoris was missing. But an hour later he was dead.

St Stephen's Church, Upper Mount Street, was thronged at the funeral service but the interment upon lonely, wind-swept Calary was private. 'He shall not hear the bittern cry ...'

A cursory glance at the *Introduction to the Practice of Medicine* written by Purser and Boxwell (the latter a grandson of William Stokes) reveals a very different situation from that reflected in Clossy's and Lendrick's books. Clossy's endeavour to relate illness to diseased organs was realised by Jonathan Osborne in the single instance of renal pathology but it was Purser's good fortune to practise at Mercer's at a time when the causes of most major diseases were broadly understood. Gout, for instance, results from disordered uric acid metabolism but instead of Stephens' milk diet Purser recommended the spas at Buxton, Aix-les-Bains and Contrexéville: '... it is open to question whether the local waters are of much more use than the equivalent amount of Vartry or Dodder, rivers of Ireland, with a morning dose of sulphate of magnesium.'[63]

Koch isolated the causative bacillus of tuberculosis in 1882; diphtheria results from infection with the Klebs Löffler bacillus; insect vectors were incriminated in the transmission of malaria and yellow fever — these infections and others are outlined in a section followed by chapters detailing the effects of the disordered function of individual organs, including the recently-recognised endocrine system and the ill-effects of vitamin deficiency.

Purser and his co-author present an excellent survey of twentieth century medicine but without clearly recognising myocardial infarction as a clinical entity and regarding cancer of the lung as a rarity. Insulin had become available but Corrigan's button and leeches remained within their therapeutic armamentarium. They did not appreciate the full diagnostic potential of x-rays and electrocardiography; the noon-time of 'high-tech' lay ahead and meanwhile fundamental Hippocratic principles were not forgotten:

> What 'Medical Etiquette' is, we confess we are not quite sure. It is certainly not medical ethics. Medical ethics is a question of honour, and the interest of patients is the foundation of its rules. It must govern all professional relations between doctor and patient. It can never be dispensed with.[64]

SIR WILLIAM IRELAND DE COURCY WHEELER

Those who called Dublin 'a city of dreadful knights' included persons envious of doctors who, as office-holders in the Royal College, or otherwise, collected knighthoods. In Mercer's the remote celebrity of Sir Henry Jebb and Sir John Lumsden's present glory would have irked Billy Wheeler until, in 1919, his record of service to the wounded earned a 'K' for Wheeler.

Sir William Ireland de Courcy Wheeler was born on 8 May 1879 at 33 Merrion Square, destined to become of the those uncommon instances in which a former president's son is elected PRCSI.[65] His father, William Ireland de Courcy Wheeler, MD, FRCSI, a son of George N. Wheeler and his wife, Williamza Florence Ireland, was born in Annesborough House, Robertstown, County Kildare, in 1844. He married Victoria Shaw (a relative of GBS) and their nine children grew up in the opulent circumstances taken so very much for granted in Victorian times by the Anglo-Irish gentry and professional class. He died from typhoid fever on 25 November 1899. By then young Billy was studying medicine at Trinity College, where he never let work interfere with tennis, dancing and other predilections of youth, yet managed to make good progress and gained some honours and prizes. At a meeting of a debating society, young Wheeler presented a bear's skull excavated in Connaught. 'The bear to which the skull belonged', he said in a modish comment aimed at the Land League, 'lived contemporaneously with primitive politicians in the West of Ireland and, if we believe in Darwin, it is hard to see why the politicians survived and the bears became extinct.'

If he was guilty of the complacency engendered by good fortune, fate supplied a drastic corrective, an accident in St Stephen's

Green in which a spiked railing damaged an eye beyond recovery. The sight of the other eye was threatened temporarily by sympathetic ophthalmia. His medical studies were interrupted by the necessary treatment and by protracted litigation in an action against the Board of Works, which was eventually settled in his favour. Then, greatly to his credit, he resumed his studies, still determined to follow a career in surgery.

Graduating in 1902, Wheeler became FRCSI in 1905, having meanwhile visited Doyen's clinic in Paris and spent three months with Kocher in Berne. Realising the value of speaking and writing in advancing his career, he learned how to excel in these arts. He also knew how much could be gained by visiting English and foreign clinics. These visits to Moynihan in Leeds, the Mayos in Rochester, Crile in Cleveland and others kept his methods in the forefront of surgery. Sir Gordon Gordon-Taylor recalled that the first time he saw de Martel's intestinal clamp used was in Mercer's Hospital. A patient with an abdominal aneurysm wired by Wheeler created a record by surviving for seventeen years and eight months.

He believed that a competent man should be a capable general surgeon but ought to develop a special interest to follow in the spirit of someone going on a holiday. His own interest, encouraged by Sir Robert Jones, was to be orthopaedics. His actual holidays invariably were brief for he disliked to be many days away from Mercer's. He married Elsie Shaw, the eldest daughter of Lord Shaw of Dunfermline, in 1909. They lived in 23 Fitzwilliam Square and had two children, Tom and Desirée. He was Surgeon-in-ordinary to the household of the Lord Lieutenant.

Wheeler's teaching drew large classes and the private 'grind' which he and T.G. Moorhead gave was a popular attraction. He was author of A Handbook of Operative Surgery (1906), which went into a fourth edition, and of Injuries and Diseases of the Bones (1928).

His personal charm made him a social success and, having a fund of stories, he became a master of a minor but important art form, the after-dinner speech. Admittedly, there were occasions when his friendliness was not in evidence and some of those in close professional contact found him demanding, irascible and overbearing. Nor did his own mishap make him sympathetic to the misfortunes of others. The anaesthetists who worked with him included a Dr Morrison, known to his colleagues as 'Sticks'

Morrison, because disablement by poliomyelitis made him dependent on two sticks. During the course of a difficult operation,
Wheeler noticed his hampered movements. 'I'm afraid, Morrison,
you're not up to this kind of case.' 'Well, Sir William, I suppose it's
a case of the blind leading the halt.'

He availed freely of the assistance of his juniors and said that
when he did a prostate operation he always had 'the finger of a
Fellow of the College in the rectum'. The late J.H. Coolican recalled going with him on a country visit and how, when the car
broke down, he helped the chauffeur to push it while the great man
sat inside.

'Competition?' Wheeler interrupted a London colleague's complaints. 'I have no problems with competition in Dublin.' And he
said he wore a crucifix to avoid, in an emergency, coming under the
care of William Pearson in the Adelaide Hospital, a Protestant
institution.

During the First World War, Major Wheeler was consulting
surgeon to the War Office. He was surgeon to the Duke of Connaught's Hospital for limbless soldiers and placed his private
nursing home, 33 Upper Fitzwilliam Street, at the disposal of the
St John Ambulance Brigade and the British Red Cross as a
hospital for wounded officers. Eight wounded officers were admitted
there from the hospital ship *Oxfordshire* on 30 April 1915 and as
the months passed, the demands on the institution increased.

Mr Ernest Guinness offered £500 to furnish an adjoining house
and by August the beds in both houses were fully occupied. The
management committee included, in addition to the honorary
surgeons, Wheeler and F.C. Heuston, such notabilities as Lady
Talbot de Malahide, the Viscountess Powerscourt, Andrew Jameson and Denis Pack Beresford. Gifts of fruit, vegetables, oysters,
salmon and flowers were acknowledged and grouse and pheasant
were donated in season.

During the summer of 1916, he arranged to visit the Front and
set out in August bearing Major General Ford's reluctant 'open
sesame':

> Major Wheeler is the bearer of the note [the DDMS, Irish
> Command wrote]. He is on his way to France. What he wants
> is a definite order to report to some authority for temporary
> duty ... and I think he ought to go somewhere near the Front
> where his attainments as a surgeon will be most usefully

employed ... He does not want to find himself wandering about without any definite job.

I hope he will not be kept too long in France as his services are really very urgently needed in Ireland as officer in charge of the 'Officers' Hospital'. It will however be an advantage to us over here that he see something of the wounded 'first hand'. I am very sorry to lose him for the time being.[66]

He visited hospitals in Boulogne and was attached to a Casualty Clearing Station at Remy Siding.

On his return to Dublin in 1916, he was involved in the organisation of the Dublin Military Orthopaedic Centre. He recalled its genesis later in a letter to General Webb:

Robert Jones wrote to me privately asking would I organise it in 1916. He then came over (incognito) and we went to the DDMS who was a patient in my hands in my private hospital! There was no escape for the DDMS, and in about half an hour we had the entire staff from OC to Hall Porter nominated, with his signature to a report for the War Office. After a few visits to London and Liverpool the organisation was complete and not a soul knew of the project until it was a fait accompli.[67]

The matron was Wheeler's former theatre-sister at Mercer's and a personal friend; W.S. Haughton shared with him the surgical duties; T.G. Moorhead, Frank Purser and T.G. Hardman were to be physician, neurologist and radiologist respectively. Such blatant adherence to sectarian and party lines galled Sir Arthur Chance, Inspector of Special Hospitals, who expressed his chagrin without delay, complaining to Sir Robert Jones that 'if the new hospital is organised in ostentatious and contemptuous disregard of my opinion, it will be impossible for me to have the influence there which is, I think, desirable, if not essential, for its harmonious and efficient working.'[68]

Sir Robert attempted to placate Chance and urged Wheeler to be more tactful. The latter protested that he had done nothing to annoy Sir Arthur: 'Our circle does not bring us into contact with Chance and he may be labouring under some misapprehension.' He promised to seek Chance's advice when patients were admitted and to be diligent in arranging the further 'polite attentions' which Sir Robert diplomatically counselled.

Before long, Wheeler was dissatisfied with his rank and went so far as to make it plain to Sir Alfred Keogh that he would like to be recommended for the honorary rank of Lieutenant Colonel, only to be told that as a member of the staff of the Blackrock Orthopaedic Hospital the appropriate rank was temporary Major. In due course, however, he was promoted and from July 1918 approval was given to Lieutenant Colonel Wheeler to receive the pay and allowances of his rank. He received approval to visit France again in November 1918.

The prospect of demobilisation in 1919 was unwelcome to Wheeler, especially as Haughton was to remain in office, and he was at pains to express his feelings to Sir T.H. Goodwin, the Director-General of Army Medical Services.

> It is now proposed to demobilize me and leave my junior colleague undisturbed.... Dublin is a small place and I am put in a very invidious position by the arrangement suggested. It will be construed in Ireland as a censure on me by the Military Authorities. This injury will be a very real one when I am endeavouring to get back the threads of private practice.[69]

He did not wish to sever his connection with the orthopaedic centre and requested that Sir Robert Jones be consulted. The latter assured him that he would be retained by the Ministry of Pensions, which was desirous of taking over the hospital.

He appears to have persuaded himself that conspiratorial forces lay behind the War Office's demobilisation order and his correspondence with General Sir Richard Ford reflects their belief that 'C' (presumably Sir Arthur Chance) was the villain of the piece. Having powerful friends, he proceeded to pull strings, as the following letter attests:

House of Commons
25 March 1919

Dear Col. Wheeler,
Sir James Craig has arranged to see you if you will call at the Pensions Office Millbank to-morrow after 4 o'clock.

Yours sincerely,
Edward Carson.[70]

Although officially demobilised from June 30th, he continued to resist the order in his correspondence with the Director-General. 'There is no idea whatever as to your "dismissal"', Goodwin assured him, 'you were no more "dismissed" than Sir Thomas Myles or any other of the eminent surgeons and physicians whose demobilisation, much to our regret, has become necessary.'[71]

Nevertheless, Wheeler refused to accept that his demobilisation was, as Goodwin would have it, 'an ordinary one of military routine', and, acting on his behalf, Sir James Craig urged the Director-General to stay his hand until such time as Blackrock Orthopaedic Hospital was transferred from the War Office to the Ministry of Pensions.

The surgeon was encouraged, too, by General Ford, who urged him not to resign — 'that is exactly what our friend C would like — he always wanted to get you out of the Orthopaedic Hospital ... I describe C as very little better than a "gas-bag" and as a surgeon beneath contempt. We have not lost the battle yet. Do not let C get an inkling of anything — not a word.'[72]

His pertinacity was rewarded and his work at the Ministry of Pensions' Orthopaedic Centre was uninterrupted until his resignation, following an illness, in September 1921.

On the Council of the RCSI, to which he was elected in 1906, Wheeler was forceful, with an exact knowledge of rules and procedures. He was PRCSI in 1922–1924. He also held the office of president of the Leinster branch of the BMA; he was chairman of the City of Dublin Nursing Institute and president of the surgical section of the Royal Academy of Medicine in Ireland.

On 1 May 1923, in his official capacity and accompanied by the vice-president, Mr R.C.B. Maunsell, and others, he visited the Vice-Regal Lodge and presented an address of welcome on behalf of the College to His Excellency, T.M. Healy, KC, Governor-General of the Irish Free State:

We, the President, Vice-President, and Council of the Royal College of Surgeons in Ireland, wish to greet you on your appointment as the first Governor General of the Irish Free State, and to express the earnest hope that your tenure of that high office may be both long and prosperous, and rendered illustrious by the establishment of peace and prosperity within the borders of the Irish Free State ...

We can assure your Excellency that the services of our

College will on all occasions be placed loyally and whole-heartedly at the disposal of the Government of the Irish Free State whenever questions arise affecting the public or the welfare of the people.[73]

Wheeler wrote and spoke on many topics, appendicitis, gastric cancer, empyema, diaphysectomy, tuberculosis of the fallopian tubes, upper abdominal palpation by the 'Dangle method', i.e., with the patient erect and stooping forward. Broadcasting on cancer and pain he said: 'Cancer comes like a thief in the night, without noise or ostentation. The medical profession is regarded by the public as the constable on duty, but he must be summoned: the alarm must be raised by the victim at the earliest moment so that drastic action may be taken while there is still time.'[74]

The three months postgraduate course with Kocher early in the century had stimulated his interest in the surgical treatment of toxic goitre, then unknown in Ireland.[75] 'In Berne we obtained a very intimate knowledge of the results. Every *Pension* was crowded with exopthalmic patients waiting their turn for operation. We lived with and had our meals with numbers of these patients, both before and after operation. The operation in Kocher's hands appeared simplicity itself. It was quite bloodless and seemed to us to be performed with the same safety as removal of the appendix. The mortality at that time was 4.5 per cent.'

He visited the Mayo Clinic when Plummer was investigating the use of iodine in hyperthyroidism. By 1930, generally using local anaesthesia, he had operated on more than 100 cases of Graves' disease and correctly regarded surgery as the most effective treatment then available.

He participated in Dublin University's annual postgraduate course and in February 1925 gave four lectures on orthopaedics at St Bartholomew's Hospital, a contribution to a series of advanced lectures in surgery sponsored by London University. He spoke at BMA meetings in Bath, Portsmouth, Manchester and London. For many years he edited the chapter on general surgery in the *Medical Annual* and his own contributions were frequently referred to in the surgical literature. He was a Vice-President in Surgery when the BMA met in Winnipeg in 1930 and was extern examiner to the Queen's University and the NUI.

The honours bestowed on him included a knighthood, the honorary Fellowship of the American College of Surgeons, and the honorary MCh of the University of Cairo which he received during the International Medical Congress in 1928 in the company of Sir Berkley Waring of Edinburgh.

A most interesting paper, 'Bennett's fracture of the thumb: a personal experience', describes how Wheeler was knocked down by a lorry outside Victoria Station in July 1931. He lost consciousness briefly and, on coming to, realised that his left hand, the dominant one, was injured. 'Only those who have experience of the injury', he wrote, 'can appreciate the helplessness which follows, nor is it generally realised how much the function of one hand depends upon the co-operation of the other. The pain at the time was of the sickening kind suggestive of fracture but not intense.' The injury had broken the proximal end of the first metacarpal bone, causing the fracture described in 1881 by Edward Hallaran Bennett, professor of surgery in TCD. An attempted reduction under local anaesthesia was unsuccessful but next day it was reduced under a general anaesthesia by Mr W.R. Bristow.

A short fishing holiday in the West of Ireland followed and, using a 'fairy' Hardy rod, which could be held against the plaster in the palm by the four free fingers, Wheeler was able to cast effectively. 'On the first evening a salmon rose in the pool, the temptation was too great, a larger fly was substituted by the Gillie, and a 20lb fish was hooked.'

Wheeler played the fish for an hour with the miniature rod and fine line before landing it. But afterwards his hand felt different inside the plaster and before long it was evident that the metacarpal had slipped. The surgeon began to fear that his thumb would never control a scissors again or tie a ligature:

> Sir Robert Jones, alas no longer with us, was consulted. He was within easy reach of Dublin. His method of approach to an enquiry of this kind was interesting and instructive. He was full of optimism, he refused to recognise defeat, he cared nothing for textbook platitudes; his experience was greater than any other living authority, he could tell the past present and future of a case of this kind with equal accuracy.

Sir Robert examined the joint under a fluorescent screen and, to Wheeler's relief, the movements were not impeded. Occupational therapy was commenced. Several times daily he immersed the hand in a basin of hot water with soap suds added. He practised using scissors and artery forceps and tying ligatures in the easeful heat. He regained his dexterity gradually and after seven weeks was able to operate again, supporting the joint with elastoplast over which he drew on two rubber gloves.[76]

Wheeler and his co-religionists had come through a troubled epoch and in an address he expressed thoughts many unionists would have shared:

> There have been times in the recent history of this country when some of us tired of the turmoil, bewildered at the outlook, anxious for the safety of our families felt inclined and were offered temptations to seek peace elsewhere. The impulse was fleeting for in the whole wide world whether in peace or in war there is no place like the city in which we live.[77]

A glittering temptation, offered by Lord Iveagh as a bishop might offer a benefice, the position of visiting surgeon to a new hospital at Southend-on-Sea, proved irresistible and on 6 September 1932, the morning of his departure from Mercer's, the staff and governors met to do him honour by their presentation.

His professional success did not falter in London, where he also held posts at All Saints Hospital for Genito-Urinary Diseases and the Metropolitan Ear-Nose-and-Throat Hospital, but it was suspected that he missed his friends and Dublin's easy-going ways. Wheeler, like many other emigrants, found platform No 13 at Euston Station to be the 'gate of paradise' leading to the resumption of felicity in a city where, unfortunately, his place in Mercer's was now firmly held by Mr Owens.

'Ah, Sir William', an old woman from the Liberties greeted him on a return visit, 'when you left Dublin the whole place shook.' Be that as it may, the shock abated, leaving Wheeler to regret his decision. He sailed for New York in the *Berengaria* in October 1932, en route for St Louis to attend the Clinical Congress of the American College of Surgeons, during which he delivered the John B. Murphy Oration in Surgery.

At the outbreak of the Second World War, Sir William Wheeler became consulting surgeon to the Admiralty with the rank of Surgeon Rear-Admiral and was posted to Aberdeen to duties which necessitated much travelling. Though by then in his early sixties, he was active enough to enjoy flights in fighter aircraft and to climb a ship's side by the pilot ladder. His death in Aberdeen when dressing for dinner on 11 September 1943, was sudden and unexpected.[78]

23.   Medical Staff, 1934.

24.   Sir William I. de C. Wheeler.

25.   Dr R.J. Rowlette.

26.   Mr T.G. Wilson.

28.   Sister Mary T. Moore.

27.   Mr T.A. Bouchier Hayes.

Chapter Five

1934–1991

BI-CENTENARY

The bi-centenary was celebrated towards the end of 1934 by an 'at Home' in the hospital; a subscription dinner for governors, medical staff and students, past and present, and their guests; a dance for the nurses, past and present, the governors, visiting staff and guests. Dr T.P.C. Kirkpatrick delivered an address in the hospital on Tuesday, December 4th and in his peroration reminded his audience that three Dublin hospitals owed their existence to women.[1] 'Grizel Steevens, Mary Mercer and Mary Aikenhead form a trinity of which any city might be proud. Today we ask you to pay your homage to the memory of one, Mary Mercer ...'

R.H. Keatinge used extracts from the minute-books to recreate those early days when Isaac Steele, the steward, was expected on Sundays to read a chapter of *The Whole Duty of Man* to the patients. 'It is a long jump from Isaac Steele's time till today — nearly two hundred years – but, the Governors of the Hospital of 1934 are unanimously of the opinion that never during the whole period ... has the charity been better served than by our esteemed friend and present Registrar, Mr Henry D. Jury.[2]

Sir John Lumsden praised the nursing and paid a tribute to the board of governors. 'The Medical Staff's relations with the Hospital Governors has latterly been of the happiest, and we have been all working in the Hospital's best interests, as one team.'[3]

Dr Rowlette stressed the need to adapt the work of the hospital to the varying conditions of the times: 'We are being reluctantly compelled to hold the view that the day of small hospitals is passing or past.' They are less efficient than larger hospitals.

That is the view taken by the Governors of Mercer's Hospital with the full support of the members of the Medical Staff, and within recent months they have decided to explore, in association with the governing bodies of two other hospitals of similar scope, Sir Patrick Dun's Hospital and the Royal City of Dublin Hospital, the possibility of an amalgamation of these three institutions into a hospital of some 450 or 500 beds.[4]

Amalgamation, or federation as it came to be called, was not to be achieved without an unconscionably protracted period of incubation. Meanwhile, at Mercer's, there were further staff changes from time to time. In 1935 J.W.E. Jessop was appointed biochemist with an honorarium of £25 per annum and Seymour Heatley's move to Dun's left a vacancy to which Mr J.H. Coolican was promoted. The latter was an unanimous choice but his election did not lack excitement. It seems that a few of the governors wished to invite Sir William Wheeler to return to Mercer's, while others, finding him over-bearing, preferred to give the younger man an opportunity to attain his full potential. Wheeler actually submitted an application but withdrew it, to avoid losing face, on receiving a letter from the acting-secretary of the medical-board predicting Coolican's election. This unwarranted communication displeased the governors who issued an appropriate rebuke for what they regarded as 'a grave act of impropriety ...'[5]

A native of Ballina, County Mayo, J.H. Coolican (1896–1964) was educated at Clongowes Wood College and Dublin University. Having graduated in 1919 he worked in London, visited American surgical centres, studied gastric surgery under Finsterer in Vienna and equipped himself with the fellowships of the Edinburgh and Irish surgical colleges.

Nigel Kinnear has described how Coolican's initial enthusiasm for abdominal surgery was replaced by the attractions of an emerging speciality. 'Perhaps it was the influence of Wheeler's restless, glittering mind which decided Coolican to launch himself into the then uncharted and somewhat choppy sea of thoracic surgery.'

Again he educated himself by travelling to Sweden, Norway and Germany as well as to the United Kingdom. There he encountered the tranquil charm of Craaford, the inspired industry of Semb, the frightening intensity and energy of Sauerbruch and the integrity and humanity of Price Thomas. From all of them he profited. Clear thinking backed by excellent technique quickly established his reputation in the speciality. His skill in chest surgery at Mercer's and Hume Street Hospitals was soon recognised by appointments to Peamount, Newcastle and later to St Luke's Hospitals. In addition to this formidable list of commitments he also held appointments at the Drogheda Hospital, Kildare and at the Countess of Wicklow Hospital, Arklow.[6]

J.H. Coolican served the RCSI as a member of Council for many years. His principal avocation was golf and he was captain of the Portmarnock Club in 1948.

When Mr Owens, who was universally popular, died in 1937 he was succeeded by Mr J. Seton Pringle.[7] F.G. Stewart left to take up a post in South Africa in 1939 and was replaced in the x-ray department by Dr Harold Pringle. Sir John Lumsden aware of his still increasing responsibilities, and also of the need to make way for younger men, resigned in November and Joseph Lewis and Brian Pringle were made full physicians.

Sir John was elected consulting physician and governor in which capacity he continued to give the hospital the benefit of his advice until his health began to fail in the summer of 1943. He died at his home, Earlscliff, Baily, County Dublin, on 3 September 1944 survived by Lady Lumsden, five daughters and a son. The latter, John Fitz Lumsden, following in his father's footsteps, was captain in command of the Trenton, New Jersey, unit of the US Army Ambulance Corps. Sir John's youngest daughter, Mrs Story, was the widow of an Englishman, George Story, a brewer at Guinness's who perished at sea in the Second World War. Shortly after his arrival in Ireland, Story was introduced to Oliver St John Gogarty who shook his hand warmly and said: 'Welcome to our rough island, Story!'[8]

'Joe' Lewis, a Jewish physician, was generally recognised as an able consultant. His contributions to medical literature included papers on pneumothorax and diabetes. He was particularly interested in diseases of the heart and his weekly evening clinic attracted students from all the Dublin schools.

The newly-introduced 'Bed Bureau' scheme was explained to the board by Rowlette on 2 November 1937 and at about this time the salary of the masseuse (forerunner of a long line of physiotherapists) and the formation of a sub-committee to consider the provision of a nurses' home also occupied the governors' attention.

On 5 April 1938, Mr J.H. Coolican discussed arrangements for blood transfusions and it was agreed 'that the sum of one guinea be paid to the St John Ambulance for each transfusion and that the Hospital recover the said sum from the patient if able to pay, if not, the Treatment to be given free.' A 'blood transfusion outfit' costing £2 was procured for Mr Coolican in January 1939; in April the sum of seven guineas was paid to the Dublin Blood Transfusion Service, a forerunner of the present Blood Bank.

The first successful blood transfusion in Ireland was given by Robert McDonnell, FRCSI, on 22 February 1870, to a young woman exsanguinated by post-partum haemorrhage.[9] The procedure could not, however, be safely applied until after the demonstration of agglutinins and iso-agglutinins by Landsteiner and Shattack in 1901 and the discovery of blood groups by Jansky in 1907. The value of blood transfusion became increasingly evident during the 1914–18 War and on his return to Dublin from France Henry Stokes, surgeon to the Meath Hospital, grappled with the problems of transfusion in civilian practice.

Stokes spoke on the subject before the Section of Surgery of the Academy of Medicine on 16 December 1921, having given twenty-nine transfusions in the previous two years. He discussed indications for transfusion, outlined the prevention of clotting by using either vessels coated with paraffin wax or sodium citrate. 'How to have a group of donors available for emergencies', he said, 'is a puzzle I have not solved, but I suggest that it is the duty of all of us to have our bloods standardized so that time need not be wasted when the demand arises.'[10]

With the declaration of war on 3 September 1939 the acronym ARP (Air Raid Precautions) became a talisman of safety even in neutral Ireland and the governors no longer found it possible to get contracts for supplies for longer than a month. The City Manager planned to evacuate patients from Mercer's in the event of a major air-raid and use the hospital as a casualty-clearing-station. He asked that twenty-five beds be placed at the disposal of the Corporation. The OC of St Bricin's Hospital requested beds for military casualties and a mobile surgical unit. Commandant Delaney was liaison officer between the hospital and officialdom; J.H. Coolican was chief ARP officer for Mercer's and Robert Rowlette officer in supreme charge of the emergency scheme for dealing with air-raids and casualties.

At individual level, Dr Gilmartin found an opportunity to show his resourcefulness as an anaesthetist when a badly burned German aviator was given facial skin-grafts by a plastic surgeon. T.G. Wilson, the ENT surgeon, believing like many that Irish 'neutrality' should favour the Allies, found himself in trouble for assisting British service-men stranded in Ireland to escape across the border to Belfast. Wilson was charged with having on 21 August 1942 assisted a person liable to internment, with intent to hinder his arrest.

In the course of his trial on October 27th, an old woman who had hidden the escaping prisoner in a garden shed refused to swear on the bible. 'Are you not a Christian?' she was asked. 'I certainly am, but I won't swear against the doctor.' When found guilty, Wilson was fined £200 and sentenced to twelve months imprisonment. The prison sentence was suspended and he was bound to the peace for two years.

On 1 November 1942 a major ARP exercise was carried out in Dublin and twenty-four 'supposed casualties' were dealt with at Mercer's. The Department of Defence requested facilities for the treatment of soldiers and their dependents which were granted at 7s 6d per day.

The purely domestic events of those years included Miss Burkitt's retirement on 31 October 1940. Her administration was adjudged to have been characterised by 'dignity, prudence and efficiency'. She was succeeded by Sister Deery and survived until 1949.

The board's congratulations to John Charles McQuaid, Catholic Archbishop elect of Dublin, were acknowledged in a letter to Henry Jury, registrar, from Blackrock College on 13 December 1940: 'I have been very much touched by the singularly kind terms in which the Board of Governors of Mercer's Hospital has conveyed to me, through you their congratulations and good wishes.'[11] Archbishop McQuaid became, ex-officio, chairman of the boards of a number of important Dublin hospitals and exerted a strong influence on medicine and education.

Dr A.H. Charles was appointed clinical pathologist in 1942 at a salary of £20 per annum and Mr Desmond Murray became temporary honorary assistant surgeon. The latter moved to Jervis Street Hospital a few years later. Mr Thomas Adrian Bouchier-Hayes, FRCSI, who was appointed temporary honorary visiting surgeon in 1944 joined the permanent staff in the following year when J. Seton Pringle took a post in Baggot Street Hospital. Dr Michael ffrench O'Carroll became 'auxiliary' anaesthetist in 1944 with a salary of £50 per annum. A young man with a long and distinguished career ahead of him, he became impatient of the role of anaesthetist, then a subservient position, and resigned in 1947 after a row with Mr Coolican.

Tommy Bouchier-Hayes (popularly known as 'the Bouch') was one of Dublin's outstanding teachers. A native of Rathkeale, County Limerick (b. 1907), the son of a veterinary surgeon, he graduated from TCD in 1930 and won his spurs when appointed assistant surgeon to the Richmond Hospital in 1933. A pupil has recalled his cherubic figure bustling around for hours teaching the elements of surgery. 'Usually late and always disorganised, he did virtually all the acute surgery and had a vast practice from the North City. He was allotted two beds but on one occasion a senior surgeon, unable to get a personal patient admitted, counted seventy patients in hospital under the care of Mr Bouchier-Hayes.'[12]

When he left the Richmond his colleagues missed his enthusiasm and optimism. Students, free to follow him, continued to attend his clinics in large numbers and his daily five o'clock 'grind' in surgery in the Dixon Hall was almost obligatory for those in the final year. The morning scene at Mercer's has been described by Dr Liam O'Sé:

In the 1940s, I was one of the fifty or more students, drawn from all the hospitals of Dublin, who made a point of attending his Thursday morning clinics. This was, in fact, a two-hour clinic, and opened with a kidney dish containing the pathological *raison d'etre* of the previous week's clinic being passed around. The clinic of the day was then presented with a fluency of expression and a clarity of exposition, dictated by the need of reaching the straining ears of students perched on chairs and rungs of beds all over the ward.

This fluency was, to my knowledge, to desert 'the Bouch' on only one occasion. On the occasion in question he was demonstrating some condition of the sternum, pointing out such landmarks as the angle of Louis. Then, in the manner reminiscent of a learned, if somewhat cloistered judge enquiring 'Who is Joan Collins?', he peered over the top of his glasses and asked: 'Who was Louis?' From the throats of the assembled multitude came the thunderous response: 'My uncle, and he was mad!'

It was, indeed, unfortunate that the question and answer constituted the punch lines of a very popular Jimmy Durante record of the day. One can only express the hope that the house surgeon was able to explain matters to his chief.[13]

A first-class surgeon, Tommy Bouchier-Hayes had many non-professional interests including music and horse-racing. In the latter sphere he was to be seen from time to time in the owners' ring. His colt, Padraig, which won a number of races, was the gift of a wealthy patient. A mare, Mkata, was a present from the Viscount de Fontarche but racing and breeding were to be expensive hobbies. His patients became his friends and it was Brian O'Nolan, better known as Myles na Copaleen, who insisted that Sean O'Sullivan should paint his portrait.

Basic to the Bouch's popularity and success were certain personality traits. 'His generosity had the abundance and richness of his native Munster and was the keystone of his personality. To give sympathy, kindness and encouragement to patients; to give friendship and instruction to students; to give advice and new ideas to administrators, were all expressions of this generosity.'[14] According to his colleague, P.A. McNally, he had strong religious feelings and 'carried the precepts of his religious teaching into his daily life through the medium of kindness and goodness to others.'[15]

His position as medical adviser to Aer Lingus and Aer Rianta led to an interest in aviation medicine and for his endeavours in this field he was to be made a Freeman of Louvain in 1958. Meanwhile, through his connection, Dublin Airport was an important source of patients for Mercer's.

A 'Lady Almoner', Miss Doreen Gannon, was appointed on 6 October 1942. When counsel's opinion was obtained regarding the powers of the governors to grant facilities for private patients the admission of such patients was considered inadvisable. The purchase of an ice-cabinet for the storage of *Penicillin* quietly recognised the advent of the antibiotic age.

A 'character' from this period, Willie Monks, merits mention though he lacked an official position. Willie's family had a little shop in the neighbourhood and every morning he brought the newspapers to Mercer's. Having delivered them, he was ready to make himself useful doing any little messages that the nurses, patients and others might require. He had gradually become indispensable and if a spare pair of hands was needed for any odd job the cry went round, 'Where's Willie Monks?' He moved about the hospital like a shadow passing freely from one ward to another. He thought nothing of taking a nurse's bags down to the bus and waiting in the long queue until she was free to come along. And if, for one reason or other, he was prevented from making his daily visit he unfailingly sent his sister to replace him.

The cessation of hostilities in Europe focussed attention on the continuation of the battle against disease and in particular on the deficiencies of the campaign against tuberculosis to which a number of nurses had fallen victims. At Mercer's, as at other Dublin general hospitals, patients with pulmonary tuberculosis were necessarily admitted to the general wards but gradually the nurses and the other patients became aware of the risks involved. A decision to exclude cases of tuberculosis was postponed in June after Dr Brian Pringle's impassioned plea on behalf of this unfortunate group.

As the physician pointed out, the lack of beds entailed lengthy delays before admission to a sanatorium was possible. And meanwhile the opportunity of inducing an 'artificial pneumothorax' — then the favoured treatment for early cases — which could be done in a general hospital, without serious risk, he believed, to nurses or neighbouring patients, was being lost.

> If the Governors decide to forbid admission of such early cases [Pringle continued], the Physician will be forced to send them home, well knowing that they lose their chance of cure, and will infect others while waiting since cough and expectoration will increase in the absence of treatment.
>
> Finally I submit that this is a Hospital for the treatment of the sick poor. If these cases are excluded the proper function of the Hospital is not, in my opinion, being fulfilled.[16]

When the discussion was resumed on August 8th the following resolution was carried unanimously:

> In view of the incidence of Tuberculosis amongst the Nursing Staff and the danger of infection to the patients, and further in view of the refusal of the Hospitals' Commission, after repeated applications, to assist the Board of the Hospital in making the proposed arrangements for the proper segregation of Pulmonary Tuberculosis patients and the

housing of their domestic staff, this Board is reluctantly
compelled to refuse all Pulmonary Tuberculosis patients,
save those in the early stages; and that this resolution be sent
to the Medical Board for their consideration.[17]

Brian Pringle's resignation in September 1945 is unlikely to have
turned wholly on the disagreement over tuberculosis. A future
president of the Royal College of Physicians of Ireland, he was
physician to Steevens' Hospital, Chief Medical Officer to Guinness's Brewery and founder of the Multiple Sclerosis Society.

A letter requesting continued admission of cases sent from
Rialto Hospital for surgical treatment was read to the governors
on 4 December 1945. The registrar was instructed to reply that the
decision to exclude such cases could not be altered. It was, however, agreed to accept cases from Peamount Sanatorium until
31 January 1946.

The decision to exclude cases of tuberculosis was not supported
by the staff and on 5 March 1946 the governors 'viewed with alarm
the number of T.B. cases in the hospital.' They asked the doctors
for a special report and when convinced of the need to provide
twenty segregated beds in a department equipped for chest surgery
a deputation requested the Hospital Commission to provide the
necessary funds. Regrettably these were not forthcoming and
when the governors learned in July that there were fourteen
tuberculous cases in the hospital they decided to delete the words
'save those in the early stages' from the resolution of 8 August
1945. The doctors protested and at a special meeting held on
18 September 1946 the two groups had diametrically opposed
viewpoints. Mr Coolican was refused permission to admit a patient
with pulmonary tuberculosis on October 1st. He suggested that
patients from Rialto Hospital requiring procedures not
necessitating admission for more than a few hours could be dealt
with as out-patients, but the concession was not granted. In
December, nevertheless, cases of tuberculosis were still being
admitted.

This episode is of singular interest and importance. One feels
that had it been possible to facilitate Mr Coolican in his efforts to
establish a surgical chest unit the hospital would have made a
considerable contribution to Dublin medicine. Thoracic surgery
was an expanding speciality just then and improved diagnostic
methods were revealing the menace of lung cancer. The resulting

frustration explains why the staff continued to seek representation on the board of governors but Lord Glenavy's judgement was invariably quoted against them.

The recruits to the staff in the late 1940s were Mr J.G. Mathews, visiting surgeon (1946); Dr W.B. McCrea, assistant ophthalmic surgeon (1946); Mr John McAuliffe Curtin, assistant laryngologist (1946); Dr P.A. McNally, visiting physician (1947); Dr J.W. Gaffney, assistant anaesthetist (1948); Professor John Dunne, psychiatrist (1949).

Dr Michael McGrath who had held posts as house-surgeon and casualty-officer in Mercer's, was appointed assistant anaesthetist in 1950 and Drs E. Thompson and Henry FitzGibbon joined the department of gynaecology. Having given twenty-five years' service to the hospital, Dr Mary Connolly resigned in 1952. Drs Desmond Douglas and Patrick Mathews were appointed ophthalmic surgeon and assistant ophthalmic surgeon respectively. Drs Rory O'Hanlon (gynaecologist), Geddes Redman (radiologist) and Mr J.E. Coolican (assistant surgeon) were appointed in 1953. Mr McA. Curtin ranked as a senior ENT surgeon from 1954 and Mr Con O'Connell was elected assistant laryngologist. T.G. Wilson retained a nominal attachment but his main work at this period was done elsewhere.

A highly competent ENT surgeon, Wilson was the author of *Diseases of the Ear, Nose and Throat in Children* (1955) but is probably better remembered for his excellent biography of Sir William Wilde, *Victorian Doctor* (1942), and for arguing convincingly that Jonathan Swift suffered from Ménière's disease.

Victorian Doctor contains sixty-one illustrations by the author, eloquent testimony of Wilson's competency in another art form. His paintings include a portrait of Denis Johnston, the playwright and author, and a study of the forecourt of Dr Steevens' Hospital which now hangs in the Colles Room of the College of Surgeons. He was professor of anatomy in the College of Art and an honorary RHA, in which capacity he was accorded an unusual distinction, being permitted to hang two paintings annually. Those familiar with his work think his forté lay in water-colours and etching.

T.G. Wilson was elected PRCSI in 1958.[18]

PATHOLOGY AND OTHER PROBLEMS

Mr Henry D. Jury resigned from the position of registrar on 2 April 1946 and was voted an annual pension of £300 free of income tax. It was generally agreed that 'Secretary' would be a more suitable title for his successor. The vacancy was advertised and from sixteen candidates three were interviewed on May 14th. Mr J.P. Little, BA, BL, was then appointed secretary with a commencing salary of £400; a pleasant and meticulous gentleman, he continued to hold the post until after the closure of the hospital in 1983. From 1 October 1961 he had the assistance of an excellent deputy, Miss Jane Rodgers.

The feasibility of building a new wing was under consideration in the late 1940s and a close eye was kept on neighbouring properties. The Department of Health approved of the purchase of 4 and 5 Lr Mercer Street (6 and 7 were acquired later) and plans for a new Nurses Home and other improvements were discussed on 15 July 1949. A contract with the builders, Messers Leonard and Donnelly, was signed and sealed in June 1954 and permission to build on the site for thirty years was sanctioned by the Department of Local Government.[19] The new Nurses Home was completed in November 1956.

Miss Deery had resigned in August 1950; she was replaced as matron by Miss Mary J. Kelly who had an instinctive flair for the selection of excellent sisters and staff-nurses, many of whom were incomparably skilled in nursing arts, each constituting in herself an 'intensive care unit'.

Negotiations for the purchase of the Widows Home continued but the vendor's price (£3,000 in 1951) was thought to be too high.[20] This property was eventually acquired in 1963. Ten years earlier, Bartley Dunne, a neighbouring publican, offered to sell his property in Stephen's Street and Digges Lane to the governors for £20,000.[21] A valuation of the property was obtained and the Department of Health consulted. The bid which was eventually made in April 1955 was declined.

On 7 December 1954 the hospital's overdraft was £28,499 16s 0d but by then the governors were accustomed to being heavily in debt to the bank with the tacit assurance that sooner or later the Hospitals Commission and Department of Health would reduce the deficit. A comfortable situation, perhaps, enabling them to face spiralling costs with equanimity and pay due attention to demands from trade unions. Had the reactionary minority who voted against the sweepstakes still been about, their abhorrence of gambling would have cut no ice. And yet, even for a voluntary hospital, there is no such thing as a free lunch.

It was not humanly possible to resist the bonanza but the control effectively imposed by the Hospitals Commission by virtue of its largesse may have sapped initiative. The system of deficit budgeting was surely a betrayal of economics. St Michael's Hospital, Dun Laoghaire, proposed in 1958 that a fund of five million pounds be accumulated for the payment of the deficits. St Laurence's Hospital sought support in 1968 for a plea to the Minister concerning the payments of deficits.

Their debts ensured that the governors must go cap in hand to their paymasters when purchases were contemplated. 'A letter from the Department of Health Approving the purchase of a cystoscope was read and noted with satisfaction.'[22] It made independent action impossible — the department of thoracic surgery that Mr J.H. Coolican and his son wished to provide was developed elsewhere. The Corporation's legitimate request for accommodation for patients with venereal diseases, a major clinical problem in the 1950s, was turned down for lack of facilities.[23] The failure to avail of Bartley Dunne's offer, however the money was raised, was a signal instance of lack of enterprise. This property was sold in July 1990 for £1.8 million.

The equipment provided was not always the best. When Dr Gilmartin requested, towards the end of 1953, the purchase of the latest anaesthetic apparatus the Hospitals Commission recommended a less expensive machine. Dr Gilmartin demurred and was given permission to write personally to the Commission. Many months later he was obliged to accept the type of machine listed by the combined purchasing section of the Department of Local Government.[24]

Additions to the staff in this period included Mr John Lanigan, consulting neurosurgeon (1956); Dr Eric Doyle, paediatrician (1956); Dr Michael Solomons, assistant gynaecologist (1956); Dr Tom Scully, assistant anaesthetist (1957); Drs T. O'Looney and A. Cowan, honorary visiting dental surgeons (1958). The almoner, Miss Gannon, resigned in 1956 and was replaced by Miss O'Toole. Dr G. Gearty's services were available as cardiologist to the Federated Hospitals (1963).

The death of Mr Bouchier-Hayes after a short illness on 29 January 1960 left a vacancy which was to be filled by Mr Richard Brenan. When Dr Lewis became seriously ill in June 1963, Dr J.B. Lyons, physician to St Michael's Hospital, was engaged as locum. Dr Lewis died on 5 May 1964 survived by his wife and a son, John, who graduated from the RCSI and now practises in Leigh, Lancashire.

When Joe Lewis was assistant physician he had also fulfilled the duties of pathologist, a not uncommon arrangement before trained pathologists were available. Later, like a number of other hospitals, Mercer's sent its specimens to the laboratory at Trinity College for examination. The inadequacy of this arrangement was appreciated and in 1954 it was proposed that part of the air-raid shelter be converted to a laboratory. A grant of £2,700 was approved by the Department of Health. The Hospitals Commission favoured a scheme under which the Trinity College Medical School would supervise the laboratories in certain teaching hospitals but in view of an established teaching connection with the RCSI the medical board recommended that the latter's pathology department should be supervisory and supply a service.

The board of governors, meanwhile, had become less enthusiastic about the conversion plan. After a long period of vacillation the Department of Health stated that because of financial strictures it was no longer possible to make a grant for pathology. In view of this set-back a meeting was held with the Hospitals Commission and a modified plan was drawn up. An appeal from the medical board on 2 February 1960 led to a request that the Department of Health should reconsider its negative attitude. The report of a meeting with the Department of Health was 'read and noted.'

The 'Path Lab affair' is another instance of difficulties faced by governors dealing with bodies whose delaying tactics rivalled those of Fabius Maximus the Cunctator. But when the General Medical Council visited Mercer's officially in June 1961 its adverse report on the pathology facilities threatened its continuation as a teaching-hospital. A great deal of work had to be done urgently to rectify the situation but finally a laboratory sufficient for the hospital's immediate needs and a small autopsy-room were provided. Dr Joan Mullaney was assigned as temporary consultant pathologist (1962) and Miss Nuala Horner was senior laboratory technician.

Meanwhile in 1955 the desirability, according to the medical board, of introducing private accommodation was discussed again by the governors. The Minister for Health was informed of the proposals and asked to approve in principle. Counsel's opinion was obtained towards the end of 1959 and it was then felt that alterations of the charter would be required if the traditional prohibition of fees was to be removed.

When the medical board sought the opinion of Mr T.F. O'Higgins, SC, in 1962 he said: '... it is in the vital interests of the Hospital that this prohibition be removed.' He believed that alterations of the charter were unnecessary. Recent social changes and the Voluntary Health Insurance Act (1957) had created a demand for the accommodation of paying patients. If Mercer's could not provide this it would be by-passed by VHI patients which could influence the intake of other patients and jeopardise seriously the standing of the hospital as a teaching institution.[25]

In the light of additional legal advice it was agreed in August 1963 that when all interested parties had been advised private and semi-private beds should be provided. A plan for converting Ward Three and Ward Four for this purpose was implemented and when, towards the end of 1965, the private section was ready for occupation it was decided that patients in semi-private beds were to be charged £17 17s per week, a sum comfortably covered by the VHI.

FEDERATION

'There are nineteen hospitals in Dublin', Oliver St John Gogarty observed in *As I Was Going Down Sackville Street*, 'and all un-mergeable into one.' He attributed the unmalleable nature of the capital's hospital system to the fact that so many endowments and grants were denominational. 'There is a greater vested interest in disease than in Guinness's Brewery.'

Gogarty's acceptance of divisions separating the hospitals may have been a reaction to the ineffectuality of a scheme of amal-gamation instigated by Dr Rowlette and others in 1920. There had, indeed, been an earlier scheme and at a meeting of the Dublin branch of the British Medical Association in 1888 Edward Mapother addressed the meeting on the subject of hospital reform.[26] He supported Lord Spencer's plan to amalgamate the Richmond and Steevens' on a site near Christchurch Cathedral 'and the simul-taneous fusion of several of the other smaller hospitals, with the view of saving working expenses and aggregating a larger number of cases suitable for scientific observation.'

Robert Rowlette took 'The Problem of the Dublin Voluntary Hospitals' as the subject of a presidential address to the Section of State Medicine in the Academy of Medicine on 6 February 1920. Having discussed the poverty and relative inefficiency of the smaller hospitals and their 'comparative failure' particularly in the sphere of research, he said: 'The suggestion has been recently made that greater economy and efficiency would be secured were all or some of these several hospitals to amalgamate into one or two large hospitals.' He then affirmed his approval of this opinion. 'I submit that by pooling their resources, their prestige, and their energy, they will provide a better service for the sick, offer a better education to the medical student and advance the cause of knowledge.'[27]

Fourteen years later at the bi-centenary celebration, Rowlette, as we have seen, spoke as an advocate of amalgamation. By then, indeed, the matter had already received lengthy consideration and on 2 December 1924 the board of governors had replied in the affirmative to the following resolution of the Board of Representative Governors of the Associated Dublin Clinical Hospitals: 'Resolved that in view of the possibility of obtaining a sufficient Grant for the erection and endowment of a Central Hospital in Dublin, the Boards of Governors of the several Dublin Clinical Hospitals are invited to consider whether, if such a grant is forthcoming, they would wish to join in discussing a scheme for amalgamation.'

In the early 1930s Mercer's appointed new representatives to discuss amalgamation and in 1934 the Hospitals Commission sanctioned the expenditure by the hospitals concerned of £1,000 to investigate legal and other questions. A special meeting of the board of governors attended by members of the medical board was held on 17 July 1934 and, as already mentioned, it was unanimously agreed: 'That the Governors of the Hospital are in favour of an Amalgamation with one or more Dublin hospitals provided that such amalgamation can be adequately financed and that the ultimate detailed scheme of amalgamation meets with the approval of the Governors.'

Throughout the 1930s, with the support and encouragement of the Department of Local Government and Public Health, the planning continued. A draft bill prepared by the Amalgamation Committee was discussed by the governors on 5 July 1938 and accepted providing the hospital was adequately endowed and contained at least 500 beds. The Minister for Local Government and Public Health agreed in 1939 to set aside £2,500,000 as an endowment fund and promised that no other hospital would be included against the wishes of the governing body of the new hospital which was to have a minimum of 400 beds, to be increased to

500 beds if a convincing case were made. (If the Meath Hospital participated the new hospital would have 550 beds.)[28]

Doubtless the Second World War contributed to the delay but in 1944 a letter from Dr T.G. Moorhead intimated that the government was now in a position to proceed with the bill and once more Mercer's pledged itself to amalgamate. On 27 May 1947 the governors elected as its representatives to the Amalgamation Committee P.J. Cahill, James Forsyth, T.M. Lyle, T. Bouchier-Hayes and J. Lewis. However, 'The best laid plans of mice and men ...' For unstated reasons, the amalgamation planned by Rowlette and his colleagues failed to materialise.

This frustrated exercise in which busy men exchanged countless hours of committee-work for unfulfilled promises is generally overlooked by chroniclers of the genesis of the Federated Dublin Voluntary Hospitals. According to one account, 'In 1957 four doctors from some of the hospitals now federated met informally and agreed that a move should be made to bring together the small Voluntary Hospitals in Dublin.'[29] Their reasoning was identical with that motivating their predecessors but their efforts were rewarded with a greater measure of success, however tardy the fruitage.

Seven hospitals were invited to participate — the Adelaide, Dun's, the Meath, Mercer's, the National Children's Hospital, the Royal City of Dublin Hospital and Steevens' — all of which agreed to do so, leading to the formation of a joint committee of lay and medical representatives under the chairmanship of Mr Robert Woods, ENT surgeon at Dun's.

When after many meetings in 1958 and 1959 it was agreed in principle that the hospitals should unite, the Minister of Health was approached. He agreed to give every assistance. Discussions were held in the Department of Health in 1960 and 1961 to enable the necessary legislation to be arranged. The Hospital Federation and Amalgamation Act became law on 8 July 1961. This created a Central Council which came into effective existence on 6 November 1961, 'establishment day'; its first chairman, Mr Arthur Chance (1961–1964), was surgeon to Dr Steevens' Hospital; it controlled capital expenditure throughout the Federation and the appointment of all future members of the visiting medical staff.

Professor Peter Gatenby's outline of the Federation's first decade, 'History of the Federated Dublin Voluntary Hospitals (1961–1971)', refers to the centralisation of pathology services —

'one of the dominant, not to say sometimes painful activities of the Central Council' — and to its main objective, the creation of a new hospital. Circumstances were to dictate that a series of sites would be considered before the final decision was taken placing the new hospital at St James's.[30]

Advised by the planning committee, the Central Council decided in 1964 that five hospitals should be merged into one at the Sir Patrick Dun's site, with the Meath (part of which was newly-built) and Steevens' (subject to a preservation order) retained as genito-urinary and orthopaedic surgical centres respectively. This choice was accepted by the Minister for Health but in the following year it was learned that another government department planned to run a major road through the proposed site.

When the Dun's site was abandoned the City Manager offered an acceptable 16-acre site in the grounds of Clonskeagh Fever Hospital, but in 1966 Mr Donogh O'Malley, then Minister of Health, frowned on this proposal. His alternative, a site at Cherry Orchard Hospital, was accepted pending the report of Llewellyn Davis, Weeks and Partners, a hospital planning firm. The planning consultants approved and provided a blue-print for a hospital of 1,244 beds.

The appointment of a project team was agreed by the Department of Health but prevented by the Minister's action in setting-up a Consultative Council to plan hospital services for the entire country. When the FitzGerald Report' was published in June 1968 it envisaged the activities of the Federation as divided between sites adjoining St Vincent's and St Kevin's Hospital at Elm Park and James's Street respectively. This recommendation was coldly received by a majority in the Federation. They had never expected to work cheek by jowl with St Vincent's and did not wish to do so.

The planning consultants at this juncture still favoured the Cherry Orchard site but the Department of Health pressed for a division of beds between Elm Park and James's Street and this was finally agreed to, providing the bulk of the beds and a priority in building should be given to the development at St Kevin's where the vast existing poor-law hospital was to be modernised and re-named St James's Hospital. The St James's Hospital Board, composed of representatives of the Federated Hospitals and of the Dublin Health Authority (now the Eastern Health Board) in equal proportions, held its first meeting on 2 July 1971.

The gradual infiltration of St James's by the 'Feds', as the newcomers were sometimes called, inevitably caused raised hackles and legal disputes. This was only to be expected for if sectarian considerations had militated against acceptance of a site close to St Vincent's the gap between St Kevin's Hospital and the Federation might have seemed even more unbridgeable. The staffs of the voluntary hospitals had argued vociferously against the development of an enlarged municipal hospital. Over the years their attitudes towards St Kevin's had been grudging and patronising. 'It is not a teaching hospital', Dr Henry Moore, UCD's feisty little professor of medicine, insisted at an Academy meeting in 1936, 'and, in my view never will be, however large it may become.'[31] Such strongly enunciated sentiments had not made for good relationships nor were they readily forgotten by later generations. Fortunately an influential minority within the Federation could see that state control blurred distinctions between 'voluntary' and 'municipal'. St James's offered an unrivalled opportunity and had a splendid educational potential.

The struggle for *lebensraum* did not materially concern Mercer's which had attained gains and encountered problems within the Federation. The principal gains related to a freedom within the Federation to pass freely in consultation from one hospital to another, and access to sophisticated diagnostic procedures; the most troublesome problem concerned pathology — Mercer's link with the RCSI, where some of its staff held professorships, became a cause for contention.

Mercer's had given its assent readily in 1958 to what was often miscalled 'the Hospitals Merger Scheme'. Captain J.C. Colville, RN, Dr P. McNally and Mr J.E. Coolican represented the hospital on the negotiating committees. The bill as drafted by the Minister and the subsequent amendments were accepted by them without demur. Mercer's first representatives on the Central Council were Captain Colville, Brigadier Stanley Clarke, CBE, DSO, Mr R.E. Jacob, Dr P. McNally and Mr J.E. Coolican. The Cherry Orchard site was acceptable in 1965 and when it fell through no objections were raised to the site at St James's.

The centralisation of pathology improved the diagnostic services immeasurably though clinicians rather regretted that they were no longer able to drop into the laboratory to discuss the significance of this test or that with the pathologist. The centralisation of the autopsy service was at first resented but there were obvious advantages.

For some years Mercer's retained the right to do the simpler blood tests, examinations of urine and spinal fluid in its laboratory, having the more complicated bacteriological and biochemical tests done centrally. Later, when this was no longer practicable, the laboratory at Mercer's became a centre for immunology.

The teaching connection with the RCSI necessitated the referral of tissue specimens, biopsies and the like to the department of pathology in the College of Surgeons. A charge was made for these examinations though the same service was available at no further cost under the financial arrangements already established with the Federation's laboratories. This 'irregularity' proved irksome to the Central Council and the moves to make Mercer's fall into line caused tensions in the hospital similar to those the nation has experienced *vis-à-vis* stronger and intransigent neighbours in the European Community. The situation eventually provoked an outburst from Professor McNally when, on 27 November 1967, he proposed a motion defending the *status quo*: 'That the present satisfactory and efficient pathological services in Mercer's Hospital which are of benefit to patients and staff alike be left undisturbed.'

It appears to us [McNally said] that all seven hospitals are to be Federated but Mercer's is to be more Federated than the others. We find it difficult to understand the expenditure of £250,000 by the Adelaide if it intends to move and we question if this expenditure fully complied with requirements of the Act.... The recent expenditure by Sir Patrick Dun's of £5,000 without even getting prior approval from the Council has surprised us as the eventual post facto approval did not. However, when a point arises vital to the professional status and financial welfare of the staff of Mercer's and costing a negligible annual sum for an efficient pathological service of benefit to the patients and staff, this arouses the necessity of a couple of committees talking and meeting over several years and not reaching any satisfactory conclusion. We do not believe that if the professional welfare of the Medical Staffs of the Adelaide, Sir Patrick Dun's, Meath, Royal City of Dublin, St Steevens or the National Children's Hospital were involved, it would arouse such opposition, controversy and discussion.[32]

McNally's aggressive argument prevailed but before long an invitation from Professor Gatenby to accept students from Trinity College coincided with a mood of disaffection towards the College of Surgeons which had sent an unrelieved group of its weaker students to Mercer's. At 'Surgeons' the students were encouraged to express a preference and those with the highest marks were given first claim on the hospital of their choice. It so happened that in a particular year none of the better students had selected Mercer's and the academic records of all those directed to the hospital were abysmal. It was regretfully decided that a time had come for a change of academic allegiance and in January 1969 the governors recommended that a teaching connection be established with the School of Physic.

The young men and women who came to Mercer's from Trinity College in the spring of that year may have seen themselves as innovators. Far from it! This was a homecoming for Mercer's which, as we have seen, had taught Trinity students in the eighteenth century, the first hospital to do so officially. The renewed allegiance had the further advantage that it was now possible fully to avail of the centralised pathology service and eliminate the anomaly requiring double payment.

Mercer's continued to support the Federation loyally but the original participants became increasingly disappointed, not to say cynical, when unpardonable delays made it apparent that the move to a new hospital was a consummation unlikely to be achieved before their retirements. The project had the blessing of the Oireachtas, the assent and approval of the Department of Health and Comhairle na nOspidéal, the good-will of the seven hospitals, some of which had been striving towards this end since 1920. What, then, was holding them back? Commercial organisations made decisions, drew up plans and went ahead completing very large projects in a few years. Did building a hospital have to be so very different?

The new recruits were content to tolerate and encourage alterations and dilution of the original aims of federation but Professor McNally and others of his generation still believed, however naively, 'that it would be a simpler matter to get one big hospital built into which everyone would move at the same time, than to build a lot of small interrupted lots which could become stagnant any time with a change in Government policy or an economy campaign.'

A situation which had, indeed, become stagnant was given fresh impetus when the board of Mercer's discussed the possibility of a piecemeal amalgamation of the Federated Hospitals and arranged for an informal meeting of the chairmen of Mercer's, Dun's and the Royal City of Dublin Hospitals. The outcome of this and other meetings is recorded in the minutes of Mercer's Hospital:

> The Boards of Sir Patrick Dun's Hospital, Mercer's Hospital and the Royal City of Dublin Hospital agree to the Principle of Amalgamation of their respective Boards with a view to a unified move to a new hospital at St James and that a joint working party be set up to investigate this resolution.[33]

With a sense of *déjà vu* the working party was formed but the cataclysmic events hidden in the years ahead included the hiving off of 'the Manch group' — the Meath, Adelaide and National Children's Hospitals — to occupy a hospital in Tallaght still as insubstantial as a castle in Spain and the premature closure of Mercer's, Dun's, the Royal City of Dublin and Dr Steevens' Hospitals. The last-named hospital, incidentally, lost its priceless Worth Library, and the wards in which Abraham Colles had worked and Sir William Wilde studied are fated to be occupied by a regiment of administrators, a triumph of sorts for the Eastern Health Board.

THE LAST ACT

When the present author was appointed consultant physician to the Dublin Federated Voluntary Hospitals in 1965 and assigned to Mercer's, his senior colleagues in the medical department were Frank O'Donnell and Paddy McNally, the latter being then the more dynamic.

Francis J. O'Donnell was born in Rathfarnham, County Dublin, in 1894. From Castleknock College he proceeded to the medical school of the RCSI and graduated in 1920. Having gained experience in the Bagthorpe Infirmary, Nottingham, he returned to Dublin and in the late 1920s was appointed MO to the Rathfarnham Dispensary District. Meanwhile he had taken the MRCPI in 1923 and was elected a Fellow in 1925. He held the office of PRCPI from 1955 to 1958.

O'Donnell's particular clinical interest was dermatology and he was extremely skilled in the handling of difficult skin problems, though woe betide the patient who made the least deviation from his instructions or ventured to seek a second opinion. He held the post of dermatologist to Hume Street Hospital; he was a Fellow of the Royal Academy of Medicine in Ireland, a member of the British Association of Dermatologists and of the North of England Association of Dermatologists, a governor of the Apothecaries' Hall with a great interest in that body. His publications included articles on empyema and malignant disease of the lung, written at a time when the latter was considered a rarity, but his most interesting paper was an account of caisson disease and its prevention, based on personal experience when a tunnel to carry water-pipes and electric cables was drilled under the Liffey in the 1920s. Discriminating students attended Frank's teaching sessions, knowing that though the latest syndromes were unlikely to be discussed, this man had important lessons to impart, lessons that he alone could teach and were not to be read in any textbook.[34]

Patrick Aloysius McNally, MD, PhD, FRCPI, the eldest of the family of Walter McNally and his wife, the former Molly Staunton of Westport, County Mayo, was born in Wardner, Idaho, USA, in 1909 but grew up in Dublin. A Clongownian and a 'Trinity man', he had the *savoir faire* that can be imparted to a son by a successful father—in his day Walter McNally had an international reputation as an 'Irish baritone' and as a cinema owner became wealthy when moving pictures replaced vaudeville. From his father, too, he inherited a love of music that made him an assiduous concert-goer and perhaps his acquaintance with the traditions of the entertainment world may have lent something to his light-heartedness.

Urbane, compassionate, knowledgeable, his accomplishments were based solidly on professional competence and he was delighted when appointed associate professor of medicine in the RCSI and later at TCD. His geniality and sincerity appealed to students and he was one of the very few Dublin teachers to have been president of 'the Bi' in two schools. His presidential address, 'Medical Care: Can We Afford It?', aroused a good deal of public discussion when published in the *Irish Times*. His choice of theme was an oblique indictment of charity as dispensed by the state. His personal efforts to help the poor and disadvantaged were implemented through chairmanship of 'Heart of Variety' by which the Variety Club of Ireland channelled its charitable funds, and through the Irish Epilepsy Association which he founded.[35]

Widely-travelled and well-read, McNally was an amusing dinner companion and a generous host in the Stephen's Green Club where for years he was a member, appreciated by those who understood the dual aspects of his character reflected by his election to the offices of Chief Barker of the Variety Club of Ireland and Vice-President of the RCPI. He resigned from Mercer's and retired from practice in 1975. The last few years of his life were first shadowed and then darkened by ill-health, a myocardial infarct preceding Parkinson's disease in a remorseless, akinetic form. Behind the impassive mask good-humour still flickered but death cannot have been unwelcome when it came suddenly on 11 August 1976.

During Mercer's last phase its surgeons were Joseph Gerard Mathews, FRCSI, John Edward Coolican, MCh, FRCS, FRCSI and Richard Brownell Brenan, MCh, FRCS, FRCSI. They practised general surgery and the excellence characteristic of Sir William Wheeler's years at Mercer's was fully maintained. Mr Mathews was particularly skilled in abdominal surgery and for many years was a member of the Council of the RCSI. Professor Coolican had additional expertise in vascular surgery and chest surgery having been surgical registrar at Harefield Chest Hospital. Dick Brenan, who joined the staff in 1965, was formerly a Surgeon-Lieutenant RNVR and surgeon to the General Hospital in Nairobi, Kenya; he was particularly attracted to the surgery of the thyroid gland.

The surgeons were well served by their anaesthetists, Tommy Gilmartin, Michael McGrath and Tom Scully. Dr Royiyah Salleh, an RCSI graduate from Malaysia, was anaesthetic registrar in the late 1960s.

Professor John Dunne was the doyen of his speciality in Ireland until his death on New Year's Day 1991. Having held a chair of psychiatry in UCD, he retired from the post of Chief Medical Superintendent of Grangegorman Mental Hospital (later St Brendan's) before coming to Mercer's. Like Edward Hill, he was endowed with exceptional genes and remained in practice until late in 1990. The 'John Dunne Medal' is awarded annually by the *Irish Journal of Psychological Medicine* to a trainee for a contribution to the journal.

The sudden and unexpected death of Geddes Redman in December 1967 from coronary heart disease shocked his colleagues. Endlessly obliging, he was universally popular. Dr James McNulty whose publications included a textbook on the radiology of the liver and other monographs, was assigned to the x-ray department in 1968.

C.D. O'Connell, MCh, died in 1968 from a bronchial carcinoma; he was replaced as ENT surgeon by Mr Thomas Wilson who, like his father, T.G. Wilson, was also skilled in the arts. Cornelius Dermot ('Con') O'Connell graduated from UCD in 1936 and worked in London and New York before returning to Dublin where he secured a number of appointments. A Council of Europe scholarship enabled him to study the management of deafness in Scandinavia and he travelled north into the Arctic Circle. John McAuliffe Curtin's obituary of his colleague referred to Con's 'strength and dependability' and said 'To have known him was an experience which added a great deal to one's view of life.'[36]

Dr Eric Doyle's resignation (1969) left a vacancy filled by the appointment of Dr Barbara Stokes as consultant paediatrician (1970). A succession of pathologists included Drs Ian Temperley, John Greally and Conor Keane.

Professor Gilmartin was invited to join the medical board in 1969 'in view of his long years of service and his particular knowledge of special problems.' Hitherto the preserve of the *honorary* medical staff, the medical board was soon to be enlarged on the advice of Central Council giving membership to all consultants.[37]

Steps were being taken in 1967 to provide the hospital with an Intensive Care Unit (ICU). Having obtained the go-ahead from Central Council, approval was sought in February 1968 from the Department of Health which requested that the proposal to place an ICU within the existing building be reconsidered. As the medical board continued to press for this vital amenity a sub-committee composed of Brigadier Clarke, Mr R.K. Talbot and Mr R.B. Brenan was formed. In due course their plans were forwarded to the house committee but for economic reasons the project was turned down flatly by the Department of Health early in 1971.

Pricked to independent action, perhaps, by the discouragement of the Department, Mercer's decided to raise the funds. With the enthusiastic assistance of a 'Ladies Committee', a modernised version of the Linen Guild, convened in March 1971,[38] this was speedily accomplished. Matron's requirements for the completed ICU in 1972 were a sister, five staff-nurses and four student-nurses. Meanwhile in November 1969 the Workers Union of Ireland's demand for a five-day week for clerical staff signalled an approaching end to Saturday-morning clinics.

When a fire in the x-ray dark-room destroyed the film processing unit in 1970 the options were either to replace it with a unit of
similar type (the cost of which was covered by insurance) or to
install a much superior automatic unit costing £3,000. The latter
would need the Department of Health's sanction and rather than
face the prospect of that slow-moving body's disapproval, after a
disruptive delay, the governors accepted the dictates of their
conservative natures.[39]

Professor Jessop, dean of the School of Physic, informed the
governors on 9 June 1970 that Professor William Watts of TCD
would be glad to serve on the board and could give time to do so in
a full capacity as well as keeping the board in touch with the
negotiating committee.[40] On July 7th W.A. Watts was elected to
the board. The secretary's completion of twenty-five years in
the hospital was noted on 7 September 1971 and Mr Little was
thanked for his courteous and competent service.

Mercer's Hospital, as the present writer recalls it, was a friendly
hospital. Disagreements at medical board level were exceptional
but a resolution in 1975 proposing the introduction of operations
to effect sterilisation in patients requiring this for medical reasons
was rejected by a majority influenced in this regard by the Catholic
ethic.

The resignation of the Matron, Miss Kelly, became effective on
1 June 1976; she was replaced by Miss P.M. Taaffe, matron of the
Drogheda Cottage Hospital.

Dr O'Donnell died suddenly in his home in the early morning of
30 January 1978, being then the doyen of Dublin's practising
physicians. His interest in dermatology had helped to fill the void
created by the death of his wife but for some years he had seemed
a lonely figure, increasingly enfeebled by age but resisting the
governors' suggestion that he should retire, suggestions unsupported by any effective move to arrange a pension for him.

His memory and intellect remained relatively unimpaired but
his cynicism had increased remarkably. He regarded as maladroit
certain administrative decisions within the Federation. It would
be unfair to say that he was reactionary for, long before many of
the administrators at St James's were born, Frank O'Donnell had
contributed a thoughtful paper to the *Lancet* (1927) describing how
a large infirmary might be modernised and converted to 'a genuine
social asset'. But he had lost patience with those who, having
tolerated the delays of an indecisive Health Department, appeared

to have forgotten the spirit in which the Federation was originally conceived.

The feelings of affection and admiration he inspired among his juniors were well expressed on the morning of his death by a Mercer's intern, growing accustomed to the deaths of patients but not to the sense of finality experienced when a personal friend passes into the abyss: 'What a pity to think that we'll never see that lovely little white-haired man again!'

For reasons difficult to comprehend the Federation had delayed taking the customary steps to advertise the vacancy left by Professor McNally's retirement in 1975. O'Donnell's death created a second vacancy. Fortunately it was now possible to strengthen the medical department by the appointment of two new physicians, Dr Joseph F. Timoney (1978) whose diabetic clinic soon attracted patients and Dr Peter Daly (1979) an oncologist who introduced the modern chemotherapy of malignant disease. Dr J.B. Lyons who maintained a special interest in neurology had succeeded Professor McNally as president of the Irish Epilepsy Association.

Desmond Douglas died suddenly from coronary heart disease on 10 October 1979.[41] After graduating from TCD in 1937 he gained experience in his chosen speciality at the Royal Victoria Eye and Ear Hospital (where at the time of his death he was senior surgeon) and Moorfields Hospital, London. With the RAMC he served in India, France and Germany where he saw the horrors of Belsen. After the war, Douglas practised successfully in Dublin. He was particularly skilled in dealing with buphthalmos and from 1968 to 1970 was president of the Irish Ophthalmological Society. He was succeeded in Mercer's by Hugh Cassidy, FRCSI.

Rory O'Hanlon, the senior gynaecologist, was taken ill in April 1979 and died in the following year. Jovial and gregarious, Rory's personality was perfectly suited both to his profession and to his avocation, yachting. An accomplished skipper, he completed many intrepid voyages including trans-atlantic crossings and was a popular Commodore at the Royal George Yacht Club. His remains, in accordance with his wishes, were taken to sea in the Dun Laoghaire life-boat and consigned to the deep.

With the passing of Dr O'Donnell, Professor Thomas J. Gilmartin, for whom the first chair of anaesthesia in this country was created in 1965, was the doyen of the medical staff. He was the first in Ireland to use curare and the leader and inspiration of a movement that ensured the availability in Irish operating-rooms of fully-trained, whole-time anaesthetists. Fortunately he was not a prophet who remained without honour in his own country. The first dean of the Faculty of Anaesthetists, he was elected honorary FRCSI in 1974 and was awarded the John Snow Silver Medal, the highest award of the Association of Anaesthetists of Great Britain and Ireland in September 1985 in which year the Gilmartin Lecture was inaugurated. He lived in Baggot Street in a house once occupied by Charles Maunsell and in an atmosphere of Georgian elegance enhanced by his personal flair and pertinacity as an art collector.

Gilmartin's roots were in Connaught. The son of James Gilmartin, JP, and his wife, Rita Coghlan, he was born in Ballymote in 1905 and educated at Summerhill College, Sligo, Belvedere College, Dublin and 'Surgeon's' where he graduated in 1929. In addition to his post in Mercer's he also was consultant to the City of Dublin Skin and Cancer Hospital, Hume Street, the Dublin Dental Hospital and Peamount Sanatorium, and held a number of academic appointments.[42]

He contributed to the social life of the College of Surgeons — president of 'the Bi' (1950) and of the Graduates' Association. He was chairman of the IMA's Anaesthetists' Group when its report on Anaesthetic Services was issued. He was a vice-president of the Association of Anaesthetists of Great Britain and Ireland (of which in 1932 he was a founder member) and chairman of a Steering Committee which created the Faculty of Anaesthetists of the RCSI in 1959.

Tommy Gilmartin died on 22 June 1986 survived by his wife, Peggy, and their son, John, a well-known art historian.

CLOSURE

The closure of a hospital is a sad occasion, discouraging for patients who have come to see it as a haven, disruptive of careers and professional relationships, heart-breaking for those nursing sisters for whom Mercer's had been a home. For many, however, the sadness experienced was of the variety that causes tears at a wedding. This was the necessary step implicit in Rowlette's desired amalgamation scheme and in the later Federation. The consummation, regrettably, had been delayed, the slow pace of development upsetting the logistics. The needs of the medical school had now become paramount and some degree of abnegation was expected.

This broader viewpoint was not attained immediately. Irritation, even anger, was experienced when rumours of impending closure began to circulate in the late 1970s, the justification then offered being a falling bed occupancy and Comhairle na nOspidéal's insistence that the city had too many acute beds. But the building of the new hospital had not yet commenced and its completion was not expected before 1987.

As the unsupported rumours were found initially to have little substance the staff was inclined to adopt a head-in-the-sand attitude, many doctors under the delusion that they were fully protected by the terms of the Act and that what was conceived in the spirit of a gentleman's agreement would even now be honoured. Early in 1977 a Federation spokesman promised that in the event of closure within two years each member of the medical staff would be given index-linked payment of his present annual earnings for life and be offered an appointment to the hospital of his choice within the group. Confirmation in writing of these attractive terms by the Department of Health was not forthcoming, the offer watered down to the intention to compensate for loss of earnings resulting from transfer. Soon after this the spokesman intimated that the 1961 Act could be amended to the disadvantage of Mercer's.

The proposition in December 1978 that transfer of the cardio-thoracic services from the Royal City of Dublin Hospital to St James's should be followed by a move from Mercer's to Baggot Street had the acceptance of a majority but never materialised. These damp squibs may have led to a false sense of security but the transfer of laboratory staff to St James's took place early in 1981 and on October 19th the chairman of the board of governors, Professor Watts, now provost of Trinity College, addressed the medical board.[43] He dwelt on Comhairle na nOspidéal's ruling that any development at St James's required a parallel reduction of activities in the Federation. If the proposed medical professorial unit were to be opened as planned in St James's there must be a corresponding closure in either Dun's or Mercer's. As the latter was the smaller and had a falling bed occupancy the chairman proposed that it should close when negotiations with Dun's permitted rationalisation of the services.

The logic of his argument was inescapable and uncontestable. The recently introduced 'common contract' would allow consultants to take up posts elsewhere without loss of earnings and it was already known that the replacement of doctors due to retire on pension would not be sanctioned by Comhairle na nOspidéal. From the narrower viewpoint of Mercer's Hospital it may have been a breach of faith but it made sense as a gesture to help the medical school endangered when the new wine was slopped into old bottles at St James's.

After preliminary negotiations with Dun's and taking into account the needs of medical students and of the nurses' training-school, the date of closure seemed likely to be in either spring or autumn 1983. A transfer group comprised of Professor Watts, Mr J.P. Little, the Matron and Dr Daly worked out with officials of Federation and the Department of Health the proposed movements of doctors, nurses, administrative staff and others. Eventually, so as to cause minimal inconvenience to student nurses, it was decided that the hospital should close in 1983 at the end of May.

It was agreed by the medical board on 21 December 1981 that Professor Watts should ask the governors to accept the following proposal:

> At a joint meeting of the Boards of Sir Patrick Dun's and Mercer's Hospitals held on Thursday December 17th, 1981, it was agreed on the basis of information provided by the secretaries of the two Medical Boards, that it was possible to accommodate the consultant staff of Mercer's in Sir Patrick Dun's with the assistance of the other Federated Hospitals, taking into account resignations among consultants under the terms of the Common Consultant Contract. The trans-location of consultants from Mercer's to other hospitals would not lead to any diminution in status, earnings or facilities for patient care during the period of transfer and thereafter. Under such circumstances Mercer's Hospital will close ...[44]

A recommendation from the medical board enjoined the governors to ensure that Mary Mercer's name be perpetuated in St James's and that monies accruing from the sale of hospital property be devoted to the establishment of a centre of excellence for the care and rehabilitation of elderly people at St James's.

Though the decision to close may thus appear to have been taken, finally, as a necessary step to expedite the transfer of the university department of medicine to St James's, a wider analysis shows that the hospital's decline was more complex, the gradual consequence of sectarian, social and technological developments.

It may, indeed, have begun long ago when Samuel Haughton, an earlier champion of the School of Physic, enticed Butcher away from Mercer's. Not only was Butcher a major loss but his departure allowed Edward Stamer O'Grady to establish ascendancy and promote disruption and discord. Harmony was eventually restored and a high standard of clinical practice regularly maintained but others, too, Seton Pringle, Purser and Abrahamson, were to leave Mercer's just as they reached their full potential.

St Vincent's Hospital, the first of Dublin's two great Catholic hospitals to open, cannot have seemed a threat when it appeared in two adapted houses on St Stephen's Green in 1834, Mercer's centenary year, yet it was a most significant and competitive outcome of Catholic emancipation. Hardly less significant, in a rather different way, the rise of the Adelaide Hospital, destined to become 'the flag-ship' of the Protestant community and entitled to generous support inevitably weakening Mercer's standing in that community. St Vincent's and the Mater Hospital were to become advantageously linked to the National University in 1908 and meanwhile Sir Dominic Corrigan (1802–1880) had emerged as the prototype of the well-educated Catholic doctor prepared to share leadership of a profession hitherto dominated by Protestants. Dun's Hospital benefited from a close relationship with Trinity College; the founders of the City of Dublin Hospital were RCSI professors and later its staff supported the School of Physic staunchly. Mercer's academic relationships were apt to be more tenuous, its staff more mixed and with divided loyalties.

The Beveridge Report, one of the great documents of the war years, provided the outline for a Welfare State. The British National Health Service came into operation in 1948 pointing the direction Irish health legislators would follow in a somewhat contentious manner. The Bishop of Clonfert's plan (1944) for an Irish health scheme on an insurance basis had already encountered what J.H. Whyte called the 'virulent opposition' of the Minister for Local Government and Public Health, Mr Sean McEntee.[45] The Medical Association of Eire also failed to win approval for its insurance scheme. The Health Act (1953) came into operation in July 1955. The Voluntary Health Insurance Act, 1957, established the Voluntary Health Insurance Board which commenced business in October. The Health Act (1970) set up health boards and regional hospital boards. Comhairle na nOspidéal was formed in 1972.

The availability of 'free treatment' created an endless demand and whatever nominal freedom the voluntary hospitals might possess they were now placed squarely under the control of a health board which became the Maecenas which provided or withheld funds for the purchase of the highly ingenious instruments which revolutionised diagnosis and treatment. The day of 'the special unit' was at hand and lacking such an amenity, Mercer's was relegated to the third division.

All this had been foreseen by Rowlette and his contemporaries. Had their plans been realised within a reasonable time, Mercer's could have closed with a sense of fulfilment and been spared a lengthy period of dismal attrition.

A meeting of the Section of the History of Medicine of the Royal Academy of Medicine in Ireland was held in the hospital on May 18th. The actual closure was phased over a few weeks, teaching and out-patient sessions continuing well into the month of May. Ambulatory patients were sent home; others were transferred elsewhere and on May 28th only one patient remained in Mercer's Hospital, a member of the staff.

Physician, heal thyself! The bitter taunt is mitigated by the acceptance that all flesh is grass; it was ironic, nevertheless, that the hospital's last patient was one of its surgeons, Mr Richard Brownell Brenan, who lay dying from cancer while the nurses deputed to tend to him moved quietly, aware that their footsteps echoed eerily in the empty building. He succumbed that evening. *Requiescat in pace*!

Miss Taaffe took up the post of matron at the Royal City of Dublin Hospital and most of the nurses went to either St James's or to Dun's. Three of the consultants retired under the terms of the Common Contract, another to take up a career outside medicine. Five moved to Dun's, two to Steevens', one to Baggot Street and Dr Peter Daly, who had represented his colleagues so painstakingly on the transfer committee, took up a post as oncologist at St James's. Mr J.P. Little and Miss Jane Rodgers were to remain in the hospital until matters pertaining to the sale were completed.

The reception to mark the closure of the hospital, to which all grades of staff were invited, was held on Sunday May 29th at Thomas Prior House, Ballsbridge. The venue, no doubt chosen for reasons of utility, did have an element of appropriateness: when Prior founded the Dublin Society in the eighteenth century he was aided, as we have seen, by others including William Stephens and Francis Le Hunte who three years later were among those into whose care Mary Mercer entrusted her stone house. The wheel of history had come full circle and on 7 July 1983 the governors agreed to place the premises of Mercer's Hospital for sale by public tender.

RENAISSANCE

Frank McDonald discussed the possible fate of the vacated hospital in December 1983 and commented on certain architectural features. 'The east elevation is particularly striking. With its tower and cupola, bay windows and parapet balustrade, it faces South King Street and is clearly visible from a good distance down the north side of St Stephen's Green. Because of this, Mercer's is something of a landmark and it would be sorely missed if it were demolished.'[46] Demolition could not, indeed, be outruled as the building was not listed for protection or preservation.

A spokesman for the estate agents handling the sale, Osborne King & Megran, had said that there were enquiries both from property developers and institutional clients. The building might be refurbished for a new institutional use as a training college or redeveloped completely for some quite different purpose. Its adaptation for offices seemed unlikely but the proposal that it should be converted into residential apartments was made by the Danish ambassador to Ireland, Mr G.F.K. Haroff. The Irish Medical Association suggested that it should be a geriatric home.

The sale was awaited with great interest. Rumours abounded including that circulated by an *Evening Herald* columnist early in January 1984 — he reported that the final price, £1,250,000, paid by the Royal College of surgeons in Ireland 'was hammered out over Christmas dinner in the Berkeley Court Hotel'.[47] The actual event was less festive, the price paid a good deal lower than the figure dreamed up by the columnist.

The governors met in the Provost's House on December 19th with representatives of the hospital's solicitors and of the estate agents in attendance. Mr A. Graham, solicitor, reported that the time for the submission of tenders had closed at noon and that an offer of £850,000 had been received from the College of Surgeons. Mr I. French, on behalf of the estate agents, recommended acceptance. The governors discussed the factors relevant to the tender and on the proposal of Mr R.G. Heather, seconded by Mr

D.F. Robinson, it was agreed to accept this offer.[48]

The necessary submission to the Charitable Commisioners proposed in summary: (1) the capital fund available to be preserved and maintained in real terms; (2) the principal immediate object of the charity shall of its nature be acceptable to the Department of Health and shall be consistent with the original charter.

The sale of fixtures and fittings realised a sum of £3,332.10. The legal formalities regarding the sale of the premises were completed in early May 1984 and the chairman, vice-chairman and Mr D.J. Dempsey, acting secretary, joined representatives of the RCSI at a luncheon to mark the completion. At this function, Professor Watts expressed the board's wish that if possible the hospital's façade and name should be retained. The College representatives promised to bear this in mind.

The Department of Finance, meanwhile, following these events covertly, signalled to the Department of Health that it should secure the spoil, a would-be act of buccaneering which the governors firmly resisted (see Appendix, p. 207) on a basis 'both of honourable behaviour and of law'. As trustees for the hospital, a legal responsibility devolved upon them to apply through the Commissioners of Charitable Donations and Bequests for a *cy pres* scheme to establish new objectives and to fulfil as closely as possible those of the original bequest. 'It would be regrettable [the chairman stated] if the Department of Finance took the view that the normal processes of law could be set aside in its eagerness to obtain a further capital subvention.' The state had not made other than minor contributions to the capital cost of Mercer's Hospital nor had the latter been compensated by accommodation in the new hospital promised long ago to the Federation.[49]

The *cy pres* scheme as tabled was approved by Judge Carroll in the High Court on 18 July 1987 and by the Commissioners of Charitable Donations and Bequests on July 28th. The Board's total assets at August 31st amounted to £1,247,000 and it was agreed to transfer the assets, having settled some minor liabilities including legal costs, to the new Mercer's Foundation. The income is to be apportioned in the following manner: Mercer's Institute for Research into Ageing, 50 per cent; RCSI's Department of General Practice, 20 per cent; TCD's Faculty of Health Sciences general practice clinic, 20 per cent; sundry charities appropriate to the general terms of the *cy pres* scheme, 10 per cent.

A final meeting was held in the Provost's House towards the end of September. The draft accounts for the thirty-two months ended 3 September 1987, having been circulated, were considered and adopted. 'This terminated the business of the meeting and of the Mercer's Hospital Board.'[50]

Under the chairmanship of Mr Dermot O'Flynn, formerly urologist to the Meath Hospital, the RCSI's Mercer's Committee has shaped the development of the newly-acquired building. The former Nurses Home, renamed Millin House to honour Mr Terence Millin, PRCSI 1963–1966, has been converted to a well-appointed hostel for overseas students and is now fully occupied. The redesigned basement accommodates the RCSI's Department of General Practice under the direction of Professor William Shannon (whose father, Dr William Shannon, of Cranny, Ennis, County Clare, was a student at Mercer's in the mid-1920s) and received its first patient on 17 September 1990.

Almost all the remaining space was allocated for the development of a new medical library under the joint auspices of the Colleges of Physicians and Surgeons and including the wide range of books and long runs of journals contained in their existing collections. The RCPI retains a historical collection in its Kildare Street premises.

Opinion, initially, was divided as to whether the RCSI's entire library should be moved to Mercer's or whether the antiquarian books might be left in the existing Victorian library, which has happy associations for some of the planners. The viewpoint expressed by Professor J.B. Lyons, who had succeeded J.D.H. Widdess as part-time Librarian, Mrs Kathleen Bishop the Executive Librarian, Gillian Smith and other members of the library staff, was that the books in Mercer's should represent as fully as possible the historical and later periods leading up to the present day.

Meetings were held with the architects, Brian O'Halloran & Associates, and plans created for a library on three levels to include a seminar room, an area for special collections and an elegantly executed rare books room where, under separate security, the library's treasures might be displayed.

With the library's long-term needs in mind, the Council, at this juncture, obtained a consultant's report and the appointment of a full-time librarian was recommended. This was welcomed by Professor Lyons and Ms Beatrice Doran was appointed Librarian in 1986. Under her direction a further series of plans was examined and she travelled widely in the United Kingdom, Europe and

North America to view the finest recent examples of library architecture.

Meanwhile it had become apparent that the existing joists would not support the sheer weight of books. The plans were modified accordingly which in effect entailed gutting and rebuilding within the façade, enduring the while An Taisce's unmerited flak. At the topping out ceremony on 1 June 1990, Mr Desmond Kneafsey, PRCSI, said that with this step the College had entered a new era. The new library opened to readers on 9 April 1991.

The Mercer's Institute for Research on Ageing, established at St James's Hospital in 1988 and directed by Professor Davis Coakley, was officially launched on 14 November 1990. It was on this occasion that the Enchiriadis Choir, under the baton of Marion Doherty, performed William Boyce's restored anthem, 'Blessed is he that considereth the sick and needy', an event that gained in symbolism by its gracious creation of a link between the ghosts of the striving eighteenth-century hospital, generously helped by Boyce and Handel, and the new institute's personnel intent on scientific research as the earth revolves towards the next millennium.

Nothing now remains of Mary Mercer's stone house unless some of the unidentified material of the original structure was incorporated in the later-build façade recently carefully preserved. The values that imbued her do survive and the buildings on York Street and Mercer Street comprise Dublin's most historic medical complex.

Sources

Manuscripts

RCSI Minutes of the Meetings of the Board of Governors of Mercer's Hospital 1736–1972
Minutes of the Medical Board
Minutes of the Central Council, RCSI
The Registry of the Surgeons appointed by Act of Parliament to examine into the Qualifications of Candidates for County Hospitals or Infirmaries 1766.

TCD Mun/P.629/1-5. Manuscript Materials for a New & Corrected Edition of Milton's Paradise Lost, by Dr E. Hill, Regius Professor of Medicine.
Mun/V/8 June 1687.
Mun/P/1/545.

St James's Hospital (Federated Dublin Voluntary Hospitals)
Minutes of the Meetings of the Board of Governors of Mercer's Hospital, 1972–1987.

Rockefeller Archives Center:
Report of Alan Gregg, 403A Ireland.

Harvard
Horace Reynolds Papers, Oliver St John Gogarty to Horace Reynolds.

Printed Sources

Abrahamson, L. Obituary/R.C. Maunsell. *Irish Times* 1930, October 10; *Irish J Med Sci* 1931, 617.
An Act (1750) for Regulating the Hospital founded by Mary Mercer, Spinster. Dublin, 1897.
'An Irishman's Diary'. *Irish Times* 9 Sept. 1944.
Anon. *A Century of Service* — St Vincent's Hospital, 1934. Dublin, 1934.
Ball, F.E. *Jonathan Swift: Correspondence*, Vols I-VI, London, 1910–1914.
Bevan, P. *Dublin Medical Press* 1847, 17:74-75.
Boerhaave, H. *Dr. Boerhaave's Academical Lectures on the Theory of Physic*. 2nd ed. London, 1775.

Boxwell, W. and Purser, F.L. *An Introduction to the Practice of Medicine*. Dublin, 1924.

Boxwell, W. Obituary/Francis Carmichael Purser. *Irish J Med Sci* 1934; 135-136.

Boydell, B. *A Dublin Musical Calendar 1700–1760*. Dublin, 1988.

Butcher, R.G.H. *Dublin Med Press* 1847, 17:90.

Butcher, R.G.H. Cases of Amputation — Use of a New Saw. *Dublin Quart J Med Sci* 1851;12:209-223.

Butcher, R.G.H. Reports in Operative Surgery. *Ibid*, 1857;24:257-282.

Calendar of Ancient Records of Dublin Vols I-XVIII. Ed. Sir John T. Gilbert & Lady Gilbert. Dublin, 1889–1922.

Cameron, Sir C. *History of the Royal College of Surgeons in Ireland*, 2nd ed. Dublin, 1916.

Casey, N. in *A Portrait of Irish Medicine*, ed. Eoin O'Brien *et al*. Dublin, 1984.

Coakley, D. *The Irish School of Medicine*. Dublin, 1988.

Cosgrave, E. McDowel. *Dublin and County Dublin in the XX Century*. Dublin, 1908.

Counihan, H.E. In Memoriam/T.A. Bouchier-Hayes. *J Irish Med Assoc* 1960;46:120.

Craig, M. *Dublin 1660–1860*. Dublin, 1969.

Crookes, G.P. Obituary/Desmond Douglas. *J Irish Med Assoc* 1979;72:533.

Curtin, J. McA. Obituary/C.D. O'Connell. *J Irish med Assoc* 1968;61:113.

Danton, S. *Nursing Times* 1987;83:53-54.

Dibble, J.H. *Napoleon's Surgeon*. London, 1970.

Doolin, W. In Memoriam/Sir William I. de C. Wheeler (1879–1943) *Irish J Med Sci* 1943;613.

Doolin, W. In Memoriam/Robert James Rowlette (1874–1944) *Ibid* 1944:583-584.

Doolin, W. Seton Pringle. *Br Med J* 1955;2:1332-1333.

Dublin Almanac & General Register of Ireland.

Dublin Hospitals Sunday Fund Report.

Erinensis. Baron Larrey's Visit to Dublin. *Lancet* 1826;10:828-829.

Evans, E. History of Dublin Hospitals & Infirmaries from 1188 till the Present Time. *Irish Builder* 1897;39:15-18.

Ewald, A.C. *The Life and Letters of Sir Joseph Napier, Bart*. London 1892.

Fallon, M. *The Sketches of Erinensis*. London, 1979.

Feeney, J. *Evening Herald* 1984, January 4.

Future Hospital Policy in Dublin. *Irish J Med Sci* 1936;241-246.

Gatenby, P.B.B. History of the Federated Dublin Voluntary Hospitals (1961–1971). *Brochure of Federated Hospitals' Meeting*, 1971, 14-17.

Gentleman's & Citizen's Almanac, 1738–1822.

Gilbert, Lady ed. *Calendar of Ancient Records of Dublin*.

Gilborne, J. *The Medical Review*. Dublin, 1775.

Gregg, A. Ms. 403 A Ire Box 1. Folder 1. Rockefeller Archives Center.

Grove. *The New Grove Dictionary of Music & Musicians*, 6th ed. London, 1980.

Haughton, S. *Med Press & Circ* 1881;80:369.

Hill, E. *An Address to the Students of Physic* Dublin, 1803.

Hill, E. *Dr Hill's Library: A Catalogue.* Dublin [1816].

Howard, J. *The State of the Prisons in England & Wales*, 3rd ed. Warrington, 1784.

Hume, G. *Observations on the Origin & Treatment of Internal & External Diseases.* Dublin, 1802.

Jessop, W.J.E. Samuel Haughton: A Victorian Polymath. *Hermathena* 1973;116:5-26.

K.N. In Memoriam/J.H. Coolican. *JRCSI* 1965;1252.

Keating, R.H. Extract from the Old Minute Books. *Irish J Med Sci* 1935; 16-18.

Kirkpatrick, T.P.C. *History of the Medical Teaching in Trinity College Dublin & of the School of Physic.* Dublin, 1912.

Kirkpatrick, T.P.C. The Origin of Some of the Hospitals of Dublin. *Dublin J Med Sci* 1914;137:99-109.

Kirkpatrick, T.P.C. Chronological List of the Published Writings of Jonathan Osborne. *Ibid* 1915;139:164-172.

Kirkpatrick, T.P.C. *History of Dr. Steevens' Hospital.* Dublin, 1924.

Lang, P.H. *George Frideric Handel.* London, 1967.

Lendrick, C. *A Lecture on the Epidemic Cholera delivered in the Theatre of Mercer's Hospital.* Dublin, 1831.

Lendrick, C. *Supplementary Observations on the Epidemic Cholera addressed to the Pupils of Mercer's Hospital.* Dublin, 1832.

Lendrick, C. *Observations on Demonical Possession.* Dublin, 1833.

L'Estrange, F. New Truss for Inguinal Hernia. *Dublin Med Press* 1844; 11:124-125.

L'Estrange, F. Description of an Apparatus for Dislocation. *Ibid* 1845; 14:60.

L'Estrange, F. Partial Dislocation of the Inferior Maxilla. *Ibid* 1846; 16:405.

L'Estrange, F. *Dublin Med Press* 1847;17:71.

Lindeboom, G.A. *Herman Boerhaave.* London, 1968.

Little, J. Jonathan Osborne: A Biographical Sketch. *Dublin J Med Sci* 1915; 139:161-164.

Lumsden, Sir J. Personal Reminiscences of Mercer's Hospital. *Irish J Med Sci* 1935, 1921.

Lyons, J.B. Mercer's Hospital 1734-1972. *J Irish Med Assoc* 1972;65:299-306.

Lyons, J.B. Obituary notice, F.J. O'Donnell. *J Irish Med Assoc* 1978;71:168.

Lyons, J.B. The Section of Medicine & Medical Developments over the Century. *Irish J Med Sci* 1983;152:14-24.

Lyons, J.B. A Notable French Surgeon in Dublin. *Irish Med Times*

18 November 1983.

Lyons, J.B. Mercer's Hospital & the College Connection. *J Irish Coll Phys Surg* 1984;13:49-57.

Lyons, J.B. *An Assembly of Irish Surgeons*. Dublin, 1984.

Lyons, J.B. The Debt that Mercer's owed to the Music of Handel. *Irish Med Times* 24 May 1985.

Lyons, J.B. An Appreciation of Professor Gilmartin. *Ibid* 25 July 1986.

McDonnell, J. Amputation of the Arm Without Pain. *Dublin Med Press* 1947;17:8-9.

McFeely, J.D. *Recollections of an Old and Observant Practitioner*. London, 1931.

McNally, P.A. In Memoriam/T.A. Bouchier-Hayes (1907–1960). *J Irish Med Assoc* 1960;46:120.

McDonald, F. *Irish Times*, 17 December 1983.

Maconchy, J. Reports in Operative Surgery from the County Down Infirmary. *Dublin Quart J Med Sci* 1868;44:335-344.

Meenan, F.O.C. *Cecilia Street: The Catholic University School of Medicine 1855–1931*. Dublin, 1987.

Meenan, J. & Clarke, D. *The Royal Dublin Society*. Dublin, 1981.

Mitchell, D. *A 'Peculiar' Place*. Dublin, 1989.

Moorhead, T.G. Obituary/Sir John Lumsden. *J Med Assoc Eire* 1944; 15:38.

Obituary. Jonathan Osborne. *Dublin Quart J Med Sci* 1864;37:249-251.

Obituary. Sir John Lumsden. *The Times*, 5 Sept 1944.

Obituary. John Morgan. *Med Press Circ* 1876;209.

Obituary. E.S. O'Grady. *Freeman's Journal* 1897;October 20; *Med Press* 1887;2:410.

Obituary. Jonathan Osborne. *Dublin Med Press* 1864;51:97.

O'Brien, E. 'From the Waters of Zion to Liffey-side'. *J Irish Coll Phys Surg* 1981;10:107-119.

O'Brien, E. Browne, L. & O'Malley, K. *The House of Industry Hospitals 1772–1987*. Dublin, 1988.

O'Brien, E.& Crookshank, A. *A Portrait of Irish Medicine*. Dublin, 1984.

O'Brien, E. *Messiah*. Dublin, 1986.

O'Brien, E. *The Charitable Infirmary Jervis Street 1718–1987*. Dublin, 1987.

O'Brien, W. ed. *Report on the Trial of Robert Kelly*. Dublin, 1873.

O'Sé, L. *Irish Med News*, 23, October 1989.

Osborne, J. *On Dropsies, connected with suppressed perspiration, and Coagulable Urine*. London, 1835, 2nd ed 1837.

Osborne, J. On the State Poison of the Athenians, used in the Case of Socrates. *Dublin Quart J Med Sci* 1853;15:329-343.

Osborne, J. On the Plague of Athens, as described by Thucydides. *Ibid* 1958;25:309-321.

Quane, M. Mercer's School Rathcoole & Castleknock. *J Roy Soc Anti-*

quaries Ire 1963;93:9-35.

Reports of Mercer's Hospital, 1925–1934.

Robbins, H.C. Landon. *Handel and his World*. London, 1984.

Rowlette, R.J. The Problem of the Dublin Voluntary Hospitals. *Dublin J Med Sci* 1920;9-24.

Rowlette, R.J. The Future of Mercer's Hospital. *Irish J Med Sci* 1935; 22-23.

Ryan, P.B. *Jimmy O'Dea the Pride of the Coombe*. Dublin, 1990.

Saffron, M. *Samuel Clossy, M.D. (1724–1786). The Existing Works with a Biographical Sketch*. New York, 1967.

Savage, R. Burke. *Catherine McAuley*. Dublin, 1949.

Shaw, Watkins. *The Story of Handel's Messiah*. London, 1963.

Smith, A. Contributions to the History of Medicine. *Dublin J Med Sci* 1840;17:210-223.

Stoker, T. *Med Press Circ* 1881;82:161.

Stott, R. Health & Virtue: Or, How to Keep out of Harm's Way. Lectures on Pathology & Therapeutics by William Cullen c. 1770. *Med Hist* 1987;31:123-142.

Synge, V.M. In Memoriam/S. Seton Pringle. *Irish J Med Sci* 1956;22.

Thom's Irish Almanac & Official Directory.

Townsend, H. *An Account of the Visit of Handel to Dublin*. Dublin, 1852.

Tufnell, J. Effects of Inhalation of Ether Vapour. *Dublin Med Press* 1847;17:25.

Warburton, J. Whitelaw, J. & Walsh R. *History of the City of Dublin*, Vol 2. London, 1818.

White, T. de Vere. *The Story of the Royal Dublin Society*. Tralee, 1955.

Whyte, J.H. *Church & State in Modern Ireland 1923–1979*, 2nd ed. Dublin, 1980.

Widdess, J.D.H. Robert McDonnell — A Pioneer of Blood Transfusion. *Irish J Med Sci* 1952;11-20.

Widdess, J.D.H. *A History of the Royal College of Physicians of Ireland 1654–1963*. Edinburgh, 1963.

Widdess, J.D.H. *The Charitable Infirmary, Jervis Street, 1718–1968*. Dublin, 1968.

Widdess, J.D.H. *The Royal College of Surgeons in Ireland and its Medical School, 1784–1984*. 3rd ed. Dublin, 1984.

Wren, W.S. Professor T.J. Gilmartin/An Appreciation. *Irish Times* 15 August 1986.

Notes and References

Introductory Note

1. P.B. Ryan (1900) traces Mrs Mulligan's origin to W.S. North's song 'Queen of the Coombe' featured in a pantomime *Taladoin or the Scamp with the Lamp* which opened at the Gaiety Theatre on 26 December 1889. Seamus Kavanagh changed the name to Biddy Mulligan the Pride of the Coombe and other comedians used it until in due course the character became inseparably associated with Jimmy O'Dea.

Chapter I. 1734–1784

1. Kirkpatrick, 1924, p 16.
2. O'Brien, 1987, p 2.
3. Gilbert, Vol II, p 545.
4. Kirkpatrick, 1935, p 1.
5. Gilbert, Vol II, p 145.
6. *Ibid*, Vol II, p 429.
7. Craig, p 40. 'Until about 1679 there were two ancient churches side by side, one certainly and the other probably ruined. The former was the chapel of the mediaeval leper-hospital of St Stephen ... They both stood in Stephen Street, which winds in a large curve round the lands of the White Friars. They are shown thus in Speed's map of 1610.'
8. An Act ... 'Whereas Mary Mercer, of the city of Dublin, spinster, being piously and charitably inclined to build, at her own charge, a house for the reception of twenty poor girls or other poor persons, proposed to build the same in the parish of St. Peter's, in the suburbs of the city of Dublin, provided the said parish would set out to the said Mary a piece of ground for that purpose.

   And whereas the ministers, churchwardens, and parishioners of the said parish of St. Peter's, in order to encourage so pious a work, did by act of vestry, bearing date the twenty-fifth day of February, in the year of our Lord one thousand seven hundred and twenty-four, direct that a lease should be made to the said Mary ... of the ground herein after mentioned, for the term of nine hundred and ninety-nine years ... for the use aforesaid, all that plot or parcel of ground situate, and being, part of the ground commonly called St. Stephen's Church-yard, in the suburbs of the City of Dublin ...'

9. TCD. Mun/V/8 June 1687.
10. TCD. Mun/P/1/545.
11. Ball, Vol II, 346.
12. An Act ... '... and also reciting that she the said Mary, had erected and built on the said plot of ground, a large stone house or messuage, with conveniences and accommodations thereunto belonging, fit for the reception and habitation of poor persons ... was disposed to settle and convert the said stone house or messuage, for the accommodation and use of such poor persons as may happen to labour under diseases of tedious and hazardous cure ...'
13. Gilbert, Vol VIII, p 135.
14. *Dublin Gazette*, 8 March 1735.
15. Swift, J., Vol I, 202.
16. Kirkpatrick, 1924, pp 114-119.
17. Meenan and Clarke, 1981, p 1.
18. Kirkpatrick, 1924, p 114.
19. Nevertheless, Stephens remained a governor when the hospital was incorporated by the Act of 1750.
20. Kirkpatrick, 1924, p 119.
21. Gilbert, Vol VIII, p 187.
22. Minutes of Meetings of the Board of Governors of Mercer's Hospital — hereafter, Hospital Minutes (Archives RCSI).
23. Kirkpatrick, 1924, p 152.
24. Hospital Minutes, Vol I, 30 March 1754.
25. Kirkpatrick, 1935, p 9. According to Alex Sakula, however, it is now clear that Relhan was practising in Brighton in 1759 (and wrote *A Short History of Brighthelmston*); in 1762 he settled in London and was elected FRCP in 1764. He acted as Censor and was Harveian Orator. Relhan died in London in 1776 and was buried in Paddington.
26. Saffron, passim.
27. Casey, in O'Brien and others, 1984, p 222.
28. Howard, p 209.
29. *Groves*, Vol 8, pp 83 and 96-97.
30. Shaw, pp 1-18.
31. Townsend, p 44. Charles Burney (1716–1814), a musician and composer, published a *History of Music*.
32. Boydell, p 74.
33. Lang, p 339.
34. Lang, p 336.
35. Hospital Minutes, 21 November 1741.
36. *Ibid.*, 12 December 1741.
37. *Ibid.*, 2 January 1742.
38. Programme of performance in RCPI, 14 November 1990.

39.   Hospital Minutes, 23 January 1742.
40.   Robbins Landon, p 181.
41.   Townsend, p 64.
42.   Hospital Minutes, 4 January 1742.
43.   Boydell, p 275.
44.   Boydell, p 89 and 276.
45.   Mercer's Hospital's music books which were deposited in the library at Trinity College on 13 May 1981 contained no original Handel material. References to Handel in the Hospital Minutes, Vol 1, pp 49, 89, 98, 101, 103, 105, 112, 132, 192.
46.   Keatinge, pp 16-18.
47.   Registry of the Surgeons Appointed by Act of Parliament (Archives RCSI).
48.   Lindeboom, passim.
49.   Boerhaave, Vol I, p 65.
50.   *loc. cit.* p 110.
51.   Stephens played a major part in forming the Society. 'If Prior was the prime mover, Stephens may well have been the earliest of his confidants.' White, p 11.
52.   With Prior, Arthur Dobbs, Rev Dr Whitecomb and John Pratt, he formed a committee which by September 1731 had drawn up the plans of several projects. (Meenan and Clarke, p 3). The dissertation on dyeing is recorded in the Society's first minutes. 'The principal Colours used in dyeing are Blew, Yellow and Red: for Blews are used Woad, Indigo and Logwood; for Yellows, Weld, Woad-Wax and old Fustick, Turmerick formerly, but not much now. For Reds, Redwood, Brazilo, Madder, Cochineal, Safflore, Kermes berries and Sanders, the latter seldom, and the Kermes not often ...' Muriel Gahan (Meenan and Clarke, p 242) points out that safflore is one of the earliest dyes and used in 6th century BC; she suggests that Stephens may have cultivated safflower on his Wexford farm.
53.   Kirkpatrick, 1912, p 98.
54.   On 5 July 1746 (*Hospital Minutes*) Mr Stone paid £10 'a benefaction given by Mr Bart Clossy.'
55.   Kirkpatrick, 1924, p 118.
56.   Saffron, p 108.
57.   Smith, p 220.
58.   Saffron, passim.

Chapter 2. 1784–1834

1.   Autograph letter O. Gogarty/Horace Reynolds: Harvard.
2.   Hospital Minutes, 17 October 1795.
3.   Minutes of the Meetings of Council, RCSI.
4.   Widdess, 1984, p 66.
5.   Kirkpatrick, 1912, pp 168-188.

6. Hospital Minutes, 17 April 1800.
7. Erinensis, 828-829.
8. Dibble, p 283.
9. Cameron, p. 382.
10. Hume, 1802, p 15.
11. *loc. cit.*, p 211.
12. *loc. cit.*, p 191.
13. Cameron, p 384.
14. *loc. cit.*, 388.
15. Cameron, p. 402.
16. Hospital Minutes, 22 February 1815.
17. Cameron, p 431.
18. *loc. cit.*, p 446.
19. *loc. cit.*, p 450.
20. Hospital Minutes, 28 November 1807.
21. *Ibid.*, 26 January 1833.
22. Hill, 1803, p 27.
23. Widdess, 1963, p 105. Hopkins was author of a Midwifery *Vade Mecum*, London, 1811.
24. Kirkpatrick, 1912, p 164.
25. Like his contemporaries, Hill would have been influenced by William Cullen who for his generation was what Boerhaave had been for Stephens. Cullen held chairs in Glasgow and Edinburgh and his *First Lines in Physic* was a popular textbook. He envisaged the human body as a mechanism involving three systems (1) the simple solids, (2) the nervous system, (3) the animal functions (the fluids). The solids gained bulk through nutrition from the animal fluids acquiring strength and vigour which gave them 'cohesion', 'flexibility' and 'elasticity', qualities that increase or diminish in different circumstances. The sensibility and irritability of the nervous system are nicely balanced in health but can be deficient or excessive requiring tonics or sedatives as medication — wine, exercise, cold and heat were stimulants whereas emetics, venesection, warm baths and opiates had an opposite effect.

The consistency of the fluids is of less importance than that of a correct degree of tension in the arterial system. Cullen was sceptical of those who directed attention to a need to alter the viscidity of the blood. 'When I was first acquainted with Physic', he wrote, 'I found physicians reasoned very boldly, they spoke of thickening or thinning the blood with as much clearness as a Scotch maid would speak of making pottage thicker or thinner.' (Stott, p 139).

Hume appears to accept Cullen's system when he writes (p xii), 'The word acrimony is frequently introduced, by which I mean the state of the solids and fluids produced by constitutional defect, existing either from inheritance or early acquired ...'

26. I am indebted to Vincent Kinane for this information.
27. Hill, 1816.
28. Ms. TCD 629/1-5.
29. Fallon, p 138.
30. Lendrick, 1831, p. 5.
31. Lendrick, 1832, p 20.
32. Here he overlooks the high mortality rates in undeveloped countries. 'In savage life we know that disease is comparatively rare, that a rude and imperfect surgery is adequate and that the assistance of the scientific accoucheur may be altogether dispensed with.' Lendrick, 1833, p 8.
33. Hospital Minutes, 28 April 1832.
34. Kirkpatrick, 1924, p 225.
35. *A Century of Service* (Anon), p 19.
36. Fallon, 128.
37. *loc. cit.*, 135.
38. *loc. cit.*, 137.
39. *loc. cit.*, 143.

Chapter 3. 1834–1884

1. Hospital Minutes, 11 October 1836.
2. *Ibid.*, 13 June 1837.
3. *Ibid.*, 21 December 1838.
4. *Dublin Med Press* 1840;3:321.
5. He contributed articles to the *Dublin J Nat Sci* and *Trans of the Assn of Fellows of the KQCPI*.
6. Lendrick, 1840, p 19.
7. *loc. cit.*, p 52.
8. Duncan, 1849, p 20.
9. *loc. cit.*, p 90.
10. Duncan, 1851, p 217.
11. Hospital Minutes, 14 October 1848.
12. *Ibid.*, 28 February 1855.
13. *Ibid.*, 26 March 1856.
14. *Ibid.*, 8 March 1862.
15. Walter Doolin was a brother of William Doolin of 23 Westland Row, the quantity surveyor who acted for the physicians when the RCPI in Kildare Street was built and grand-uncle of William Doolin, PRCSI 1938–1940.
16. Hospital Minutes, 3 June 1863.
17. *Ibid.*, 13 January 1864.
18. *Ibid.*, 29 March 1867.
19. Obituary 1864; Kirkpatrick, 1915; Little, 1915.
20. Widdess, 1963, p 206.
21. Osborne, 1837, p 33.

22. *Ibid.*, p 19.
23. Osborne, 1835, p 57.
24. Lendrick, 1840, p 84.
25. *Dublin Medical Press*, 1852;27:415.
26. Kirkpatrick, 1924, p 199.
27. Danton, p 53.
28. Obituary, 1864.
29. Kirkpatrick, 1915.
30. Little, 1915, p 163.
31. Osborne, 1853, p 340.
32. *Dublin Quart J Med Sci*, 1854;18:457.
33. Meenan (1987) names the early 'Cecilians' who attended Mercer's giving the year of qualification: Wm Ashton, 1857; J.T. Crean, 1858; John Fulham, 1858; Thos Murray, 1859; P.J. Murray, 1860; J.J. Mullen, 1860; Chas O'Lomasny Ronayne, 1863; Henry King, 1863; P.J. Cunningham.
34. Coakley, 1988, p 68.
35. Hospital Minutes, 14 November 1859.
36. *Ibid.*, 19 and 26 October, 4 November 1859.
37. McDonnell, pp 8-9.
38. Tufnell, p 25.
39. L'Estrange, 1847, p 71.
40. Bevan, p 74.
41. Butcher, p 90.
42. Cameron, p 480.
43. Butcher, 1851.
44. Butcher, 1857.
45. O'Brien, 1873, passim.
46. Jessop, p 23.
47. Jessop, p 25.
48. Cameron, pp 629-630.
49. Obituary, 1876. Kirwan was sentenced to death in 1852 for the murder of his wife but the sentence was commuted.
50. Cameron, p 799.
51. Obituary, *Medical Press*, p 410.
52. *Medical Press*, 8 April 1868.
53. *Saunder's Newsletter*, 12 March 1868.
54. Hospital Minutes, 26 June 1868.
55. *Ibid.*, 8 May 1869.
56. Moore was the author of 'Infantile Mortality' (1859); 'Idiopathic Tetanus'; 'Paralysis and Atrophy from Lead Poisoning'; 'Clinical Lectures on Diabetes' and other articles written during the tenure of his post in Mercer's which he left when appointed to Dun's Hospital in 1862.
57. These included 'A Case of Leucocythaemia' and 'Hospital Reports of

"Ileus", "Pericarditis", "Ataxia", etc.'. He was a member of the Pathological Society and Hon Sec to the Medical Society of the College of Physicians of Ireland.

58. His publications included 'Treatment of Strangulated Hernia', 'Lupoid Ulcer', 'Locomotor Ataxy of Syphilitic Origin and its Treatment'. He was Senior Surgeon to the Westmorland Lock Hospital and Hon Surgeon to the Sailors' Home.

59. Cameron, pp 670-673.

60. Maconchy, pp 335-344.

61. Haughton, p 369.

62. Stoker, p 161.

63. Hospital Minutes, 18 August 1873.

64. *Ibid.*, 11 March 1874.

65. *Ibid.*, 18 March 1878.

66. *Dublin Hospital Sunday Fund Report*, passim.

67. Hospital Minutes, 19 March 1879.

68. *Ibid.*, 13 April 1881.

69. *Ibid.*, 19 December 1882.

70. Ewald, p 308.

71. Hospital Minutes, 29 September 1875.

72. *Ibid.*, 28 September 1875.

73. *Ibid.*, 14 April 1875.

74. *Ibid.*, 14 May 1879.

75. *Ibid.*, 15 October 1883.

Chapter 4. 1884–1934

1. *MP&C*, 1884;89:186.

2. *Ibid.*, 1887;94:102.

3. *Ibid.*, 1887;94:132.

4. Hospital Minutes, 11 March 1885.

5. *Ibid.*, 21 March 1887.

6. *Ibid.*, 11 May 1887.

7. *MP&C*, 1887;95:38.

8. *Ibid.*, 1887;95:411.

9. Hospital Minutes, 28 November 1887.

10. *Ibid.*, 16 December 1887.

11. *MP&C*, 1887;95:606.

12. *Ibid.*, 1887;95:628.

13. *Ibid.*, 1889;98:342.

14. The custom of purchasing staff appointments was widely practised. On 2 July 1821 the Standing Committee of the Meath Hospital noted a vacancy for a physician and two weeks later referred to a report 'that a bargain has been made between two Medical Gentlemen whereby a consideration in money was to be paid on the appointment of a Physician ...' The medical board assured the

Standing Committee 'that in electing a Gentleman of Doct^r Graves Character and qualifications they conceive they have considered the best interests of the Hospital.' They denied that there had been any pecuniary transactions between 'the Candidate and the Electors' but agreed to meet the committee in conference to guard against possible future irregularities. Three dissentients—Whitley Stokes, Cusack and Thomas Roney — objected to the election believing that 'practices alluded to' should have been checked 'in the present instance'.

15. *MP&C*, 1891;102:207.
16. Lumsden, p 19.
17. *MP&C*, 1896;113:531.
18. Hospital Minutes, 6 April 1897.
19. *MP&C*, 1897;114:394.
20. *Ibid.*, 1897;114:394.
21. *Ibid.*, 1897;115:171.
22. *Ibid.*, 1897;115:221.
23. Hospital Minutes, 3 August 1897.
24. *MP&C*, 1899;119:468.
25. *Ibid.*, 1897;114"364. Mr Ball, Mr Justice Madden and Mr Henshaw resigned.
26. *Ibid.*, 1897;115:48.
27. *Ibid.*, 1897;115:121.
28. McFeely, pp 65-66.
29. Later Dr Wentworth Taylor practised in Rathdrum, County Wicklow and was MO to Rathdrum Workhouse and St Kyran's Industrial School.
30. Hospital Minutes, 1 February 1898. Richard Lane Joynt, FRCSI was surgeon to the Meath Hospital and a member of the Roentgen Society. O. St J. Gogarty speaks of him as a metallurgist in *I Follow St Patrick*. 'He knew all about the archaeology of Irish swords, spears and bells.'
31. Lyons, 1984, pp 68-69.
32. Hospital Minutes, 4 October 1898.
33. *Ibid.*, 1 November 1898.
34. *Ibid.*, 2 January 1900.
35. *Ibid.*, 12 January 1900.
36. *Ibid.*, 3 April 1900.
37. *Ibid.*, 5 June 1900.
38. *Ibid.*, 3 July 1900.
39. *Ibid.*, 1 January 1901.
40. *Ibid.*, 8 April 1902.
41. *Ibid.*, 17 June 1902.
42. *Ibid.*, 20 June 1902.
42a. McFeely, p 72.

43. Obituary, 1944.
44. Lyons, 1984, pp 88-90.
45. Wm Geoffrey Harvey, FRCPI, was appointed physician and dermatologist to the Adelaide Hospital; he was author of 'Sex and its Relation to Evolution' and 'Cases of Precocious Sexual Development'. Henry W. Mason was Registrar to the Apothecaries' Hall and radiologist to Jervis Street Hospital. Joseph T. Wigham was pathologist to the Royal City of Dublin Hospital and assistant to the professor of pathology in TCD.
46. Hospital Minutes, 4 May 1909.
47. Lumsden, p 21.
48. Doolin, 1944.
49. O'Dwyer, W.F., in Widdess, 1968, p 25.
50. Lyons, *Irish J Med Sci*, 1983;14-24.
51. O'Brien, 1981, p 117.
52. Solomons, p 71.
53. Later Dr Joseph P. Brennan was physician to St Michael's Hospital, Dun Laoghaire; he was elected to the Dáil as Clan na Poblachta deputy in 1948. He became Coroner for County Dublin in 1922 and held this post for more than forty years.
54. Hospital Minutes, 6 December 1932.
55. *Ibid.*, 6 March 1917.
56. *Ibid.*, 7 March 1922.
57. Ms Rockefeller Archives Center.
58. Hospital Minutes, 7 April 1925.
59. *Ibid.*, 12 May 1931.
60. *Ibid.*, 8 September 1931.
61. *Ibid.*, 17 July 1934.
62. Boxwell, p 136.
63. Boxwell and Purser, p 855.
64. *loc. cit.*, p 884.
65. Lyons, 1984, pp 55-67.
66. Ms RCSI Wheeler papers. Letter from Major General R.W. Ford to Lt Gen Alfred Keogh.
67. Wheeler papers.
68. Sir Robert Jones to Wheeler, 20 March 1917.
69. Wheeler to Sir T.H.Goodwin, 23 March 1919.
70. Sir Edward Carson to Wheeler, 25 March 1919.
71. Gen T.H.J. Goodwin to Wheeler, 8 August 1919.
72. Gen R.W. Ford to Wheeler, 1919.
73. Minutes RCSI, 2 June 1923, p 150.
74. Wheeler papers.
75. Wheeler, Sir W.I. de C. Observations on the Surgical Treatment of Graves' Disease. *Irish J Med Sci.*, 1926;216-224.
76. Wheeler papers.

77. Lyons, 1984, p 66.
78. Doolin, W. In Memoriam Sir Wm I. de C. Wheeler. *Irish J Med Sci.*, 1942;613.

Chapter 5. 1934–1991

1. He overlooked Catherine McAuley. The Order of Mercy which she established founded Dublin's Mater Hospital and several other hospitals in England and North America.
2. Keatinge, p 18.
3. Lumsden, p 21.
4. Rowlette, p 22.
5. Hospital Minutes, 7 January 1936.
6. Kinnear, p 252.
7. John Seton Michael Pringle (nephew of Seton S. Pringle) held the chair of surgery RCSI 1952–1961. Frederick Gordon Stewart was also radiologist to Steevens' and Hume Street Hospitals.
8. *Irish Times* (An Irishman's Diary), 9 September 1944.
9. Widdess, 1952, pp 11-20.
10. Lyons, 1984, p 103.
11. Hospital Minutes, December 1940.
12. Counihan, H.E., in O'Brien and others 1988, p 65.
13. O'Sé, 23 October 1989.
14. Counihan, p 120.
15. McNally, p 120.
16. Hospital Minutes, 5 June 1945.
17. *Ibid.*, 7 August 1945.
18. Lyons, 1984, pp 141-147.
19. Hospital Minutes, 10 August 1954.
20. *Ibid.*, 1 May 1951.
21. *Ibid.*, 8 September 1953.
22. *Ibid.*, 4 May 1954.
23. *Ibid.*, 4 April 1950.
24. *Ibid.*, 7 September 1954.
25. Ms RCSI.
26. *MP&C*, 1988;96:125.
27. Rowlette, p 24.
28. Lyons, 1972, p 305.
29. Gatenby, P., p 14. The four doctors were Peter Gatenby, Stanley McCollum, John Sugars and George Fegan.
30. This phase is well described by David Mitchell, pp 238-245.
31. Future Hospital Policy, p 242. Moore's recommendation (p 247) 'that the municipal hospital should be reserved for incurable, untreatable and very chronic cases and that the poor patients, whose diseases offer a fair chance of improvement or cure within a reasonable length of time, should be sent to the voluntary hospitals,'

would have had the unanimous support of his voluntary hospital colleagues. William Doolin, an urbane and broad-minded surgeon, predicted that 'the "Union" stigma would cling to St Kevin's for at least a generation' after its rehabilitation (p 255). T.G. Moorhead asserted that 'the building of a municipal hospital as an alternative to the extension of the voluntary general hospitals would be a disaster.' (p 259).

32. Ms RCSI — Memorandum re Pathology Services.
33. Hospital Minutes, 25 November 1971.
34. Lyons, 1978, p 168.
35. The Irish Epilepsy Association was founded in 1967.
36. Curtin, p 113.
37. Later Professor Gilmartin and Mr J.G. Mathews were elected non-voting members of the board of governors. Dr Michael Solomons joined the board of governors as representative of the Royal City of Dublin Hospital on 1 August 1972.
38. Hospital Minutes, 2 March 1971.
39. *Ibid.*, 7 April 1970.
40. *Ibid.*, 9 June 1970.
41. Crookes, p 533.
42. Wren, August 15.
43. Minutes of Medical Board, 19 October 1981.
44. *Ibid.*, 21 December 1981.
45. Whyte, pp 101-114.
46. McDonald, December 17.
47. Feeney, January 4.
48. Hospital Minutes, 19 December 1983.
49. *Ibid.*, 25 February 1985 and Professor Watts' letter, 6 February 1985.
50. *Ibid.*, 29 September 1987.

Appendix

The Governors in 1734

Lord Bishop of Cork, Dr Clayton
Dr Jonathan Swift, Dean of St
    Patricks
Archdeacon Whittingham
Dean Madden

William Stephens, MD
Rev Mr James King
Hannibal Hall
W. Dobbs
John Stone

The Governors named in the Act of Incorporation

1. Lord Primate
2. Lord Chancellour
3. The Speaker
4. Lord Archbishop of Dublin
5. Lord Archbishop of Tuam

All for the time being.

6. The Earl of Kildare
7. The Earl of Blessington
8. The Lord Laneborough
9. The Bishop of Kildare
10. The Bishop of Clogher
11. The Bishop of Elphin
12. The Lord Tullamoore
13. The Lord Mornington
14. Lord Chief Barron Bones
15. The Right Hon Mr John Ponsonby
16. Right Hon Mr Luke Gardiner
17. Hon Mr Thomas Butler
18. Lord Rawdon
19. Robert Ross Esq.
20. Robert Downs Esq.
21. Bolyn Whitney Esq.
22. William Tighe Esq.
23. Thomas Le Hunte Esq.
24. Thomas Pakenham Esq.
25. Sir Charles Burton
26. William Woodworth Esq.
27. Alexander McAulay Esq.
28. John Rochford Esq.
29. John Putland Esq.
30. Robert Stannard Esq.
31. Richards Baldwin Esq.
32. Columbine LeeCarre Esq.
33. Dean Hutchinson
34. Dean Madden
35. Dean Owen
36. Archdeacon Pococke
37. Dr Wynne
38. Dr King
39. Dr Bradford
40. Rev James Jackson
41. Dr Le Hunte
42. Dr Stephens
43. Dr Anderson
44. John Stone
45. George Daunt
46. Rice Gibbons
47. Rathborne Mills
48. Joseph Shewbridge
49. George Whittingham

The Governors in the Year of Closure

W.A. Watts (Chairman)
J.W. Brooks
E.K. Carter
A.C.S. Clarke
M.H.M. Clarke
C.W. Fulcher
T.J. Gilmartin
A.F. Grey

R.G. Hall
R.G. Heather
J.W.P. Hoblyn
J.G. Mathews
D.F. Robinson
M. Solomons
R.M. Wolfe
Secretary — J.P. Little

Governors of Mercer's Hospital Foundation, 1987

W.A. Watts (Chairman)
J.W. Brooks
M.H.M. Clarke
A.F. Grey
R.H. Hall

R.G. Heather
J.W.P. Hoblyn
J.G. Mathews
D.F. Robinson
Secretary — D.J. Dempsey

MEDICAL STAFF 1734–1983
Compiled by Mary O'Doherty

Physicians

William Stephens
1734–1747

Francis Le Hunte
1734–c1745

John Anderson
1740–1762

Richard Woods
–1752

Anthony Relhan
1753-1757

Francis Hutcheson
1759–1761

Samuel Clossy
1762–1763

Archibald Hamilton
1764–1777

James Span
1768–1773

Plunkett Lhoyd
c1770

Edward Hill
1773–1830

Charles William Quin
1783–1785

Francis Hopkins
1786–1811

John W. Boyton
1812–1826

Charles Lendrick
1827–1841

Jonathan Osborne
1835–1864

James F. Duncan
c1847

E. Steele
1853

William Moore
1861–1868

Thomas Peter Mason
1865–1900

Henry Eames
1869–1873

G.F. Duffey
1877–1882

C.F. Knight
1882–1889

H.A. Auchinleck
1890–1898

Edward L'Estrange Ledwich
1897–1913

John Lumsden
1897–1939

John Magee Finney
1904–1922

Arthur Norman Holmes
1913–1914

Francis Carmichael Purser
1913–1919

Robert James Rowlette
1919–1944

Leonard Abrahamson
1920–1930

Thomas Gillman Moorhead
1924–1925

Francis J. O'Donnell
1928–1978

Joseph Lewis
1930–1964

Brian Pringle
1933–1945

Patrick Aloysius McNally
1947–1975

John Benignus Lyons
1965–1983

Francis Joseph Timoney
1978–1983

Peter A. Daly
1979–1983

Surgeons

Hannibal Hall
1734–1741

William Dobbs
1734–1741

John Stone
1734–1756

George Daunt
1738–1786

Rice Gibbons
1740–1773

Joseph Shewbridge
1744–1767

George Whittingham
1747–1773

Rathborne Mills
1747–1759

Richard Blundell
1759

Gustavus Hume
1760–1812

Henry Morris
1760–1786

Michael White
1765–1776

Vernon Lloyd
1773–1787

Francis Foreside
1775–1783

James Graisett
1775–1777

Andrew Blackhall
1777–1778

Henry Jebb
1778–1811

Rice Gibbons
1779–1799

Francis L'Estrange
1782–1836

Richard Daniel
1783–1788

J. Taylor
1789–1798

James Grasett
1791–1799

Patrick Dillon
1796–1797

Gerard Macklin
1796–1830

Frederick Jebb
1801–1809

Samuel Wilmot
1807–

Mathew Quinlan
1809–1821

Alexander Read
1809–1851

James Smith
1812–1814

William Auchinleck
1814–1848

Francis Hopkins
1818–1819

William Taggart
1822–1824

William Daniell
1822–1842

Abraham Palmer
1823–1848

William Frederick Macklin
1831

William Tagert
1835–1861

William Jameson
1843–1867

Philip Bevan
1849–1867

Richard George Herbert
  Butcher
1851–1868

Francis L'Estrange
c1860

Edward Ledwich
1861–1879

Edward Stamer O'Grady
1867–1897

John Morgan
1867–1876

Benjamin F. M'Dowell
1869–1879

Montgomery A. Ward
1879–1897

Frederick Alcock Nixon
1880–1898

Joseph D. McFeely
1897–1904

Henry Moore
1897–1900

Robert Charles Butler
  Maunsell
1898–1930

Henry Croly
1901–1904

Seton Sidney Pringle
1903–1918

William Ireland de Courcy
  Wheeler
1904–1932

Dorothy K. Milne Henry
1922–1925

T.H. Croly
1922–1945

J.E. Deale
1926

A.B. Brooks
1928

James Owens
1928–1937

John H. Coolican
1931–1964

Seymour F. Heatley
1932–1935

J. Seton Pringle
1937–1945

J.O.P. Hayes
1938–1951

Thomas Adrian Bouchier-
Hayes
1945–1960

Joseph Gerard Mathews
1946–1983

John Edward Coolican
1953–1983

John Lanigan
1956–1983

Richard Brownell Brenan
1965–1983

Anaesthetists

J. Beckett
1913–1919

J.P. Brennan
1919

P.J. Gaffney
1923–1953

A.B. Brooks
1927–1931

T.J. Gilmartin
1932–1983

M. ff O'Carroll
1944–1947

J. Gaffney
1948–1960

M. McGrath
1950–1983

T.A. Scully
1961–1983

Bacteriologists

E.S. Horgan
1927

R.A. O'Meara
1928–1931/2

E. Marjory Booth
1940–1951

Biochemist

W.J. Jessop
1937–1973

Dental Surgeons

J. Cockburn
1915–1931

W. Stewart
1933–1945

T.C. Coleman
1945–1949

A. Cowan
1958–1983

T.G. O'Looney
1958–1966

Gynaecologists

John H. Glenn
1897–1909

Gibbon FitzGibbon
1909–1911/1926–1956

A. Holmes
1911–1914

B. Solomons
1911–1926

John M. Gilmor
1924–1942

Henry FitzGibbon
1952–1959

E.W.L. Thompson
1957–1959

M. Solomons
1956–1983

R.H. O'Hanlon
1960–1983

Laryngologists

Horace Law
1926–1940

T.G. Wilson
1928–1966

J. McAuliffe Curtin
1946–1966

C.D. O'Connell
1960–1968

G. Fennell
1969–1973

T.D. Wilson
1974–1983

Ophthalmologists

J.B. Story
1899–1925

R.H. Mathews
1926–1929

Mary F. Connolly
1927–1952

W.B. McCrae
1946–1959

D.H. Douglas
1960–1979

P. Mathews
1960–1983

H. Cassidy
1983

Paediatricians

E. Doyle
1956–1969

B. Stokes
1970–1983

Pathologists

W.G. Harvey
1906–1910

J.T. Wigham
1910

J.H. Pollock
1921–1923

E.C. Smith
1924–1926

J. Lait
1927–1932

J. Lewis
1933–1939

D.M. Mitchell
1940–1951

A.H. Charles
1940–c1944

R.A. O'Meara
1952–1959

I. Temperley
1961–1965

J. Mullaney
1962–

B. Wallace
1967–1973

C.T. Keane
1971–1983

J. Greally
1974–1982

Psychiatrist

J. Dunne
1949–1983

Radiologists

W.G. Harvey
1906–1910

H.W. Mason
1910–1914

T.G. Hardman
1914–1932

F.G. Stewart
1932–1939

H. Pringle
1939–1959

E.G. Redman
1953–1967

J.G. McNulty
1968–1983

Radiotherapist

M.J. Brady
1952–1959

Senior Nursing Staff in Closing Year

P. Taaffe	Matron
A. Dunne	Assistant Matron
C. Conroy	Home Sister
M. Dodd	Outpatients Sister
N. O'Donnell	Theatre Sister
M. Fitzgibbon	Sister male surgical ward
E. Doorley	Sister female surgical ward
M. Daly	Sister semi-private wards
N. Taylor	Sister male medical ward
S. O'Leary	Sister female medical ward
T. O'Connell	Night Sister
I. O'Mahony	Night Sister
M. O'Connell	Sister Intensive Care Unit
Helen Murray	Pastoral Care Sister
Brigid Wall	Tutor
Mary Moore	Tutor

29.   Topping-out. (Mr D. Kneafsey, PRCSI,
      and Mr J. Hegarty, Contractor.)

[Letter from Chairman of the Board of Governors to Secretary, Department of Health]

Mercer's Hospital

ADDRESS FOR CORRESPONDENCE:
P.O. Box 795,
JAMES'S STREET,
DUBLIN 8.
TEL. 532335

WAW/AS   6th February, 1985

Mr. P.W. Flanagan,
Secretary,
Department of Health,
Custom House,
Dublin 1.

Dear Mr. Flanagan,

I reply to your letter about the disposal of capital arising from the sale of Mercer's Hospital. I understand from your letter that the Department of Finance considers that those monies should be transferred to the Minister for Health for use at his discretion. I think you will already be aware that the views expressed in your letter are not acceptable to me or to my colleagues. There are several reasons for this.

The first is that the Board of Mercer's Hospital are Trustees for the Hospital established on the initiative of Mary Mercer more than two hundred years ago. The Board is responsible for continuing to serve the purpose of the original bequest to the best of its ability. This is a question both of honourable behaviour and of law. In law, when a bequest has ceased to serve its original intention, the trustees of the bequest proceed to make a new application through the Commissioners of Charitable Donations and Bequests for a cy pres scheme which will enable new objectives to be established as close as possible to the original bequest. The Board of Mercer's Hospital has been proceeding in this way and intends to continue to do so. They, and not the Department of Finance, have the right to propose a new cy pres scheme. It would be regrettable if the Department of Finance took the view that the normal processes of law could be set aside in its eagerness to obtain a further capital subvention.

Secondly, the State has not contributed, except in minor respects, to the capital cost of Mercer's Hospital, which was provided by the Board of the Hospital managing the income and capital available to it from time to time. The State has used the facilities provided by the Hospital and paid for them. I have never heard that this would entitle the State to assume that it had become the owner of the property also.

Thirdly, the ethos of Voluntary Hospitals is that members of the Board give a great deal of voluntary service without expectation of reward. I myself have spent many hours in the service of Mercer's Hospital for more than ten years. Some of my colleagues have given even more time. When the question of the closure of the Hospital arose, members of the Board, and I was particularly closely involved myself, were responsible for taking the decision to close, for transferring nearly two hundred jobs elsewhere without dispute with the trade unions, for conducting a complex sale, and for subsequently conducting complex legal business. That the Department of Finance should now expect that the capital sum involved should be simply given to it without the smallest sense that any duties have been carried out or any valuable work done is, I find, insulting to people who have put in years of work without any financial reward.

Finally, the original intention in the development of Dublin hospitals was that the Federated Hospitals should, over a period of years, close and be provided with a new hospital in compensation for that. In fact, Mercer's Hospital has not received new alternative accommodation which it controls. It does not exercise any control over St. James's Hospital. It does not own any of the property there and is not represented on its Board. The suggestion from the Department of Finance that funds should be simply given to it is rather a long distance from the suggestion of Mr. Erskine Childers when he was Minister for Health that a new hospital should be built for the Federation.

In all these circumstances, the Board of my Hospital has chosen, in accordance with routine legal procedures, to develop a cy pres scheme by which the funds of the Hospital will be applied to the health needs of the citizens of Dublin. It is probable that the decisions of the Board will in fact be supportive of the general objectives of the Department of Health and may well prove entirely acceptable to the Department, but the Board itself must take those decisions and has no intention of delegating its authority to anybody else.

In writing in these firm terms it would be proper for me to thank you personally for the assistance that you and your immediate colleagues gave to Mercer's Hospital at the time of closure. Such practical co-operation and consideration of the views of others points the way to future joint endeavours.

Yours sincerely,

W.A. Watts
Chairman of Mercer's Hospital

Index

30. *Department of General Practice. (Professor William Shannon.)*

31. *The Mercer library, 1991.*